the lady rode
Bucking horses

THE STORY OF FANNIE SPERRY STEELE, WOMAN OF THE WEST

Dee Marvine

TWODOT®

A · TWODOT® · BOOK

To my father, Gerald Hamilton Hall, who loved horses

Fannie Sperry Steele

Contents

PART THREE

Preface

Tona Freeman Blake deserves most of the credit for bringing this book into being. She and another Montana horsewoman, Elizabeth Stiffler Wells, befriended Fannie Sperry Steele during her final years and, with Fannie's enthusiastic support, began researching her remarkable life. Fannie gave them access to her letters and scrapbooks, old newspaper clippings, magazine accounts, and early stampede and rodeo programs, and they conducted extensive interviews with Fannie, her family, neighbors, and old-timers who knew her. Looking for a writer to help them tell the story, they brought me into the project, and Fannie became a part of me, too, during the two years I relived her life in the writing of it.

This book depicts an era of the American West when capturing renegade horses from the hills above the homestead served as training ground for extraordinary horsemanship. It documents the outstanding girl who outrode all others at stampedes and roundups, long before these contests of skill and stamina on a bucking horse came to be known as rodeo, and the woman she became, her spirit undaunted throughout a life marked with courage and adventure, triumph and heartache. Though dramatized to convey the full import of her unique life, I have tried to tell the story as Fannie lived it. Except for a few minor characters, the fictionalizing of scenes, and story devices added for continuity, the people, places, rodeo events, dates, and diary excerpts are real. Italics are used throughout for all direct quotes from primary sources such as newspaper accounts, promotional flyers, and Fannie's diary.

Acknowledgments

For the privilege of meeting and talking with Fannie Sperry Steele during her last months in a Helena nursing home and the adventure of vicariously living her life while writing this book, I want to thank Tona Freeman Blake and Elizabeth Stiffler Wells, who introduced me to Fannie and her world; Fannie's nieces Amelia "Babe" Hilger, Hallie Alexander, Bea Krieger, and Vi Nelson, and nephews Dan Hilger and Bryan Hilger, who shared family stories as well as Fannie's photos, scrapbooks, letters, and papers; Fannie's sister-in-law Fleta Isham Sperry, who showed me the Sperry homestead; all of Fannie's extended family; neighbors Otto and Jennie Eder, Charlie and Norma Hughes, Mrs. Daniels, and Gene and Wendall Copenhaver, who supplied reminiscences or old letters; the Montana Historical Society, for filling in some gaps in Fannie's newspaper clippings; my writer friends, for their encouragement and inspiration; and my husband, Don Marvine, for his enthusiasm while we experienced Montana through Fannie's eyes.

Prologue

The gold rush of the 1860s tarnished to silver, then to copper. But the vast territory of Montana still rolled arid and raw across endless grasslands, rising in its western third into the rugged and serene Rocky Mountains.

In the 1870s a final decade of Indian wars ebbed into history, and as the last shot cracked through the truce, the lifeblood of the native nations sank into the sand along with that of their spirit brothers, the buffalo. Longhorns moved onto the ranges. Cattlemen cursed interloping sheepherders. Rustlers and other opportunists appeared. Towns were chartered in makeshift post offices, and homesteaders plodded overland or took steamboats up the Missouri to file claims on barren but potentially beneficent sections of the new land.

It was at the river town of Fort Benton on a June day in 1879 that Rachel Schrader, arriving to become the bride of Datus Sperry, embraced this awesome young country. The couple had met in Detroit on an estate where both were employed. Rachel, a petite twenty-five-year-old seamstress, had been brought to America as an infant by her German-immigrant parents. Datus, twenty-nine, of hardy English farming stock, had migrated with his family from Otsego County, New York. He was a tall, gentle man, big-shouldered and big-hearted with a quiet humor that attracted the quick-witted Rachel. They fell in love. And for two years they dreamed of going West.

But Datus felt he couldn't ask Rachel to brave the hardships and hazards of the frontier until he had some idea of how they could earn a living.

Fannie's parents, Rachel and Datus Sperry, 1879

So early in 1872 he headed west with his brother, Miles. He might have reconsidered had he known it would be seven years before he would see Rachel again.

The Sperry brothers worked their way across the prairies and then crossed the Rocky Mountains into Utah Territory, where they joined a wagon train northbound into Montana Territory. The brothers claimed squatters' rights on a parcel of land in Seven Mile Gulch, west of Helena. They built a cabin and purchased tools, a team, and a fresh heifer. Then Datus wrote Rachel, asking her to join him.

Her journey took her over the Northern Pacific railroad line to Bismarck, North Dakota, where she embarked up the Missouri River on the steamboat *Montana* for Fort Benton. Among her baggage was her treasured sewing machine and a pink floribunda rosebush, which she carefully tended during the forty-three days it took the ship to make its way up 1,300 miles of the muddy Missouri River between Bismarck and Fort Benton.

To Rachel the weeks of travel seemed an exciting adventure. She delighted in the sights along the Missouri as the boat moved steadily upriver. She found the lush prairies beautiful and the wide-open skies inspiring. She saw deer, antelope, and other small game bounding along the riverbank, and at one point the *Montana* had to shut down its engines overnight to avoid collision with a gigantic herd of buffalo crossing the river. But Rachel saw few homesteads, only the occasional small cluster of log sheds that marked the wood yards where the ship refueled.

On the afternoon of June 23, 1879, the *Montana* steamed into Fort Benton, bustling gateway to settlement of the Northwest. Rachel's journey, thus far, had been the thrill of her life. She knew that many a pioneer woman endured unspeakable hardship on the trip overland and often faced the new country sick at heart and in body. But not Rachel. She arrived refreshed, her spirit, wit, and ambition intact.

Datus was waiting. They were married the following morning by a Fort Benton justice of the peace and started at once for the homestead, a dusty, three-day trip with Datus's team and wagon over the rocky Mullen Road. Rachel was awestruck by the bigness of the land, the sky, and the mountains. A tinge of snow still remained on the upper peaks, and patches of lodgepole pine, juniper, and fir swept down to meadows fresh with sage and bunchgrass. Yellow balsam and blue lupine spread swatches of color across the middle slopes.

They followed the rutted wagon track across the sweeping valley, finally turning their eager, sweat-streaked faces toward the forlorn homestead beside a small creek. Rachel, her legs wobbly from the long ride, ran toward the cabin where a single window reflected the twilight, and with Datus offering the last water from their canteen, planted the rose bush.

Their first winter in Seven Mile Gulch swept heavy snow through the valley, but Datus and Miles had put up enough buffalo grass to see their animals through the harsh months. They hunted deer and rabbits for meat and trapped coyotes and wolves for the cash their pelts brought. The fireplace kept the cabin cozy, and Rachel felt their only real hardship was enduring the steady diet of rutabagas.

Spring greened early with plenty of moisture. The milk cow produced a heifer calf, and Datus bought a saddle horse for Rachel. Even though she was expecting a child, Rachel soon rode expertly with Datus across the valley and up into the mountains. They welcomed their daughter, Carrie Amelia, on April 7, 1880.

The second winter proved mild with only a trace of snow, and cattlemen trailed huge herds up from the Southwest onto Montana rangeland.

Rachel gave birth to another baby girl, but the child died after two agonizing weeks. The next year, the birth of a third daughter, Bertha Lovina, helped to ease that loss.

Through those challenging years, Rachel's courage never wavered, and though her eyes showed a trace of weariness, they still lit her wind-chapped face as none other Datus had ever seen. To accommodate their growing family, Datus worked out a tenant agreement with Judge Nicholas D. Hilger, owner of a ranch 20 miles north of Helena at the Gates of the Mountains. At that scenic landmark, the ambling Missouri flows between towering bluffs into a deep, cool-shadowed canyon before stretching out again in a wide arc across the territory. There, too, a mountain in the Big Belt range crests in a craggy formation that can be seen for miles, called the Beartooth by the Indians, and later renamed the Sleeping Giant by settlers.

Early in the spring of 1884, after giving Miles the land at Seven Mile Gulch in return for the livestock, Datus and Rachel packed up their two daughters and their few belongings, dug up the floribunda bush, and trailed the livestock up Prickly Pear Valley to the Hilger ranch at the Gates of the Mountains.

Surrounded by this spectacular natural beauty, the Sperrys found life idyllic in their comfortable cabin. Winter brought light snows that disappeared quickly with the warming chinook winds that swept over the Beartooth. And spring came early, unseasonably warm. But no rain fell, and a summer drought settled across the rangeland. The Sperrys' first son, Arthur Datus, was born in October 1885 at the peak of the autumn dryness.

The following spring, word came that still more cattle and sheep were being brought into the territory. Datus worried that the parched grasslands could not sustain the increasing herds. But during the summer he and Rachel cut and stacked enough hay to winter their own stock and the Hilger herd. They felt secure on this bountiful land along the river, though they both yearned for a place of their own.

Riding one day up into the hills, they came upon an abandoned homestead nestled in a narrow valley directly beneath the Beartooth mountain. A sod-covered dugout stood at the edge of a meadow of wild grasses, greened by a sparkling creek that ran full despite the drought. The Sperrys gazed up at the crest of the mountain, where fir and jack pine feathered against the sky, then down the creek valley at the lone wagon trail winding among the evergreens and out onto the Prickly Pear flats beyond. Both knew they had found their home. They purchased the rights to 320 acres for $100 and, with the help of a neighboring rancher, built a four-room log house and a small barn.

The drought continued. By September they noticed geese migrating early. Their cattle haired out sooner than usual, too. And for the first time, Rachel saw a white Arctic owl, another sign of a severe winter ahead. But they moved into their snug new home before the first snowfall, and Rachel was pregnant again.

The fierce winter of 1886–1887, recorded in weather annals as one of the harshest ever to hit Montana, ended the era of big cattle drives. Large outfits could neither feed nor shelter their immense herds, and nearly 80 percent of all cattle and sheep in the territory perished. Dead stock lay everywhere, along the streambeds, in coulees, and on the open ranges. As snow melted and grass grew luxuriantly around the rotting carcasses, Datus fetched a midwife over the mud-mired road and settled her in at the Sperry ranch.

On March 27, 1887, Fannie Amanda Sperry was born.

Montana Territory matured into statehood in 1889, the same year that Rachel gave birth to their fifth and last child, Walter Charles. Six miles across the Prickly Pear flats, the settlement of Mitchell sprouted next to the Northern Pacific branch line. And the Sperry roots deepened into Montana soil.

PART ONE

Homestead and Horses  I

The wild horses moved across the ridge. It was a small band, three mares with new foals and two yearlings, headed by a buckskin stallion. All looked sleek in the July sun, their bellies bulging from buffalo grass.

At the first sound of the approaching rider, the buckskin arched his neck and squealed a warning. The lead mare, a big bay, turned and broke into a run up the far edge of the draw. The other mares and foals followed, while the wary stallion nipped at the flanks of one of the yearlings to hurry it along.

Fannie Sperry, riding her fastest gelding, Brownie, galloped up the embankment, leaning into the climb as she guided her horse among the rocks. Catching sight of the wild herd, she reined to a stop and held up her hand to signal her younger brother, Walter.

"It's only that buckskin and his family," she said, taking off her scruffy hat and wiping her faded calico sleeve across her forehead.

"No, Fannie, look!" Walter hauled back on the reins as he pulled alongside and pointed across the ridge where a glint of silver flashed through the stand of jack pine at the edge of the draw. A young stallion galloped from the trees after the retreating band. Close behind him ran two other three-year-olds, both bays.

"Holy Moses! It's Chinook!" Fannie touched the heels of her boots to Brownie's flanks. "I'll head him off. You get Ma."

"Don't let him get away," Walter shouted, starting Elsie, his dappled mare, at a gallop back down the trail.

Fannie gave Brownie his head, and the gelding sprang forward after the fleeing stallion. She had wanted to get him corralled since the first time she'd seen him, a sturdy chestnut colt frisking on the high range. As the weeks passed, she noticed his dark coat changing. He lost his foal hair, turned a rosy color, then, finally, a luminous silver-gray.

"Some colts are foaled dark," her mother explained, "but then the lighter color comes over them like a warm chinook wind blows over the Rockies to change a spell of freezing weather." Chinook. Fannie felt a tinge of pride as she settled on the name for the wild colt.

The Sperrys kept an eye on the feral bands that ran in the foothills above their ranch. In the spring, competition for the mares compelled the dominant stallions to drive off maturing males. Usually, these young horses continued to graze nearby, out of range of the stallions' fierce nips and thrashing hoofs. They were content to engage in playful mock battles among themselves or halfhearted attempts at worrying the dominant stallions. But when danger threatened, they were allowed to rejoin the safety of the band. That spring, the dominant buckskin had challenged Chinook, driving him off, and forcing him to join the two young bay stallions that would be his companions until each was able to win mares of his own.

Narrowing her keen blue eyes against the wind as they raced up the draw, Fannie murmured to Brownie, "This time we'll get him corralled for sure."

The Sperrys had rigged a blind corral around a rocky spring 3 miles above the ranch by constructing a rough fence surrounded by brush. Open at both ends, the enclosure had a concealed gate at each end, and wild horses, accustomed to entering and leaving freely as they went to the spring for water, could be trapped by closing the gates as they drank. Brownie had been captured that way. Now his ears pointed straight ahead, alert for sounds of the wild herd, and Fannie bent low over his neck, keeping out of sight below the ridge as she neared the top of the draw.

Fannie had learned to ride almost as soon as she could walk. Her mother, Rachel, had ridden with each of the five Sperry children in the saddle in front of her when they were babies. The two older girls, Carrie and Bertha, were first, then Arthur, and, finally, Fannie and Walter. They had taken their first solo rides on Old Bob, a bunged-up, white horse that their father, Datus, sometimes put to harness. If a child slipped from Old Bob's broad back, Rachel boosted the toddler aboard with instructions to hold on tighter.

As the years passed, Rachel would shake her head with both trepidation and pride, claiming the children rode like "wild Injuns." They loved to chase the scattered bands of wild horses that roamed the foothills near the homestead. Some folks called the feral bands mustangs, but descendants of that early Spanish-bred stock hadn't drifted that far north. Most of Montana's wild horses had come from domestic stock lost or abandoned by homesteaders or cattlemen, and the unbranded offspring were mavericks, free to anyone who could catch them. Each year the Sperrys added several to their string.

Fannie concentrated on the task ahead, her mouth pressed into its usual determined line at the prospect of capturing the best of them yet, the silver-gray stallion. Nearly fifteen hands, she guessed, and as well-formed as a purebred. Harsh winters and sparse grazing stunted many of the feral horses, and inbreeding destroyed most of the characteristics of specific breeds, leaving the animals small and shaggy, some little more than runty scrubs. But fresh blood from more recent strays produced enough of a mix of desired traits to make their capture worthwhile. Some of the herds even bore the marks of racing blood attributed to a Thoroughbred stallion that had roamed the range years before.

Datus Sperry was always pleased when he found the weight and strength of a Percheron, or the quickness of a Steeldust among the wild bunch, but he grumbled and passed up any with pinto, piebald, or calico markings. He disliked what he called "those Injun ponies."

But Fannie liked the Injun ponies. Pintos were her favorites.

Now her face flushed in the hot sun as she worked her way behind and downwind from the band, watching patiently until Chinook began to move back toward the draw. If he'd just keep moseying that way, she could cut him off and drive him down to the corral. Deciding not to wait for Walter, she turned Brownie off the trail and spurred him in a wide arc, cutting the silver-gray horse off from the others. "Yeeeeow!" she yelled, fanning her hat above her head.

Chinook pranced sideways, his neck arched, then bolted down the trail. Fannie urged Brownie after him, and as she charged onto the trail, she heard a faint call from below. Good old dependable Walter was on his way with help. "I got him," she hollered. Down the mountain she raced, Brownie's feet swift and sure as a mountain goat's over rocks and around scrub juniper as he veered to one side, then the other, to keep Chinook on the trail.

But the wild horse widened his lead. Skittering off the trail down a slide of loose shale, he jumped a rocky creek and headed up along the bank toward higher ground. Fannie pulled up. The creek was impossible to ford, and though Brownie was fast, he wasn't a jumper. She grimaced her disappointment.

Then she heard her mother shout, "We'll bring him down." Rachel had ridden up on the other side of the ridge and was coming down along the creek. The clash of hoofs against the rocks sounded as if her sisters, Carrie and Bertha, must be up there, too. The wild horse hesitated, then Fannie could hear him thundering back down. Brownie whinnied and pulled at his bit, eager to join the chase, but she held him till Chinook came into view again.

"Head him onto the trail," Fannie yelled, glimpsing Walter off to the side among the trees. The young stallion pounded toward him, nostrils flared, the flying mane and tail glinting silver in the dappled sunlight. Walter waved his hat, hazing the renegade horse straight for the blind corral. "We got him!" he shouted.

"Not yet we ain't," came their mother's shout. "But Arthur's down below." The petite woman, her skirt flapping, crouched over her mount as it sailed over the creek, followed by both Carrie and Bertha on their big, swift horses.

Fannie grinned. She admired good horsemanship. She was pleased, too, that her older brother had come along. Usually he was too busy with ranch chores to chase wild horses. What fun! The whole family helping haze Chinook into the corral. All but Pa.

She held her breath as the young stallion thundered into the hidden enclosure. He galloped past the spring, discovered the far end was blocked, then whirled and raced back toward the entrance. Arthur sprang from the brush and pushed the gate shut. Fannie and the others converged on the corral and dismounted as the trapped horse reeled back and forth, squealing his distress.

Fannie, near to bursting with delight, ran to the fence, her dark braids bobbing over the shoulders of her faded shirtwaist. "Don't be afraid, Chinook."

Carrie fanned her neck with her hat, lifting the sweat-soaked cluster of light-brown curls tied back with a leather thong. "Think it'll hold him?"

"It's solid." Arthur twisted the heavy wire that held the gate shut.

"Let him cool down," their mother said. "There's water and plenty of grass. Now we better get back. Your pa will be wondering why we rode off like we was half crazy."

The family often rode off without him. Fannie realized when very young that, despite his expertise with draft horses, her father never rode horseback. "Pa," she had asked, "don't you like to ride?"

"It hurts me too much," was his response. Yet, he knew more about horses than anybody. She had seen him break to the harness even the orneriest critter, and stockmen were always stopping by the ranch to buy or trade for his well-trained teams. When logging operations began nearby, his draft horses were employed skidding logs to the river. The logs were then floated downstream for use in the building of a new town, Great Falls. And he was particular about the care of his livestock. "We always take care of our horses before we take care of ourselves" was a rule that none of the children ever broke.

Fannie would take care of Chinook all right. Still tingling from the excitement of the chase and the thrill of capturing the wild horse, she couldn't wait to begin breaking him. He would make a fine saddle horse, the envy of every family in the valley. But first, she decided, she would ride him in a real bucking-horse contest. It was time she proved to a few of those conceited, clumsy cowboys, who won the prize money at local roundups, that a girl could ride as well—or even better—than any cowboy.

"I'll stay here for a while and make sure he don't jump the fence," she said.

Rachel, mounting up, motioned toward the ranch. "We got to get ready for tomorrow's big doings." To Fannie, her mother's small, commanding figure astride—faded dress tucked around her well-worn boots, strands of her dark, gray-streaked hair flying from its bun—represented the finest of western womanhood.

Carrie gave her sister a stern look. "If you're goin' to the Fourth of July picnic, you gotta help fix. You can peel potatoes."

Fannie shrugged. She hated kitchen chores, but now that she had Chinook corralled she guessed she could take on any burden, even peeling potatoes. With a last fond look at her prize, his coat glistening with sweat as he paced in the shade of the rock overhang, she spurred after the others.

"Do I have to go tomorrow?" Fannie pouted. "I could start breakin' him."

"It's time you got your mind off horses once in a while," Carrie scolded. "Here you are, fourteen years old, and you're hardly ever out of the saddle."

Bertha agreed. "There's more to life than horse biscuits, you know." Bertha's warm, brown hair highlighted a glowing skin, and her posture in the saddle gave her a regal look, even in her work clothes, much like their mother.

"Oh, all right. I'll go." Fannie pulled her hat down tight. "Come on, Walter, I'll race you." The two youngest Sperrys took off down the mountain, Brownie and Elsie neck and neck. Fannie couldn't imagine a time when she would stop thinking about horses. They had always been her best friends—hers and Walter's.

Her earliest memories were of the wild horses. At night, snuggled on her cot in the girls' small bedroom behind the kitchen, she would hear the pounding of hoofs as the wild bands raced down from the high ridges toward the salt lick beyond the Hilger ranch, and she would listen for their faraway whinnying.

One afternoon when she was only two years old, she saw them drinking at the meadow creek. Excited because they rarely came that near, she ran after them, trailing a long scarf in her tiny fist. "Gonna catch me a white-face horsie," she called to her mother. The horses galloped away, but she waited beside the creek all day hoping to capture a passing bronco if one came back that way. Her mother had remarked, "I never saw a kid so crazy about horses."

That observation strengthened one evening a few months later. One of the Sperry mares had just foaled, and as the spring twilight followed her father into the log house, Fannie heard him say, "It's a damn pinto. Might as well kill it."

Her mother, placing the chimney on the lamp that would light supper chores, glanced up. "Oh, Datus, a pinto? What a shame."

"No good Injun cayuses," he muttered, tossing his hat onto a peg behind the door. "Can't afford to have 'em croppin' the range."

Little Fannie's cheeks flushed. She jumped up from the floor where she sat playing with baby Walter. Grabbing his small quilt, she slipped past her father and ran out into the April dusk. A cold wind swept down from the Beartooth, stirring the pines huddled around the Sperry meadow. The little girl shivered in her rumpled serge dress as she crossed the corral to the barn and struggled with the door. Once inside, surrounded by the familiar animal smells, she heard the mare's soft whuffle in the near stall. In the darkness, she could barely make out the spotted foal lying at its mother's feet. Slipping in beside the mare, she knelt in the straw to place Walter's quilt over the still-wet colt. Murmuring softly, she patted the spotted nose and stretched her short arms around the colt's neck. "I won't let Papa hurt you," she promised.

Lantern light flickered across the stall as her parents followed her into the barn. The sorrel sidled to shield her foal and little Fannie crouched over the newborn. Her father smiled down at her as he eased around the mare's rump.

"By golly, that *is* a mighty pretty little pony. Maybe I was too hasty." He lifted Fannie into his arms while her mother shook the straw from Walter's quilt. Fannie snuggled against her father. His arms, as much as his words, told her he was not going to hurt the pinto. They watched as the mare nuzzled her foal. At first, its spindly legs buckled when it struggled to get to its feet. Then, awkwardly, it stood and began to nurse.

"She looks plenty healthy," her father said.

"But she's a calico." Her mother frowned at the irregular patches of brown, tan, and white that marked the foal. "She's every color of the rainbow."

"That's a good name for her," her father said. "Rainbow. Do you like that, Fannie?" And Fannie gazed up at the smile beneath his mustache.

But her mother looked worried. "With a colt on that mare, we'll have to buy more feed till the grass greens up." She sighed as she picked the loose straw off Fannie's dress. "Supper's almost ready, Datus. You better go in and help Carrie. There'll be folks by tomorrow wanting cream."

Carrie, then age ten, had become her father's top hand. Recently, while he was down with the flu, Carrie had milked all nine cows by herself. She stood cranking the cream separator as they came back into the kitchen. "Are we gonna keep the pinto, Pa?"

"It'll be Fannie's," he said.

The oldest Sperry daughter smiled approval as she shifted the crock of fresh cream under the separator spout and raw skimmed milk fell from a second spout into a bucket on the floor. Carrie had had her own full-size horse since she was six. Bertha, too.

"I got a pinto horsie," Fannie announced as she wiggled from her father's arms and ran to five-year-old Arthur, who sat oiling an old bridle. Arthur, proud of his own Welsh pony, Blackie, had his own opinion about useless pintos.

"Aw, who wants a silly old pinto?"

Fannie's lips pressed into a thin line. "I do." She took a defensive position beside the baby playing on the floor. "Me and Walter do."

Now, with the wild stallion secure in the high corral, Fannie wished she and Walter could stay on the Beartooth the next day and begin to gentle him. But no. The Hilger boys were coming to take them to the Fourth of July celebration. Joe and his brother, N. D., sons of Judge Nicholas D. Hilger, had asked to take Carrie and Bertha. Carrie insisted that Fannie come with them.

Fannie wrinkled her nose at the thought of being such a tagalong. Seeing the bronc riding and the fireworks would be fun, but she would just as soon skip the dance. She couldn't stand any of those gangly boys who couldn't ride for sour apples, let alone dance. She didn't much like dancing anyway—unless it was on Rainbow, the pinto she had taught to sidestep.

She could ride as well now as her mother, Rachel. And Rachel was the best horsewoman in the valley. The fact that her father's hernia kept him from riding may have had something to do with her mother having become such a fine rider. But mostly, Fannie was certain, her mother's skill came from a remarkable strength of will.

For as far back as Fannie could recall, her mother's energy sparked the Sperry ranch, where work took first priority. In good years, haying on the two meadows produced a surplus that could be sold at the hay market in Helena. Milking the cows, a mix of dairy breeds, always provided salable quantities of milk products. Rachel and the girls spent hours at the big barrel churn, and the fresh butter and cream were kept cool in crocks immersed in the creek or, in winter, stored in the old-homestead dugout. Twice each week, Datus and Arthur hauled the dairy products to ranchers along Prickly Pear Valley from Wolf Creek to Unionville.

Customers often stopped by the ranch, too, to deal with Datus for draft horses or with Rachel for new-broke horses from the hills. The Sperry children would come running when they heard the hoofbeats of a visitor's horse or the jingle of a team and wagon coming up the road. But usually they amused themselves. The valley rang with their shouts and laughter as they dashed across the meadow to check on Rainbow and Blackie, then to the corral to size up a new bronco.

On the evening air the children's excited calls sounded in the gathering dark, a counterpoint to the quiet voices of the grown-ups inside the house. When lamplight beckoned, the youngsters drifted inside, boys bedding down in the front room, girls cuddling beneath summer quilts in their small bedroom, muffling giggles for a few minutes before falling silent. Fannie always listened for the drop of her father's boots, which told her the grown-ups, too, were ready for sleep.

With the first light, they awoke to the sound of meadowlark song. After chores and a breakfast of hot biscuits with sidepork and gravy, they saddled Old Bob. "Let's play Buffalo Bill," Carrie said. The others shouted agreement.

"I'll be Annie Oakley." Bertha swung beneath the horse's belly, hanging upside down, one shoe wedged into a stirrup, her fingers gripping the opposite stirrup.

"I'm Buffalo Bill," Arthur announced, climbing into the saddle. His boot pinched Bertha's fingers on the stirrup.

"Ouch! Can't you see I'm doing a trick."

"How can I be Buffalo Bill if you got your hand in the stirrup?" Arthur snapped back.

"Arthur, put your feet up on the withers." Carrie sounded exasperated. She handed the reins to Arthur, who raised his knees high onto the horse's neck and urged Old Bob into a trot, Bertha dangling beneath the belly for a few paces before dropping onto the dirt. Old Bob stepped carefully to avoid brushing her with his big hoofs.

Fannie and her little brother held up their arms to be boosted aboard.

"Here, you can be trick riders, too." Carrie gave them a leg up behind Arthur, with Fannie barely clinging on above Old Bob's tail, her bare legs tickled by the twitch of his hide. Carrie led them across the rocky creek before complaining, "I'm tired of these baby games. Let's play stagecoach robbery."

"Yeah." Arthur leaped from Old Bob and ran to catch their saddle ponies, while Carrie harnessed a draft horse, Nell, to the two-wheeled cart their father had made to transport them to school. Then, with little Fannie and Walter riding shotgun in the cart to thwart pursuing bandits, and Bertha and Arthur bareback on their ponies, bandanas tied over their faces, Carrie cracked the lines and Nell stampeded down the dusty wagon-track road toward the flats. Before the make-believe outlaws overtook her, Carrie had raced halfway to the schoolhouse, nearly 6 miles away.

Classes at the two-room Mitchell school convened only from April through November. Subzero winters loomed unpredictably over the Montana rangelands December through March, and homesteads were too far spread apart to risk sending the children such a distance to school during those months. Since the Sperrys depended on the three older ones to help with the heavy workload in the more moderate weather, their school attendance, like that of the neighbors' children, proved sporadic at best.

In April of 1895, just after Fannie's eighth birthday and when Walter was five, their turn came to adjust to the classroom. Though Fannie learned quickly and liked the songs and poems, she could see little sense in wasting the warm months in the stuffy schoolroom when she could be working with her horses.

But one daily event kept her enthusiastic—racing to school on horseback with her classmate Christine Synness. Christine lived across the valley from the Sperry ranch. The only girl in a ranch family of boys, she knew her way around horses as well as Fannie did.

"Hey, Chris, I'll race you," Fannie called each day as she caught sight of her friend's blond curls bobbing in the wind.

"Bet you can't beat me" was the invariable reply. Rainbow and Sandy, Christine's bay, knew the routine. As soon as the girls came abreast, the horses took off at top speed, enjoying the run as much as their plucky riders. Before long the whole valley knew about the two pretty young girls who met each day on the flats to race their ponies to school. The cloud of dust they raised could be seen from Mitchell to Clark Creek.

One day as Fannie galloped home from school still tingling from a fast race with Christine, she saw her mother coming across the meadow. She was leading two green broncs down from the high corral when, suddenly, the animals balked. Her mother gave a startled cry and dropped to the ground grasping her ankle. Her face contorted and her lips formed a word that caused Fannie's heart to leap into her throat. "Rattlesnake!" The stricken woman struggled to loop the ropes holding the wild horses over a scrub pine.

"Pa, come quick! Ma's been snakebit!"

Datus appeared at the barn door. He saw his wife stumbling toward them and ran to her. "Fannie, get Doc Hansen! Hurry!"

Fannie had never heard fear in her father's voice before. She turned Rainbow and galloped down the road, looking back only once and seeing her father carrying her mother into the house.

The distance to the doctor's home near Mitchell seemed far greater than ever before, but at Fannie's frantic urging Rainbow never slackened. When she reached the doctor's house, she jumped from the lathered horse, ran through the picket gate onto the porch, and pounded on the screen door, calling "Doc Hansen!"

The doctor hurried to the door, his shirtsleeves rolled up in the afternoon heat. "What's the matter, Fannie?"

"A rattlesnake bit Mama. Pa says come quick."

"Tend your horse," he said, "while I get the buggy." After an agony of time, she was seated in the doctor's carriage behind his Morgan pacer retracing her route. Her father ran from the house when he heard them approaching.

"Doc, Rachel's swallowed some rubbing alcohol. She was out of her head with pain, and when I tried to disinfect the bite, she grabbed the bottle and gulped some down before I could stop her." He pulled the doctor toward the house as his words poured out. "I cut the wound and sucked out some of the poison, but I couldn't get her to throw up the alcohol."

Rachel, pale and breathing with difficulty, was lying on the sofa. The doctor examined the two purple puncture marks on her puffed ankle, checked her pulse, and looked under her eyelids.

"About all we can do, Datus," he said finally, "is to try to keep the fever down. She could die from the snakebite or go blind from the alcohol. Depends on how much she took. All we can do is make her comfortable as possible. I'm sorry, Datus."

While her mother lay delirious, Fannie sat by her bedside and pressed cold cloths to Rachel's fevered forehead, whispering, "Please don't die, Mama."

On the third day, the sick woman opened her eyes. Squinting against the light, she tried to raise her head. "What's happened?"

"You've been sick, Mama. A rattler bit you." Fannie spooned cool water between the parched lips.

"Are the broncs all right?"

"Yes, Mama. Carrie put them in the corral."

"Take care of the horses, Fannie." She lapsed into another deep sleep that would shield her from some of the pain of her slow recovery.

"I will, Mama."

During the days that passed before Rachel was up and around, the family gathered around her bed after supper, and Arthur read aloud to them. One evening she placed her hand on his book to delay the start of the story.

"I always thought these mountain rattlesnakes too timid to do much harm," she said. "They always got out of my way when they could. But from now on, I want all of you to be careful." She sat up, her square chin thrust forward. "And I want every last rattler out of this valley."

After Rachel's recovery, when the family gathered in the evening after their supper chores, they took up a new pastime—making hat bands and belts from rattlesnake skins.

One evening Arthur began to read *The Son of the Wolf*, by a new author he'd discovered named Jack London. Rachel thought it the finest story she'd ever heard, but Fannie and Walter paid little attention. They were mulling over a worn newspaper clipping they'd discovered in Rachel's scrapbook.

A Helena lawyer, S. A. Balliet, stopping by the Sperry ranch to outfit a party of hunters with Datus's packhorses, saw twenty-year-old Carrie rounding up cattle. A few days later, he wrote the short article for the *Helena Herald* praising the horsemanship of *the young Miss Sperry*. The piece described her *rounding up stock on a fat, sleek, wiry, half-trained horse, which was bounding and dancing in a manner that would interest the full-fledged cowboy*. The article concluded,

Miss Sperry sat his back, swaying to the motion of his body as gracefully as a rose nodding in the morning breeze.

"She was only rounding up the cows same as usual," Walter said, "but this fella says her riding would interest a full-fledged cowboy."

"Those cowpokes don't do anything we can't." Fannie's lips pressed into a thoughtful line. "Walter, I can ride better'n most of them now. But I intend to be the best. Be wrote up in the paper, too, like Carrie."

That was before she had Chinook. Now she knew nothing could stop her.

Riding with the Cowboys  2

Early next morning, dressed for the Fourth of July picnic in her new riding skirt, Fannie swung to the top rail of the blind corral to size up the gray stallion. He was spirited all right. But was he a bucker? And if she rode him as a bucking horse, would he be any good for the saddle later on? He watched the girl approach, his ears laid back above the silvery mane.

"Easy, boy." At the sound of her voice, he whirled and galloped to the far end of the enclosure. Fannie squinted against the sun filtering through the pines and pulled down her hat to shield her eyes. Keeping close to the safety of the fence, she edged slowly toward the big horse. "Easy, Chinook. I won't hurt you." The young stallion stood, nostrils flared, as she crept closer, her hand outstretched. Chinook reared, towering above her, his front legs thrashing the air. Fannie stood, momentarily transfixed. He seemed the most beautiful horseflesh she'd ever laid eyes on. Then, in one agile movement, she rolled under the lower rail just as the powerful hoofs slammed into the ground.

Safely outside the fence, she got to her feet and, brushing the dust from her skirt, she slipped Brownie's reins from the rail and swung into the saddle, calling back over her shoulder, "See you tomorrow, you pretty thing."

As she came along the creek toward the barn, she heard her sister Carrie calling from the kitchen door. "Fannie, where are you? It's time to go."

Fannie unsaddled Brownie in the corral and brushed his back and legs.

"Hurry up, Fannie," Carrie called again. "The folks already left, and Joe will be here any minute." She frowned as Fannie came into the kitchen. "You're not going in that, are you?" Petite Carrie wore a pretty blue-and-white-checked gingham, her puffed hair topped with a perky straw hat.

"What's the matter with my new riding skirt?"

"It's . . ." Carrie hesitated. "It's so heavy looking. Aren't you going to dance tonight? Don't you want to look pretty?" Fannie hadn't given it much thought. Carrie was always trying to get her to "enhance her natural beauty."

Fannie scuffed into the bedroom, where Bertha, tall and attractive in a pale-green dress that showed off her figure, stood before the bureau mirror arranging her hair beneath a tiny yellow bonnet. Fannie felt awkward. She was as tall as Bertha, and whenever she put on a dress, her wrist bones seemed to hang out of the sleeves. Dresses looked silly with her heavy boots, and she didn't feel right in high-button shoes.

"Maybe I could wear your shirtwaist again, Bertha." The white dimity she'd borrowed on at least two other occasions would pretty up her outfit just enough.

Bertha brightened at the idea and took the freshly done-up garment from her drawer. "You'll look nice in this," she said, smiling at her sister. Taking off the faded calico, Fannie slipped into the cool shirtwaist and buttoned the small buttons at the neck. "Here, let's look at you." Bertha held Fannie at arm's length and brushed back a wisp of hair that strayed from one of the dark braids. Fannie reached for her scruffy hat.

"No, wait." Bertha took the hat and tossed it into the corner. Rummaging in the highboy, she found her own straw bowler, the one with the artificial cherries pinned to the brim, and placed it on Fannie's head. "Wear this." She adjusted it to a becoming angle. "All the girls will be wearing pretty hats."

Fannie gazed blankly at her reflection in the mirror.

"Now, let's get a little color into your face." Bertha lightly pinched Fannie's cheeks until a warm glow spread across the fresh-scrubbed skin. At that moment they heard the Hilger's team coming up the road, and Fannie ducked away from her sisters' scrutiny.

Outside the house the two Hilger boys sprang from the wagon to help the girls with the lunch basket. "Say, don't you look nice," Joe said, squeezing Carrie's hand. N. D. stowed the basket on the loose hay in the back of the two-seated spring wagon. "Fannie looks almost ready for Sunday," he teased, noticing the cherry-trimmed hat. "I hear Albert Synness is aimin' to dance with you tonight, Fannie."

Fannie grinned. "Well, then, he better dance better'n he rides." They all laughed, and Joe helped Carrie onto the front seat while N. D. and Bertha seated themselves behind them. Fannie climbed up onto the front seat next to Carrie. She figured since Carrie and Joe were courting, they wouldn't mind a little crowding. Joe picked up the lines and they were on their way, all talking at once as they bumped down the road and out onto the flats toward Mitchell.

Nearing the village, sounds of bellowing livestock mingled with the pleasant clinking of bridles and harnesses, and the friendly shouts of neighbor greeting neighbor rose from the open field in front of the Northern Pacific depot, where the festivities would take place. A row of wagons at one side formed a spectator area, and a rope corral for the bucking horses had been strung in the aspen grove next to the schoolhouse.

Small groups of ranchers and cowboys clustered here and there exchanging news. Women setting up picnic lunches under the trees by the creek chatted happily, keeping an eye on children who darted about among the parked wagons and buggies. Fannie wanted to run down to the grove to look over the bucking horses, but the dimity shirtwaist and cherry-festooned hat reminded her she should stay with the other ladies.

Fannie and the others found a spot to spread the picnic and then trouped into the schoolhouse, where the needlework exhibition and bake sale had been set up. Noon signaled the picnicking and, after what seemed an eternity to Fannie, folks finished eating and began drifting toward the field where two men were hazing a bucking horse. A muffled, megaphoned voice announced the first event.

"Hurry! The bronc riding's startin'." With Fannie leading the way, they scrambled up onto an empty wagon just as the first horse let go. "Look at that dish-face!" she shouted. The horse bolted across the field, bucking straightaway, a lanky cowhand rigid in the saddle. Bowing up, the bronc came down stiff-legged, then bucked again, head low, nostrils blowing dust. A quick half-twist by the dish-faced bronc and the cowboy went off over the left flank. The horse bucked on, scattering a row of ranchers standing nearby before he could be hazed off toward the rope corral. Applause and shouts rose from the onlookers.

Fannie whispered to Carrie, "Did you see that? He grabbed the saddle horn."

The starter raised his megaphone and called the next rider. "Number two will be Tom Cooper of Wolf Creek, riding Pigeon." A black bronc, eared down by a wrangler, snorted in protest as Cooper eased himself onto the saddle and tightened his grip on the lead rope. "Ready!" The wrangler released his hold on the ears, and Cooper dug his spurs into the bronc's flanks. The black sunfished, dipping the right stirrup to the ground. For a moment Fannie thought the cowboy's boot was hung up, but it broke loose, and Cooper hit the ground rolling. The crowd groaned.

Fannie applauded politely. Heck, I can ride better'n that, she told herself.

"Folks, may I have your attention?" The starter walked onto the field. "We're short a few riders here this afternoon. Any of you cowboys interested in riding a bucking horse should talk to Karl Hager. There's five dollars in prize money."

Fannie glanced at Carrie, who was perched on the wagon tongue talking to Joe, and at Bertha and N. D., who had strolled past the line of buggies. Seeing that they were absorbed in their own activities, Fannie scooted off the tailgate and made her way among the spectators. She found Hager making notes on a tablet.

"Mr. Hager." Hager paid no attention, so Fannie tugged his sleeve. "I'd like to sign up for the contest."

Hager turned his ruddy face toward her. "The women's exhibit is over there." He extended his arm in the direction of the schoolhouse.

"No, I mean the bucking contest."

"Cowboys have to sign up in person," Hager barked.

"It's me," Fannie said. "I want to ride."

Turning slowly, Hager looked at her for the first time and broke into a broad grin as his gaze reached the cherries on her hat. She sheepishly snatched the bowler from her head and held it behind her back.

"Now, what makes you think you can ride a bucking horse, little lady?"

"I can ride."

Hager chuckled and shook his head. "Well, now, I couldn't take a chance on your gettin' hurt, could I? Who's your pa?"

"Datus Sperry. I'm Fannie."

"So you're Sperry's girl. Bought a team of Percheron from your pa once. Still got 'em. Good horses. As I recall, all you Sperrys are pretty fair riders."

Fannie nodded, rocking on the heels of her boots.

"Just the same," Hager continued, "we don't have no women riding. And you're not even a woman yet. Why, you're not hardly dry behind the ears."

"Please give me a chance," Fannie persisted.

"Not this time, I'm afraid." Hager moistened a blunt pencil with his tongue and began checking the names on the tablet.

Fannie saw Andreas Synness walking toward them. "Mr. Synness," she called, wondering why he wasn't home haying with Christine and the boys.

"Well, hello, Fannie." Synness seemed surprised to see his daughter's pal among the cowhands.

Hager jerked his thumb toward Fannie. "Hey, Andreas, whatdaya think of this? This little lady wants to ride the bucking horses."

"Tell him it's all right," Fannie begged.

Synness shrugged. "She's a heck of a rider, Karl. I don't see no harm in lettin' her ride."

"Don't think I should." Hager looked sternly at Fannie. "You know, little lady, this is different than riding around the ranch. These ornery broncs go plumb wild."

"I can vouch for her, Karl," Synness said. "I've seen her ride some pretty tough broncs up at my place."

Hager still wasn't sure.

Synness went on. "She breaks wild horses for her pa. Neighbors, too. I'd say she can handle herself on 'bout any horse."

"Well . . ." Hager seemed to be coming around. "If you say so. I guess we can pick an easy one for her."

"No!" Fannie's voice was firm. "I'll draw for my bronc same as the rest."

"Jehosephat!" Hager shook his head. "I'll put your name on the list, but you better know what you're doin'." He handed her a square of oilcloth, painted with the number five. "Here's a number. Be ready when you're called."

Fannie, plopping the cherry hat back on her head, grabbed Hager's hand in both of hers and shook it vigorously. "Thanks. I can ride all right. You'll see."

She drew a bay named Spitfire. Hager, still skeptical, warned it was a green horse, fresh from the mountains, and as the riding continued Fannie hurried down to the grove to get a look at him.

"Careful. Don't spook them broncs." Two young wranglers sprawled nearby. One picked at his teeth with a piece of hay.

"I'm riding Spitfire in the contest," she told them. Then, seeing the smirks on their faces, she added, "I'm Fannie Sperry." She could see they hadn't heard of her.

"Well, now, Fannie. Ain't you scared of them ornery cayuses? A pretty little girl like you."

"I've rode a few before," she snapped. "Never seen a horse yet that scared me."

"You intendin' to ride in that hat?" The hay chewer doubled over, holding his sides and pretending to snicker.

"Holy Moses!" Fannie muttered under her breath. Again she grabbed Bertha's bowler from her head. Only this time she slung it in a wide arc onto a pile of hay. In the same sweeping movement, she scooped up the startled hay chewer's battered sombrero. "How about loaning me this," she said, pulling the hat tight over her brow. The wrangler, hands atop his newly bared head, laughed good-naturedly.

"I'd be much obliged if you'd pin on my number, too," she said, handing the oilcloth square and its attached safety pin to the wrangler and turning her back to receive it. He rubbed his thumb and forefinger together, mimicking a delicate touch. "Be glad to." He winked at his pal. "We can't have you womenfolk ridin' the bucking horses without a number."

A megaphoned voice announced, "Folks, we got a surprise for you this afternoon." The starter again stood front and center. "We got a young lady ridin' today. First up will be number five. Miss Fannie Sperry. A hometown girl, ridin' Spitfire." Fannie ran out onto the field to where her bronc stood spraddle-legged, straining against the wrangler's grip on his ears. She heard a hushed murmur, then scattered applause as the crowd caught sight of her.

Someone said, "Who's that?" Another answered, "It's that Sperry kid."

Datus and Rachel saw their youngest daughter bounding toward the big bay horse and looked at each other with surprise. Fannie, feeling a rising tension in the pit of her stomach, heard only the words of encouragement.

"I've seen this girl ride. She's good."

"Let 'er buck, Fannie!"

She nodded to the cowhand holding the bay horse. "Easy, boy," she murmured. Another wrangler boosted her into the saddle and she settled the toes of her boots into the stirrups. Spitfire struggled to free his head from the handler's grip. Doubling the lead rope around her hand, Fannie adjusted the pull to just the right distance above the horse's neck, neither too long nor too short. She could feel sweat collecting beneath the oilcloth square that hung heavy on the back of her thin blouse. She tugged the borrowed sombrero tighter over her brow, took a deep breath, and glanced at the cowhand holding the bay's ears.

"Ready?" he asked.

Fannie swallowed. Her mouth felt dry as dust. "Ready." The wrangler released the horse and jumped back.

Spitfire left the ground in a hurry. His head went down, jerking Fannie forward. She tugged the lead with her back arched, her braids flapping. Again the horse bucked high, twisting as his feet slammed into the ground. Fannie waved her free arm.

"Ride 'em, girl."

Spitfire's head plunged between his legs. He whirled a quarter turn and dug in to a sudden stop. Fannie stayed with him. Then the bay heaved skyward in a frantic effort to unseat his rider, his neck stretching higher with each leap.

"That bronc's tryin' to chin the moon."

"Stick with 'em, Fannie."

She grasped the borrowed hat and waved it above her head as Spitfire tired, crowhopping toward the row of wagons. She knew she had him. As she jumped to the ground, the hazer grabbed the lead rope.

"You rode like you was part of that horse," he said. Fannie smiled and waved to the onlookers as, head up, her braids bobbing above the number five on her back, she strode from the field.

"Where'd you learn to ride like that?" one of the cowboys asked.

"Good goin', Fannie." Karl Hager was there, too. And Andreas Synness raised his hand in a knowing salute. Fannie waved back.

"Hey, can I have my hat back now?" the hay chewer called to her. "There's gotta be some magic in that dog-eared son-of-a-gun." She had almost forgotten the hat. She tossed it to the wrangler. "Nice ride," he said.

Fannie grinned as she saw Carrie, Bertha, and the Hilger boys making their way through the crowd. "You were great, Fannie," Carrie said, hugging her. Joe clapped her on the back. "Rode like a champion."

"Ladies and gentlemen," the starter shouted. "Our prize money today goes to Number Three. Jim Dawkins of Ovando. I think that guy must have glue on the seat of his pants. He sure did show us a ride today." A shout went up from the crowd. Whistles and applause. The starter continued, "And let's give a hand to Number Five. Fannie Sperry of Mitchell. A young lady who knows how to ride a bucking horse."

"Wave, they're clapping for you," Bertha said. Fannie grinned. It was a good ride but not that special. Still, she raised both arms above her head to acknowledge the applause around her.

"Fannie, you got rope burns." Bertha took her hand and turned the palm up. Fannie hadn't noticed, but now the raw flesh began to smart. Carrie offered her handkerchief. "Let me tie this around it."

"It's nothing," Fannie said. As they left the field, she retrieved Bertha's cherry bowler from its nest in the hay.

The fireworks that evening reflected Fannie's mood. She fairly sparkled as she and the others entered the schoolhouse for the dance. The young cowboys, eager to talk about her ride, kept her surrounded. She danced every dance, Carrie's hankie tied around the abrasion on her hand. Finally, she had to say her feet hurt, and she went to talking horses with the young cowboys. Before she realized how late it was, Carrie came to fetch her, saying Joe had brought the team around.

Heading back to the ranch through the warm July darkness, Fannie stretched out on the straw in the back of the wagon and gazed at the stars. In the moonlight she saw Carrie resting her head on Joe's shoulder. N. D. had his arm around Bertha.

"Fannie," Joe called back to her in a teasing voice. "I hear a couple of the boys asked you to the house dance at Wolf Creek next Saturday. You gonna go?"

"Nope," Fannie answered. "I'm taking Chinook over there for the bucking exhibition."

Wild Horse to Bucking Bronco   3

Sunrise over the Beartooth chased wisps of fog into the pines and cast a golden light on the silver-gray stallion and the young girl perched on the gate of the blind corral. Fannie still felt a glow of pride from her bucking-horse ride the day before.

"Come on, Chris, hurry," she called when she saw her friend coming up the trail on the big bay, Sandy. Chinook raised his head and whinnied at the approaching gelding.

"Say, that's some horse." Christine swung down and looped Sandy's reins over the rail. Chinook stretched his neck over the gate to nuzzle the bay, just as he had done with Brownie when Fannie arrived at the corral. Then with a snort he whirled and galloped back toward the spring.

"Are you going to ride him over at Wolf Creek Saturday?"

"Yup. And you can bring your black horse. He's a dandy bucker."

"Weasel bucked John off yesterday. Pa says he'll never be broke."

"Then you've got the perfect bronc." Fannie felt a growing excitement. "I told Mr. Anson—he's organizing the exhibition—we'd both ride. Please, Chris. Bring Weasel and ride, too."

Christine smiled slyly. "I'll ride if you'll go to the dance afterwards."

"It's a deal." Fannie grinned, shaking Christine's hand to seal the bargain. "Now, I got to get back and help Ma churn." As she stepped up onto

Brownie, the hem of her divided riding skirt, soaked with dew from the grass, clung to her boot tops. "These blasted long skirts." She swatted the ample material with her reins. "Sometimes I think I'd like to swipe some of Walter's pants."

Christine giggled and patted her own tousled hair in mock conceit. "Pants? Why, Fannie Sperry, how you do carry on."

"See you in Wolf Creek," Fannie called as they reined their mounts in opposite directions. "Better watch out, 'cause I'm going to beat the pants off you—I mean, the skirt."

Christine waved her hat. "Don't be too sure about that." The girls' laughter floated back over the high corral.

When Fannie got back to the ranch she found that two horse buyers, who had ridden over from Craig to do business with her father, had accepted her mother's invitation to share their noon meal. "You all coming over to Wolf Creek and watch me ride next Saturday?" Conversation stopped at Fannie's unexpected brashness. "Chris and me are going to ride bucking horses at the exhibition Mr. Anson is getting up."

Rachel, passing a bowl of gravy, held it suspended in midair. "What bucking horses?"

"Chris will ride her black bronc, Weasel. He's a real ornery cuss, and I'll ride Chinook, my new wild stallion. Walter can help ear him down. Arthur, too, if he's back from his shoeing job by then." Fannie speared a bite of potato onto her fork. "Well, don't any of you want to come?"

"No, Fannie." Her mother wore the frown that always meant business. "You girls can't go over there and ride with the men."

"Why not? We ride as good as any of those cowpokes."

"Fannie!" Bertha chastised as she carried the coffeepot around the table, filling empty cups. "What will people think?"

"They'd think we knew a thing or two about horses."

"Now, don't get snippy," her father cautioned. "We know you can ride. It's just that it doesn't look right for a girl to be exhibiting herself like that."

"But I promised Mr. Anson . . ." Fannie pleaded. She turned to her mother. "Please, Ma. Just this one time."

Rachel looked at Datus. Datus shrugged. Rachel shook her head. "Fannie, what are we going to do with you?"

"Let her ride, Ma," Walter piped up, excited at the prospect of seeing Fannie ride the young stallion.

"I'd sure like to see it," one of the horse buyers said, helping himself to a slab of Bertha's lemon pie. He winked at Datus. "Maybe we can scare up a wager or two."

"It's easy money if you bet on Fannie," Walter offered. "Never seen her throwed yet."

"Don't be too sure," Datus said. "Christine can sit a bronc as well as anyone I know."

Fannie could see her parents were getting used to the idea. "Chris's pa won't let her ride unless I do."

Rachel sighed. "Well, just this once. But you'll have to halterbreak that stallion first to get him over there."

Fannie beamed. "Sure, Ma."

After chores that evening, Fannie and Walter rode up to the blind corral. They found Chinook sleek and testy, his coat luminous in the twilight. Fannie rode into the corral, tossed a lasso over his neck, and dallied the rope to Brownie's saddle horn. The wild horse pulled back, digging his feet into the rocky soil. Walter, on Elsie, approached with a hackamore, but each time he tried to get it over the nose, Chinook reared, shaking his head and squealing in defiance.

"Don't be that way, Chinook," Fannie coaxed. "We don't want to have to choke you down." But before long she could see that was the only way they would ever get a hackamore on him, and she nudged Brownie back to tighten the lasso around the stallion's neck. Chinook struggled, straining against the rope, but Brownie stood rigid, keeping it taut, slowly edging backward. The wild horse bellowed, his nostrils flared. Then, deep guttural noises came from his throat. The lasso was cutting off his air. Fannie glanced at Walter. "Get ready with that hackamore."

Eyes wild and nostrils flared, Chinook reared in panic, thrashing his head from side to side, wheezing as the rope constricted his windpipe. Suddenly, he went down, out cold. Fannie slackened the rope, while Walter sprang from Elsie to slip the hackamore over the prostrate horse's head and buckle it.

"Stand back," Fannie said. "He'll be madder'n ever when he comes to." She swung onto Brownie once again, dallying the hackamore's 12-foot lead rope around the saddle horn as Chinook regained his senses and clamored to his feet.

He reared, hoofs thrashing the air, then planted his feet firmly, irritated by the strange straps around his nose and ears. But Fannie kept moving, first to one side, then the other, gently playing Brownie's weight against the rope. The horse soon discovered that the pressure on his head lessened when he moved forward. And each time he eased his feet toward her, Fannie rewarded him with slack. Before darkness crept up the mountain from the valley below, Chinook warily began to follow the slackened rope around the corral.

"He's smart, all right," Fannie said, riding in close to flip the buckle and pull the hackamore away. The wild horse snorted, then raced to the far end of the corral. "We'll get him over to Wolf Creek just as easy as pie."

The day before the exhibition, Fannie led Chinook down to the ranch and into the home corral. "I'm putting a saddle on him right now," she announced as she snubbed him to the center post and went to the barn to fetch her saddle. "You better saddle up Elsie in case I need some help."

Walter looked surprised. "Don't you want to save him for tomorrow? He'll do his best bucking when he first feels the saddle."

"Maybe, but what if he's a weak bucker? You know how easy he took to the lead."

"Ma, you better get out here," Walter shouted toward the house. "Fannie's fixin' to ride the gray stallion." Rachel hurried from the kitchen, drying her hands on her apron.

The wary animal stood motionless, ears laid back, as Fannie cautiously approached and hoisted the saddle into place. A shiver twitched his hide when she caught the cinch beneath his belly and half-hitched the latigo. After a quick tug on the cinch, she stepped up into the saddle. The wild horse's eyes rolled back, his legs stiffened.

"Let him go!" Fannie cried. Walter released the lead rope from the snubbing post and thrust it into Fannie's hand. Chinook's head dropped. He bucked into a quick and powerful high roll that nearly toppled his rider. Fannie leaned into the move, tugging the lead to raise his head. Up it came. He reared, twisting, churning the dust, then bucked again, higher than the fence, arching to the left.

Fannie's body whipped. The tug on her shoulder and arm jerked her off balance, but she continued to grip the lead as the horse managed another frenzied lunge to the left. Fannie's head bobbed. She couldn't see. She felt her equilibrium going. She grabbed for the saddle horn.

"Get me off," she yelled.

Walter spurred Elsie in close. Before Chinook could begin another fierce effort, Fannie grabbed Walter's saddle horn and pulled herself from the wild horse onto Elsie's dependable withers. She clung there while Walter reined the mare to the opposite side of the corral.

Chinook bucked toward them, bellowing and kicking, empty stirrups flapping. Rachel, waiting with the lariat, threw a loop over his neck, and Walter soon had him snubbed to the post once again. While Fannie slipped off the hackamore and lasso, Walter released the cinch and pulled the saddle away. Chinook snorted, shook his mane, and trotted along the fence, kicking both hind legs defiantly one last time.

"Well, what do you think?" Fannie grinned.

"He'll do," Rachel said, ". . . if you're set on making a spectacle of yourself."

Walter grinned. "Only tomorrow, Fannie, don't grab the saddle horn."

That night, as a bright slice of moon cast its light across the floor of the back bedroom, Fannie lay awake listening to her sisters' quiet breathing in the double bed next to her cot. What great luck, she thought, to have a bronc like Chinook to ride in the exhibition. What a bucker. When Fannie finally slept, she dreamed of bucking horses.

"Fannie, time to get a move on." The sun was well up when she heard her mother's call. The aroma of frying bacon wafting from the kitchen told her Rachel was fixing breakfast for her, long after the others had eaten. She jumped up and hurried into the kitchen.

"Why did you let me sleep so late?" She poured hot water from the teakettle into the washpan and added cool water from the water bucket to wash her face before taking her usual place at the big table.

"You need your strength today." Her mother placed a steaming plate of bacon and eggs in front of her. "Chinook tends to veer to the left on those high bucks."

"I noticed." Fannie gulped her coffee.

Rachel fetched Fannie's riding skirt from a pile of mending on the sewing machine. "Here, I cleaned up your skirt. You had mud on it from here to Sunday."

Walter poked his head in the kitchen doorway. "Hurry up, Fannie. I got a rope on him."

Datus came in and took his turn at the sink. "Do you think Fannie can handle that stallion?" he asked, reaching for the towel.

"She'll be careful." Rachel cleared Fannie's plate from the table. "Arthur and Walter will be there to help if she gets in trouble." But Datus's worried expression remained.

With the team hitched to the two-seated spring wagon, and the food hamper, a tall crock of lemonade, and hay for the horses stowed in back, Arthur took the driver's seat beside his father, while Rachel, Carrie, and Bertha climbed onto the rear seat. Datus flicked the lines, and the team started off.

Fannie, on Brownie, dallied the rope that anchored Chinook to the procession. Walter rode Elsie beside the stallion's right flank.

They wound among the pines down the mountain slope and onto the flats. With the wagon and the wild horse, they couldn't go directly to Wolf Creek over the Beartooth and across the Herrin ranch as they often did on horseback. This time they would have to go around past Mitchell and through the pass, a distance of about 15 miles. Bumping along Prickly Pear Valley next to the Big Belt range, the Sperrys scanned the sharp outline of the landmark mountain that rose above their ranch.

"Folks in Helena are calling our Beartooth 'The Sleeping Giant'," Datus said. He gazed up at the crest. "From a distance it does sort of look like a giant resting on his back. A sleeping giant's a fit symbol for this part of the country." Datus drew a deliberate, invigorating breath of the early morning air. "After twelve years as a state, Montana's still dozing, still dreaming of things to come."

"Yeah," Arthur agreed. "But it's going to wake up one of these days and become a state to be reckoned with."

"You're right, son. And not just in mining and ranching. There'll be opportunities for business, even national politics . . ."

"It's happening already, Pa. More and more people . . ."

"Let's not encourage any more settlers. It's overcrowded as it is."

Fannie veered out of earshot as Chinook balked, and she and Walter had to urge the stallion along the dusty road. She was glad she didn't have to listen to another discussion between Arthur and her father. They were forever spouting facts and figures they had read, then getting hot under the collar as they disagreed on what it all meant. Arthur didn't love horses the way she and Walter did. She couldn't see why. She felt alive with a good horse under her, and she knew every fox den and prairie-dog hole, every prickly pear patch and rock outcropping, every gully and creek bed in the area. Still, even with Walter's help, getting the wild stallion over to Wolf Creek challenged all her skills.

Wolf Creek lay in a deep valley, its few buildings clustered on either side of the wide, swift current that tumbled over a rocky streambed toward the Missouri. Fannie's excitement heightened as they joined the gathering of horses, wagons, and buggies maneuvering into position around an open field at the edge of the settlement. At one side, a stock pen had been constructed, and Fannie spotted Christine's bronc, Weasel, milling among the bucking horses confined in it.

"Howdy, Datus. Miz Sperry. Howdy, Fannie." Dave Anson, the Mitchell station master, called to them from where he stood talking with a group of ranchers near the gate. Joe and N. D., pulling their family's carriage into the spectators' circle, waved to the Sperrys. While Arthur drove the spring wagon to an empty spot beside the Hilgers, Fannie and Walter headed for the stock pen and turned Chinook in with the other broncs.

Christine, out of breath, came running to meet them, her blond curls tied back in a loose cluster above a bright blue shirtwaist. "We had a devil of a time getting Weasel over here."

"Chinook wasn't much interested in coming, either." Fannie brushed at the dust on her skirt and boots, rolled down the sleeves of her calico shirt, and flipped the red ribbons tied to the ends of her braids back over her shoulders. As the girls walked toward the field, they passed a group of neighboring ranchers leaning against the fence.

"Them are some broncs," one said, nodding toward the pen. "That silver-gray and the black together are just about as pretty a pair as you two girls." He took a puff on his pipe. "I seen you ridin' to school for years now. When I'd spot that cloud of dust coming across the flat, I knowed right away it was the two of you."

Fannie felt herself blushing, but the man continued. "The more you growed and the prettier you got, the better you was ridin' them horses."

Another man with a grandfatherly smile nodded. "I wouldn't miss this here exhibition for nothin'."

Fannie and Christine smiled at the warmth of the comments as they strolled on toward the wagons. "Lots of folks seem to know about us." Fannie returned a nod from the two Craig horse buyers. She also noticed but ignored the young cowboys poking fun at each other near the gate. Some, including N. D., would ride broncs in the exhibition.

The girls exchanged glances expressing how wonderful it all was. At the Sperry wagon, they found Carrie and Bertha had draped a tablecloth over the tailgate to lay out sandwiches, and they joined the family, chatting and joking with folks in the nearby wagons while they ate their midday meal.

Then Anson stepped up onto a buggy shaft, beating on a tin bucket with a stick. "I hope you've all had time to finish your eats," he called out. "We're gonna start the bucking-horse riding."

Fannie felt a ripple of goose bumps as N. D. strode onto the field, the first cowboy up. He'd brought a wild pinto fresh from the mountains. Joe, on a big roan, hazed the rangy brown-and-white bronc that trotted along the line of onlookers. The bronc bellowed as Arthur grabbed his ears and a third wrangler secured the hackamore and saddle in place.

Fannie and Christine edged forward to get a better look. "That's about the mangiest pinto I ever saw," Christine commented.

"You can't judge a bucking horse by his hide," Fannie cautioned.

Joe kicked his boot from his right stirrup so N. D. could step up into it and be carried into position to lower himself onto the saddled bronc. When Arthur released the pinto's ears and scrambled back, the pinto exploded, his legs spread-eagled high above the ground. N. D. clutched the lead, his right arm flopping. A high jackknife from the bronc, and N. D. hit the dirt. He bounded to his feet, shaking his head, and the spectators applauded his effort.

The second rider lasted only a few seconds longer on a snuffy brown horse.

Christine had drawn the number three spot. Her brothers, Albert and John, hazed Weasel onto the field. While John held a grip on the black's ears, Al cinched up the saddle. Then he took a piece of rope and tied the stirrups together beneath the horse's belly.

"What's he doing?" Fannie cried. "Why is he hobbling Christine's stirrups?" The alarm in her voice was lost in the noise of the crowd eager to see the young girl ride.

"Now, Fannie. If she wants to ride with her stirrups hobbled, it's not your concern." Rachel looked worried, too.

"But it is! She could get hung up." Fannie felt a wave of panic. "And she can't compete with the cowboys if her stirrups are strapped down. That makes it too easy."

"Her legs ain't as strong as yours," Rachel said.

"But she always rides slick saddle." Fannie nibbled at her fingernails. "She never told me she was going to hobble her stirrups."

Joe's roan moved in, carrying Christine to the black bronco. The men scattered and, at Christine's signal, John unhanded the ears. Christine's blue sleeves fluttered behind the flying mane as Weasel reared, his front feet churning the air. His hind legs buckled.

"He's going over!" Fannie gripped her mother's arm. But Weasel righted himself and came down with all four feet tight as a dime.

"Ride 'em, Chris!" The young cowboys hooted their delight.

"What's a young girl doing on a bucking horse?" someone said.

Again Weasel pogoed up. Fannie could see the horizon of the far mountains beneath his belly. "Holy Moses," she murmured.

The black bronc came back to earth, twisting and snorting, the graceful rider's body whipping with each lunge. But Christine stuck till the horse began to tire. At her signal, Joe rode in to pull her from the saddle and set her down on firm ground. Albert hazed Weasel back to the pen. The crowd cheered. The young cowboys stomped and cuffed each other. Fannie ran to Christine.

"Chris!" She felt on the verge of tears. "How come you hobbled your stirrups?"

"Pa made me." Christine didn't seem happy about the restriction. "He wouldn't let me ride Weasel unless I hobbled."

"But, Chris . . ."

"I know how you feel, Fannie, but I had to."

"But you could have been hurt. Weasel almost went over backwards. If you'd got your boot caught . . ."

"You can get hurt riding slick saddle, too, Fannie." Christine seemed defensive. "Besides, all lady riders hobble their stirrups these days."

"Not all," Fannie said, defiantly.

More determined now to show that she could ride slick saddle with the best of the cowboys, Fannie's heart pounded wildly as her turn came. Walter and Arthur had blindfolded Chinook to calm him while they eared him down and cinched up her saddle. The stallion's only movement was a tense rippling of muscle beneath the cinch.

Fannie stepped onto Joe's stirrup and was carried into position beside the silver-gray horse. Grasping the lead rope, she swung her leg over the saddle and settled her boots into the stirrups.

"Ready!" she called. Her red ribbons flashed as Chinook whirled away. He bucked, twisting to the left, then heaved into an unexpected sideways plunge. She tugged the lead to get his head up, and he responded with another high jump, again to the left. Fannie was ready for this. She sat the savage twist, her right arm high above her head.

"Let 'em buck, Fannie."

"Watch that left twist." Her mother's voice drowned in the uproar.

Chinook bellowed, straining against Fannie's hold on the lead, his head chopping between his forelegs. He pitched high into a merciless snapping roll. Fannie's seat left the saddle for a brief moment, but her long legs quickly regained their grip as the bronc thudded to earth, whirling and snorting.

"Good Lord, she's riding slick saddle, just like the men."

"She's got grit, that girl."

Fannie stuck through another series of savage twists before the wild horse slackened. One glance from her told Joe to make his move. He swooped in, grabbed the back of her belt, and dragged her from the frenzied stallion. She clung to his saddle horn, her feet dangling along the ground beside the roan until Joe could get her out of range and release his grip. She gained her balance and waved to the crowd. Shouts of approval rose from the spectators. Whistles and hoots came from the cowboys.

Christine came running up. "Fannie, what a ride! That Chinook is something."

"Weasel didn't exactly fizzle out," Fannie said.

Rachel grasped her daughter's shoulders, studying her eyes. "Are you all right?"

"I'm fine, Ma." Fannie grinned. "But I thought he had me there for a minute. That left twist is a doozie."

Rachel sighed. "Thank heavens it's over."

They cheered the remaining riders, then waited as Anson and two ranchers huddled to determine the winner. There seemed to be disagreement. Finally, the three men turned and walked toward them.

"Fannie's the winner," Anson shouted, taking her hand and holding it above her head. "She stuck the longest and gave as fine a demonstration of bronc stomping as I've seen in a long time."

Fannie knew she was grinning like a possum, but she couldn't stop.

Anson continued. "Folks, I think we should show our appreciation for this fine young rider." He dug into his pocket, then took off his hat and dropped a coin into it, passing the hat to the front row of spectators. After the hat had circulated, he counted out the proceeds, and Fannie had to cup both hands to hold the money he poured into them. "Two dollars and thirty-five cents," he announced.

"Look, Ma," Fannie said as they left the field. "They gave me money."

"Well, make it last," Rachel said curtly, "because this is the last time you're going to do anything so foolish again."

"Foolish? What do you mean? I rode him, didn't I, just like I said I would?"

"I mean you've got to stop thinking about bucking horses. I heard some rude remarks when you climbed onto that bronco. Riding and breaking horses for the ranch is one thing. A public display is another." Rachel's chin had that determined slant. "Besides, it's too risky."

"Risky? But, Ma, I've never been hurt . . ."

"Fannie, you're through riding bucking horses, and that's that."

A Horsewoman's Dilemma  4

Though Fannie didn't ride in any other bucking-horse exhibitions that summer, her reputation as a horsewoman grew. And so did she. Her figure rounded to a slender five-foot-seven. Many a young cowboy's head was turned by her earnest blue eyes under thick dark brows, her high cheekbones, square jaw, and attractive mouth. She blushed when visitors commented on her blossoming beauty, but she glowed with pride when talk turned to her strength and grace in the saddle.

Summer browned into a brisk autumn, and once again the Sperrys prepared for the coming cold. But this year would be special. Carrie and Joe planned a January wedding. Rachel stepped up her hours at the sewing machine, and Carrie took instruction in Joe's Catholic faith. The week before the ceremony, Carrie sorted and packed her things to be taken to Judge Hilger's ranch, where she and Joe would live with his brother through the winter taking care of the stock while his parents and sisters spent the cold months at their home in Helena.

The morning of the wedding, January 29, 1902, the Sperrys rose early, and while Arthur and Walter did chores in the frosty predawn light, the girls dressed for the ceremony. Carrie's fingers trembled as she fumbled with the tiny buttons on the bodice of her pale-gray wool dress.

"Here, let me help you," Bertha offered, buttoning the handsome dress for her sister and adjusting the white-lace collar that framed Carrie's flushed face.

"You look real nice," Fannie said, pulling her old blue serge middy over her new union suit, lifting the skirt to tuck the underwear legs into her boots.

When everyone was finally ready, they climbed into the straw-filled wagon. The 20-mile wagon ride to Helena behind the high-stepping team seemed long and cold despite lap robes and the hot stones Rachel had prepared to keep their feet warm. "We're lucky there's not much snow," Datus remarked.

At the tiny St. Andrews church, on a hillside overlooking Helena, Fannie paused outside to gaze over the town. Through the winter-bare branches of trees lining the streets, she studied the brick business buildings, the stone mansions of leading citizens, and the frame houses of the working people. In the distance she could see the Beartooth, its Sleeping Giant outlined against the cold sky. The familiar mountain seemed far away from this bustling community, this church.

Inside, stained-glass windows filtered the pale light into prisms of color, and Fannie studied the gilded crucifix that hung above the altar. At one side, surrounded by carved angels, a life-size statue of the Virgin Mary stood with arms outstretched. As Fannie seated herself with her family on one of the rough pews, a woman wearing a prim black dress and small round eyeglasses sat down at the foot-pedaled organ. Music and the smell of incense filled the church and, as the bridal couple knelt at the altar, Fannie's heart swelled with the beauty of it all.

She listened to the words the priest offered for the bride and groom and for their families and the few friends who had traveled through the cold to attend the ceremony. And all at once, Carrie and Joe stood smiling at each other, and Fannie realized the ceremony had ended. She saw tears in her parents' eyes. Carrie cried, too, as she hugged them all, while Joe gave out cigars to the men. After coffee and cake served by the church ladies in the vestibule and a flurry of hugs and well-wishes, the newlyweds climbed into their new one-horse shay, a gift from the Hilgers, pulled by a fine-looking sorrel mare, a gift from the Sperrys.

The happy good-byes quieted to the sound of Rachel clearing her throat and announcing they should start for home, too. When they arrived, long after dark, the house seemed emptier. Fannie and Bertha sat down on

Carrie's side of the bed as if to fill the empty place. After a while, Bertha got up and began to rearrange the drawers in the highboy.

In the days that followed, Fannie felt the impact of her sister's departure. Carrie's outdoor work became her responsibility. Walter, taller than Fannie now, slim as a lodgepole pine and strong, had taken over for Arthur, who had hired out to a blacksmith in Townsend. Walter would not return to school that spring.

"But it's not fair," Fannie protested. "You're the one who should be going back to school. You may be only thirteen, but you understand things. You like to study."

"It's okay, Sis," Walter assured her. "I read better'n the teacher anyhow." And it was true. He spent hours each night with his books beside the kerosene lamp in the front room. "Sometimes we have to do things in life that we don't want to," he said, trying to conceal his disappointment.

With Carrie gone, work piled up fast for Walter and Fannie. And Datus sold the silver-gray stallion.

For once, Fannie said little. She knew that it was the only way her father could meet mounting expenses. Chinook was ridden away by his new owner shortly before her fifteenth birthday on March 27, 1902, just as her mother began the annual mending and remaking of clothing for the new school term.

"I'm almost the oldest kid in the school," Fannie grumbled, standing on the woodbox so her mother could pin the raveled hem in her riding skirt.

"I know." Rachel held several straight pins between her lips. "But you'll soon have your eighth-grade diploma."

"But why me?" Fannie pleaded. "Why not Walter? He's the one who should be going to school. Let him get the diploma."

"Walter must help his father." Fannie heard the regret in her mother's voice and pursued the matter no further. There *were* things in life that we didn't like, but had to do. When the term began the first week in April, she and Rainbow began the 6-mile ride morning and afternoon that had once been the highlight of each school day. But this year, Christine did not return to school. She, too, could no longer be spared from home duties. Without Christine and Walter, school was no longer fun.

One day in late June as Fannie rode Rainbow home from school, Dave Anson stepped from the depot porch and called to her. "Hey there, Fannie. How's the ridin'?"

"Still in the saddle." She rode over to the stocky railroad man.

"We're gettin' up another roundup over the Fourth." His big hand shielded his eyes from the sun as he gazed up at the girl on the sleek pinto. "We want you and the Synness girl to ride those broncs again this year."

"Pa sold the gray stallion," Fannie said. "And Chris's dad won't let her on Weasel since he threw Al and busted his collarbone." But Fannie had another idea. "How about us putting on a pony-express race instead? We can do it just like Buffalo Bill does in his Wild West show."

"Well, now, that would be an attraction," Anson said. "'Specially with you two girls doin' the ridin'. Got the horses for it?" Fannie nodded. "Then why don't we plan on it?"

"Thanks, Mr. Anson." Fannie galloped Rainbow back toward the Beartooth. Life suddenly looked brighter.

"Mr. Anson wants Chris and me to ride a pony-express exhibition on the Fourth," she announced as she entered the log house.

"As long as it's not bucking horses." Rachel bustled about the kitchen.

Datus, washing up for supper, grinned over his towel. "Do you think folks'll turn out just to watch you and Christine jump on and off of horses in front of the schoolhouse?"

"You betcha," Walter said. "They're pretty doggone fast."

"We'll have our horses saddled and ready." Fannie's words poured out as she imagined the action. "I'll start on Brownie 'cause he's quick as a jackrabbit, and he'll get me out ahead. When we come around, I'll switch to Elsie. We'll ride four rounds altogether."

"That sounds swell." Walter's eyes were bright with excitement. "And I'll be your relay man."

The timothy and wild grasses on the Sperry place stood dry and ready for cutting, so when the next day dawned bright and hot, Datus gave his weather assessment as usual. "Good weather for haying." He drove the Percheron team pulling the sickle mower to the upper meadow, Walter trailing him with the mule team hitched to the dump rake. All day the buzzing of flies and honeybees combined lazily with the whir of the mower blades as Datus mowed back and forth in the warm sun and Walter raked the swaths of new-mown hay into long windrows that lay across the meadow in plump piles.

That evening, father and son appeared at the supper table with two-toned faces—beet-red below the hat line, pale as a turnip above.

"It'll make a fair crop," Datus remarked, coughing from the hayfield dust. "Maybe one of these days we'll get ahead enough to buy that adjoining quarter-section of railroad land."

"We could sure bring in a crop then," Rachel agreed.

"We all got to be at it bright and early tomorrow," Datus said, "if we're to finish while the weather holds." Then glancing at Fannie, "And if we're to make that pony-express race in Mitchell on the Fourth."

Fannie grinned. Her father always seemed to find a way to make things work out right.

Next morning the Sperrys again drove the two teams up to the high meadow. Datus hitched the Percherons to the wooden-toothed bull rake that would sweep the windrows of cut hay onto the beaver-slide stacker, and Walter harnessed the mules to the stacker, driving them forward to activate the pulley that lifted the hay and dropped it into a pile. Atop the growing haystack, Rachel and Fannie, wearing work-worn dresses and battered straw hats, forked the fragrant crop into a strong, compact loaf shape that would shed water and withstand wind.

By late morning the stack stood nearly 10 feet high. As Datus pulled up to the stacker with another load, he heard a sharp cracking sound, and hay began to clog the rake. "Tarnation," he muttered. "Busted a rake tooth."

"I'll get it, Pa." Walter left the mules standing and hurried over to clear the rake.

"Don't move, Walter!" Datus's warning came sharp. "Rattler!"

Walter froze. He heard the whir of the snake's rattle somewhere near his feet. Before anyone else could move, Rachel slid from the stack, pitchfork in hand, and ran toward Walter. She raised the fork high and stabbed it into the windrow directly in front of her son.

Fannie, who had scrambled down behind her mother, saw the snake curling around the pitchfork. One tine had pierced its body. Deadly fangs convulsed from the gaping jaws. While her mother held the speared snake against the rake shaft, Fannie smashed at the head with the handle of her pitchfork until the writhing stopped. Walter, pale through his sunburn, sank onto a pile of hay.

Datus climbed down off his machine, pulled a pocketknife from his overalls, and sliced off the snake's rattle. "Twelve buttons," he said, holding it up for all to see. He handed the trophy to Walter, then picked up the limp snake by the tail and put it into the rake's toolbox. "This old granddaddy will make a nice belt for you, Walter."

Datus coughed and wheezed uncomfortably throughout the day but refused his wife's suggestion that he let the others finish the job. They worked until sunset despite the cracked tooth on the bull rake, then pulled the ailing machine down to the barn. While Fannie helped her father unharness and grain the horses and mules, Rachel lifted the dead snake from the toolbox.

"I'll skin this after supper," she said, hanging it over the clothesline next to Bertha's washing, before heading for the house to peel potatoes. Walter let the waiting cows into the barn for milking, and Datus went to work on the rake. Fannie fed the chickens, and later, cranked the separator. The long July twilight had deepened to darkness when she finally poured the fresh cream into a can and took it to the creek.

At supper Datus labored for breath, his asthma heightened by the day's dust. "Arthur will be back tomorrow," he wheezed. "I guess I better have him take over for me."

In the stifling heat that hung over the Beartooth the following morning, Arthur came riding up just as the family made ready to start for the high meadow.

"It's about time you showed up," Bertha teased. Ready to replace her ailing father in the hayfield, she had hitched up her long skirt and petticoat above her knees by rolling them at the waist.

"What's this? You look like one of those naughty dancing girls I saw in *The Police Gazette*." Arthur gave her skirt a playful tug as he boosted her off the mended bull rake and climbed onto the seat himself to maneuver the clumsy machine to the upper meadow.

"I'd like to see you wear these hot skirts." Bertha tossed her head haughtily. "See how you'd stand the heat."

Fannie grinned to think of her sister as a naughty dancing girl. But hitching up the skirts was a good idea. She, too, hitched hers up to her knees.

Rachel frowned. "You girls pull down your skirts. Someone might see you."

"Oh, Ma, it's hot. And who'll see us out here?" Bertha tied a handkerchief around her brow to keep sweat out of her eyes.

"Someone might come." Their mother fastened her straw hat to the bun of her hair with a long hat pin. Then she opened the collar of her high-necked calico and pushed up the long sleeves as if to show her daughters the proper amount of ventilation allowed. "Besides, Arthur and Walter are here," she whispered. The girls exchanged looks of resignation as they let their skirts fall to their ankles and climbed onto the mended rake for a ride up to the field.

"Wait," Datus said as he came from the kitchen. "Take this." He put his Colt 45 in the rake's toolbox. "You might see some cousins of that critter we killed yesterday."

The family finished stacking in the early afternoon, encountering no more rattlers. With another cutting before fall, the upper meadow's twenty acres assured a bumper crop.

The Sperry women spent the rest of the afternoon in the kitchen preparing food for the next day's festivities in Mitchell. Arthur groomed Brownie and Elsie, the horses Fannie would ride in the pony-express race, and replaced a missing nail in Elsie's shoe. Datus, away from the dusty field, breathed easier, and after supper he helped Walter make a firecracker by packing gunpowder into a small ginger tin. Walter would be allowed to set it off during the celebration.

Again that year Mitchell's Fourth of July celebration centered around an exhibition of bucking-horse riding. The crowd, seated on wagons and buggies lined up along the Northern Pacific track, showed the usual enthusiasm for each event. Fannie thought Anson would never get around to calling the pony-express race, and she began to wish she were riding a bucking horse instead. But finally, as the long rays of late-afternoon sun streaked across the flats, she and Christine stood front and center awaiting the starting signal. Christine's yellow shirtwaist and her own blue gingham provided accents of color against the dry, brown grasses and muted sage.

Anson droned the rules. "Now you girls will ride four rounds, changing horses at the end of each round. You must clear the markers we've put out to show the course. Your helpers will stand by with the fresh mounts, but you must dismount, take the reins of the next horse, and remount by yourselves. Remember, every second counts."

The crowd stirred expectantly, giving full attention to this added attraction. Anson held a red handkerchief in the air. Nearby, Walter stood holding Brownie's reins. John Synness held Christine's Sandy.

"When I drop this, that's your signal to get goin'," Anson instructed the girls. Fannie's dark brows knitted into a determined frown, and Christine bit her lower lip in anticipation of the exertion required.

The red handkerchief dropped. Fannie dashed forward, snatched the reins from Walter and swung onto Brownie's saddle, digging her spurs into the horse's flanks. Just as quickly, Christine was aboard Sandy, and the big bay galloped onto the course. A whoop of encouragement rose from the onlookers. Christine took the lead at the first turn, but Fannie pulled alongside on the straightaway. The two horses pounded around the markers. Into the stretch, they vied neck and neck.

"Come on, Fannie!"

"Come on, Chris!"

Brownie nosed across the change mark ahead of Sandy, and Fannie, quickly dismounting, required only two steps to grab Elsie's reins, swing onto the mare, and spur out onto the course. But Christine, remounted on a chestnut named Buster, soon closed the gap between them, pulled ahead, and arrived first at the change point to end the second round. In an instant, she was off Buster, aboard Sandy once more, and heading onto the course.

Fannie galloped into the change, hauled Elsie to a stop, and bounded onto Brownie. She felt the horse surge ahead with all the speed he could muster. But he couldn't catch Christine's bay.

At the last change, as Fannie started to swing off, a cowboy at the edge of the crowd threw up his arms, and Brownie shied. Fannie lost her balance and dismounted awkwardly. "Whoa, boy." Patting the horse's neck to settle him, she caught up Elsie's reins and jumped into the saddle.

"You can do it, Elsie," she shouted. The faithful mare galloped onto the course. But Fannie had lost time. Buster was fast, and Christine rode expertly around the markers, finishing a few lengths ahead. She dismounted as Fannie came into the finish and jumped to the ground.

"Nice going, Chris," Fannie said sincerely. "That Buster can really move."

Christine grinned. "I've been workin' him."

Dave Anson raised his hand to quiet the onlookers. "I think we've got a winner here, folks." He took Christine's hand and held it above her head. "Here's our champion. Christine Synness by 4 lengths." He placed four silver dollars in her hand. Then he turned and took Fannie's hand and held it high. "And here's our second-place winner." The crowd laughed.

Fannie laughed, too, but Anson placed two coins in her hand saying, "Just the same, here's two silver dollars that says you rode a fine race, Fannie."

"Gee, thanks." She hadn't expected this.

"Girls, I'm helping out with the bucking events down at the state fair," Anson added. "You two want to sign up?"

Fannie and Christine glanced at each other. Ride at the state fair? Now that would really be something. Christine shrugged her shoulders. "Why not?"

Rachel, who had overheard, looked sharply at her daughter.

"Please, Ma," Fannie said quietly, leading her mother aside. "I can't quit riding. You know that. Besides . . ." She looked around to be sure no one could hear, then continued in a whisper. ". . . I'm the best. Everyone says so. Even slick saddle, I can beat them all. I'm a horsewoman, Ma." Fannie had never spoken more convincingly or sounded more mature. "Don't you see? I can't quit now."

Rachel tenderly touched Fannie's cheek. "I know you're the best."

And Fannie knew she had her mother's permission.

Anson waited for an answer. "Well, girls, how about it?"

"Sure, we'll ride," Fannie said, rejoining the group. Then, under her breath to Christine, she added, "Wild horses couldn't keep us away."

A muffled explosion cracked through the noise of the crowd. Startled spectators tittered, and Fannie knew that Walter's firecracker, sounding from behind the depot, celebrated her new opportunity.

In October the Montana State Fair in Helena added two fifteen-year-old girls to its roster of bucking-horse riders. Though Fannie and Christine took no prize money, they rode well, and word spread to other communities. They received invitations to ride in bucking events at the Powell County Fair in Deer Lodge and at other local roundups and stampedes. When classes at the Mitchell school conflicted with these riding dates, Fannie played hooky, and the following summer her formal schooling ended without the coveted eighth-grade diploma when she left school to ride in a succession of bucking-horse competitions.

Over Labor Day 1903, she and Christine rode broncos at the Gallatin County Fair at Bozeman, the first of what was to become an annual event. The girls were a novelty in the otherwise all-male bucking-horse event, and they drew for their horses right along with the other bronc busters.

One seasoned buster grumbled after Fannie finished her ride on a spunky Appaloosa. "Should put you women in your own event. You're gonna get your britches dirtied if you try to ride these outlaws."

Another agreed. "It don't make us look too good when you sage hens ride our broncs."

The girls ignored the comments, but lost out on the prize money.

After riding at a Billings roundup in September, Fannie and Christine felt like seasoned troupers when the Montana State Fair again rolled around in October. The Sperrys camped out of their wagon on the open field behind the grandstand, along with others who had come to take part in the fair. The girls looked forward to the bucking events, which featured veteran-rider Jake Ross from Toston, Montana, who was generally acknowledged to be the number one bronc buster in the West. Around the first evening's campfire, Fannie and Christine sat with Datus and Rachel in the firelight glow listening to the wranglers talk.

"Yes, sir," one said, "I've known ol' Jake Ross more years than you can shake a stick at. He's held the championship of Montana for years now."

"Yup," another leathered cowpoke agreed. "Put ol' Jake on a tough bronc, and you've got yourself a show."

"They say he's the only buster ever rode that Belgrade Bull."

A third cowpoke hunkered down beside them. "I saw that ride. That

Holstein weighed sixteen-hundred-and-fifty pounds. Good riders'd travel two, three hundred mile just to try him. He'd throw 'em before they got seated, and with his head snubbed to a post." The cowboy stared into the fire as if seeing a reenactment of Ross's ride. "But ol' Jake rode that bull to a dog-raw finish."

"Jake's good all right. An' they got a mean bunch of broncs and steers for him here. Advertised for ones with killer reputations, the worst there is."

Fannie nudged Christine. "I can't wait to see Jake Ross tackle a bronc. Do you think he can outride *us*?"

Christine whispered back. "Not a chance—unless he draws the Belgrade Bull. That critter's gained four-hundred pounds since we heard the story in Bozeman."

Fannie and Christine received favorable comment on their performances in the bucking events. But Ross remained the main attraction. He rode twenty broncs to a standstill, seven head in thirty-five minutes. Fannie watched his spectacular performance from the sidelines next to Jake's pretty wife, Emma, a small sturdy woman with an earnest manner.

"So you're Fannie Sperry." Emma pushed back the sombrero that shielded her pale green eyes. "I've heard about you."

"You have?" Fannie stared in amazement.

Emma smiled. "Hope we can ride together sometime."

Fanny savored the compliment. "Emma Ross is swell," she told her mother as they headed the wagon back toward the Beartooth. "Rides good, too."

"I'm glad to see there are *ladies* riding at these events." Rachel gave Fannie a sharp look.

"Ma, you know I'd never do anything you and Pa wouldn't be proud of."

Fannie dreaded the coming months of isolation and hard work on the ranch. With winter approaching, the stock had to be brought in where they could be fed and sheltered, and, during the cold months, repairs put off during the busy summer had to be tended to. Fannie and Walter mended and oiled harness and saddle tack. They cleaned out the barn and fixed fence. In February they calved out the heifers, and, in March, the dairy cows.

They set up a line of coyote traps and checked on them every day,

Fannie and her brother Walter exercise their saddle horses.

covering the 4-mile distance on Brownie and Elsie. When snow drifted too deep, they made the rounds on snowshoes, carrying their rifles to finish off a trapped animal or to bring down a predator they spotted skulking the upper woods. Fannie could sight and shoot a wolf almost before Walter could spot it. Though his aim was quick and true, his distance sight was not as keen as his sister's.

"Wish I had your sharp eyes," he said one day. "Then maybe I'd at least get off the first shot once in a while." So Fannie sometimes held her aim until Walter had a chance at the first shot. If he missed, her bullet invariably found its mark.

Relay Racing  5

Fannie spent the morning of her seventeenth birthday, March 27, 1904, sacking out a wild horse in the home corral. She had found the small buckskin mare, weakened from sparse winter grazing, in a snow-filled coulee and had no trouble bringing her in. With gentle handling, the mare accepted the halter, then the bridle and saddle blanket and, finally, the saddle.

Fannie enjoyed this part of breaking a green horse. She flapped a gunnysack around the buckskin's legs and rump, making sudden movements, all the while talking in a quiet reassuring voice. After the mare learned that the motion of the sack was harmless, Fannie tied it to the saddle and let it flap as the buckskin moved around the corral. Later she would tie her old rain slicker to the saddle, allowing it to snap in the wind. Finally, Fannie herself would mount. When a bronco graduated from her training, a dependable saddle horse was added to the family string.

Absorbed in her work, she didn't notice a rider on a palomino coming up the valley until he called to her. "Is this the Sperry place?" She looked up to see a well-dressed man in a sheepskin coat and fine Stetson. Still holding the gunnysack, she came from the corral. The activity had warmed her, despite the chilly March wind, and her heavy denim jacket hung open above her mud-splattered long, divided skirt.

"Yes. I'm Fannie Sperry."

"You're just the young lady I want to see." The small man with reddish mustache wore a muffler knotted below his prominent Adam's apple. He tipped his hat. "I'm Will Johnson from the Capital Stock Food Company in Helena." He held out his hand, and Fannie offered hers, first wiping it on her jacket sleeve.

"My company is sponsoring a relay race this summer, and we'd like to hire you to ride for us. We'll supply a string of Thoroughbreds."

"Thoroughbreds?"

"Yes, our relays will be similar to Buffalo Bill Cody's pony-express races, except, of course, Cody never uses Thoroughbreds."

Rachel appeared from the house, pulling on her mackinaw.

"They want me to ride in women's relay races this summer, Ma." Fannie tossed the gunnysack over the top rail. "Mr. Johnson, here, is offering to pay me."

"I been hearing about your daughter, Miz Sperry. Thought I better sign her up before somebody beats me to it."

"Just where will these races be run?"

"First one will be part of the Wild West show Jake Ross is putting on in Helena July Fourth. After that, we race in Anaconda and Missoula."

"That's pretty far from home." Rachel turned up her collar against the wind.

"We'll arrange accommodations for the girls in each town," Johnson continued. "You're welcome to come along to chaperone if you like."

"I just might do that," Rachel said. "Come on in, Mr. Johnson, and let's hear more about this over some of Fannie's birthday cake. Fannie, call your pa from the barn."

As they gathered around the big kitchen table, Will Johnson explained that the Capital Stock Food Company had agreed to lend their name to the team, but the financing and Thoroughbreds were to come from backers in Butte. "All first-class events," he assured them. "A good opportunity for a rider like Fannie."

"A women's relay race in Jake Ross's show sounds all right. But I know horses ain't the only fast things at them races." Rachel glared at Johnson.

"Mrs. Sperry, I assure you . . ."

"Mr. Johnson, *I* assure *you* . . ." Rachel emphasized her words as she placed a piece of birthday cake before him, "that Fannie will make this trip only under my personal supervision."

So it was arranged. Fannie began her professional career on July 3, 1904, in Helena's Central Park. The Sperrys arrived a day early so she could try out the Thoroughbreds selected for her. She found them fine, sleek animals, fast and responsive. To add to her delight, she learned she would be competing with Emma Ross in the relay.

"Well, Fannie, here we are, riding together just as we hoped." Emma, looking professional in a fringed brown-buckskin outfit, reached over playfully to tilt Fannie's new sombrero to a more becoming angle.

"I'm sure glad to see you, Emma." Fannie felt awkward in the presence of the seasoned racer.

Noise from the crowd nearly drowned out the sound of the announcer's megaphoned voice calling the relay race. Fannie followed the figure in the brown buckskin onto the track that circled the park's baseball diamond. Two large rectangular stalls, open at the long front side where they would make their relay changes, had been set up in front of the bleacher seats. Their first mounts stood waiting, held by attendants.

"Good luck, Fannie." Emma adjusted the wide-buckled belt that adorned her slim torso. Though Fannie was taller, her twenty-two-inch waist rivaled the trim measurements of Emma Ross.

"Good luck to you, too." Fannie smoothed her new navy-serge riding skirt. She had thought it quite spiffy with the white middy and navy neckerchief until she'd seen Emma's buckskins. She adjusted her new sombrero with sweaty hands. The 1-mile track looked smooth and solid.

A voice from the platform began. "The relay race will be in three segments of four miles each. One segment will be run this afternoon, one this evening, and one tomorrow afternoon." The crowd quieted as the starter raised his pistol. "Mounts will be changed every mile, four changes in each segment. Each rider must mount and dismount unassisted. Ready, ladies?"

The starting pistol sounded, and the women swung into their saddles. Fannie's Thoroughbred surged onto the track close behind Emma. Grimacing at the dust and grit flying from the pounding hoofs of Emma's mount, Fannie applied her quirt to close the gap. The horses were well matched for speed, and Fannie knew that the difference would come in the agility with which she changed from one horse to another.

Fannie dons a new hat to begin her professional career riding Thoroughbreds for the Capital Stock Food Company in Helena.

Then her worry shifted. Her horse was running so fast in the stretch, she wasn't sure she could stop him at the stall. But making an educated guess as to when to pull him up, she slid into a stop by her waiting mount, bounded off the tired horse and onto the fresh one, urging the second animal into a fast clip onto the track.

Emma followed her in, but when she jumped from her horse her foot caught in the stirrup. She fell. She got up but didn't remount. Fannie continued around the track, crossing the finish line just as the announcer, shouting through the confusion, confirmed that Emma was injured and could not continue. The crowd groaned.

"I'll be all right," Emma said to ease Fannie's concern. "Just a little bruised." Fannie herself felt stricken as she watched Emma being escorted from the field.

The starter tapped her on the shoulder. "Your time is recorded, Fannie, and we'll try to find a replacement for Mrs. Ross tomorrow."

But no replacement was found, and Fannie's relay event was canceled. Will Johnson walked along with her to the wagon. "I'll see you here next month at the fair before we go on to Anaconda," he said. "We'll pick up some prize money yet." He tipped his Stetson to the Sperrys and was gone.

A week later Walter made the trip to the post office in Mitchell and returned with a stack of newspapers.

"Land sakes!" Rachel exclaimed as she scanned the *Helena Independent*. "Says here you helped introduce the sport of relay racing in Montana." She folded the paper so Fannie could see the article. "Your pa and me won't know how to act with someone famous in the family." She began bustling about the kitchen and, in the way of a celebration, soon had cold tea, fresh-baked bread, butter, and plum preserves on the table.

"Here's something here in the July tenth *Butte InterMountain* that might interest you, Fannie," her father said. Fannie poured the tea, sat down beside him, and read aloud the item he pointed out.

> *Miss Getts Sets World Record Relay Time. The feature of the last day of the carnival of sports at the Anaconda race track yesterday was the [exhibition] race of Miss Margaret Getts, against time, to establish a new world's record for relay racing. Her sister, Miss Dorothy, also a splendid rider, [showed her] fine . . . horsemanship in the two miles she rode to pace Miss Margaret.*

"I hear the Getts sisters are the best," Fannie said. "Listen to this. '*When Miss Margaret left the paddock for the last mile, she was jolted against a post and injured her nose, that member bleeding all the way around the course. Mounted on Good Eye, she went the course like a phantom, her steed never slacking his terrific pace until the wire was passed at 8:18½, a new world's record for the four-mile segment.'*"

Fannie was impressed. "A new world's record! And she kept on going even when she was hurt and bleeding."

Rachel stepped around the table and took the paper. "It was only an exhibition ride, but we'll keep this in the scrapbook," she said, "so you'll remember what time you have to beat."

Cowboy relay races are a new and novel event, the *Independent* reported after Fannie won a second-place gold medal in the Cowboys Relay Race at the Helena State Fair on August 10, 1904. A cowboy from Butte on a fast Thoroughbred had taken first in the race, which featured a mix of Thoroughbreds and cowponies. Rachel displayed the medal on the fireplace mantel and again clipped the item for the scrapbook.

Four days later Fannie and her mother took the train to Anaconda for the opening day of the Montana Circuit Races. Fannie felt some apprehension about riding at the famous Anaconda track. But she felt lucky, too. Not everyone had such an opportunity. Her sombrero, now appropriately broken in, felt comfortable above the large blue bow tying her braids in a loop at the back of her head.

Will Johnson met Fannie and Rachel in Anaconda and drove them in a shiny surrey pulled by two fine black horses to a small rooming house, where the landlady led them up the narrow staircase, opened a door at the end of the hall, and showed them into a high-ceilinged room. Centered on one wall was a huge brass bed, covered with a crazy quilt. Above the bed hung an embroidered sampler that read FORGET ME NOT. A washstand holding a pitcher and bowl with a stack of fresh white towels, a chifforobe, and a rocking chair completed the furnishings. When Rachel nodded her approval, Fannie set the grip at the foot of the bed.

"We serve breakfast at five." The landlady stood with her hands on the hips of her starched apron. "We have a lot of you racing folks here."

Fannie saw a frown come over her mother's face as if she were about to deny they were racing folks. But the moment passed, and Rachel said nothing as they hurried down the stairs to the waiting surrey. Soon, however, her mouth gaped open as they entered the gate of the landscaped racetrack grounds. Before them loomed the largest grandstand she had ever seen, extending nearly the complete length of the track.

"We can thank Marcus Daly, one of the Copper Kings, for this," Johnson said. "He even brought in special dirt for the track."

Fannie knew about the Copper Kings, Marcus Daly and William A. Clark, who had feuded over mining rights and political control of Butte and Anaconda. Her father and Arthur had argued through many a long winter evening about the two entrepreneurs of the mining communities and the right of miners to unionize.

"It's sure better'n that dusty old fairgrounds in Helena." Rachel was delighted by the numbers of women in light summer dresses that added a pretty touch of color to the grandstand crowd.

"There's a Cowboy Tournament before the races," Johnson explained as they found seats in the stand. "Then they'll have the trotters before you're up for the relay." His mustache jutted this way and that as he, too, craned his neck to view the lavish racing facility. "More'n a thousand paid admissions so far." Amazed at the large turnout, Fannie was also impressed with the presentation of roundup events, well organized by director Walter R. Wilmot.

As time for the women's relay drew closer, Johnson led the way to the paddock. "You'll be racing against Margaret Getts and Hester McDonald," he explained. "They're good riders, so do your best."

Fannie's heart beat faster at the thought of riding against Margaret Getts, who had topped the world's record time for the 4-mile relay.

"Here's Margaret, now." Johnson indicated a young woman coming toward them, waving her hand in greeting. Her dishwater-blond hair was parted in the middle and swirled into two puffs behind her ears. She carried a large-brimmed sombrero that matched her black-twill shirt and riding skirt. She shook hands with Johnson. "Margaret," he said, "this is Fannie Sperry."

"I'm happy to meet you." Margaret's wide smile showed dazzling white teeth. "Sorry I missed you at the rooming house."

"Pleased to meet *you*," Fannie said. "I read about your record time. Congratulations."

"Thanks. I'm pretty thrilled about it. Hope I can do even better today."

As they spoke a commotion broke out near the betting booth in front of the grandstand.

"This is terrible," gasped an elegant lady in an organdy hat. Her frock-coated escort was even more irate. "I'm going to speak to the governor about this." They strode past Fannie toward the main gate. Others milled about the booth.

"Scandalous!"

"How dare they insult the fine people of this community by putting the betting booth right in front of the grandstand?"

An angry racing fan in a straw skimmer shook his finger in Johnson's face. "Out there in front of God and everybody. No track has ever allowed the betting ring in such a conspicuous spot. Only dyed-in-the-wool gamblers will take a chance right in full view of the ladies and children."

Fannie, bewildered by the hubbub, had never seen betting on such a scale before, whether in full view of the ladies or not. It seemed a far cry from the two-bit wagers between her father and the Craig horse buyers.

Fannie and Margaret waited near the paddock for several minutes before their competitor Hester McDonald arrived. She nodded coolly to them as she took her place in one of the three stalls. She was a pretty, auburn-haired woman, wearing a white-silk shirt with a fawn-leather riding skirt and matching hat. Her belt buckle flashed silver. Fannie's eyes widened at Hester's costly outfit.

"She's the hometown favorite," Margaret whispered to Fannie as they moved toward their stalls. "Most everyone will bet on her."

At the starting gun, Hester was first away. The crowd rose, shouting encouragement and waving hats, parasols, and handkerchiefs. They had bet on Hester, all right. In each heat the fawn-clad rider rode her best at the beginning of the mile, leading by 5 lengths or more at the halfway mark. Obviously, her mounts had been selected for their fast starting speeds. But eating her dust didn't appeal to Fannie and Margaret, who overtook Hester each round in the stretch.

Then, at the end of the third mile, Margaret's mount ran into the wrong stall. By the time she drove him into the proper one and changed horses, Hester had the lead for the final heat, with Fannie a close second. They pounded into the finish neck and neck. Fannie was sure they had tied. Margaret trailed by several lengths.

The announcer barked their times. "Mrs. McDonald, 8:22. Miss Sperry, 8:22½. Miss Getts, 8:36. Hester McDonald's time sets a new world record for relay racing."

The crowd went wild as Hester took bow after bow before the stands. It was clear that only a few of the Anaconda race fans preferred to support the upstart Miss Sperry, who had made a fine showing against the favorite.

"Half a second," Rachel grumbled as they made their way back to the rooming house. "Half a second from beating Miss Fancy Pants. She barely nosed in ahead of you."

"The crowd was rooting for Hester all the way," Fannie said. "But Margaret's already beat her time in exhibition. Too bad that doesn't count."

"It's only natural," Margaret said. "She's local. And she rides a good race." Margaret was a generous loser.

"You would have beat her if your horse hadn't acted up," Fannie said. "You came back like a house afire in that last heat."

"You'll both beat her tomorrow." Rachel led the way up the rooming-house steps and found places for them around the big supper table.

Next morning, while the girls worked their mounts, Rachel picked up a copy of the *Anaconda Standard* that had been left in the stables and saw the newspaper's report on the betting-booth controversy and the races. The part about the women's relay, she read to the girls.

Mrs. McDonald, entry of Johnson & Burke, was first yesterday by a narrow margin of one-half second. Miss Sperry, entry of the Capital Stock Food Company of Helena, was second. Miss Getts, the entry from Cascade, third. Miss Getts had a little bad luck, and it is claimed, too, that her horses are not so well bred, and therefore, not so fast as the others.

"That's ridiculous." Margaret's eyes flashed in anger. "My mounts are as good as any. Good Eye is the best of them all."

"Who writes that stuff anyway?" Fannie said.

The newspaper accounts heightened interest in the races, and attendance at the track doubled the next day. Hester McDonald took the lead in the first two heats, with Fannie and Margaret closing the gap in each stretch. But Hester faltered getting out of the stall for the third mile, and Fannie took the lead. The determined Hester pulled up fast on the outside, passing Margaret and pounding hard after Fannie. As they rounded the far turn, she edged ahead, crowding Fannie's mount into the rail.

"Watch out!" Fannie yelled. Too late. Fannie's horse stumbled and went down against the fence. She managed to jump free, falling away from both horse and fence. Margaret, close behind, couldn't move out. She hauled on the reins, but her horse tripped over the downed mount and fell, his neck doubled under his body. Margaret, too, was thrown to the track.

Fannie, covered with track dirt, jumped to her feet. Her cheek had scraped the ground and a bloody knee showed through a tear in her riding skirt. But as her horse struggled to its feet, she was aboard and running again.

Margaret did not get up. Spectators strained to see the girl lying next to the fence beside her injured Thoroughbred, and gasps blurred into noisy confusion as Hester flew across the finish line. Fannie came in a few lengths behind, dismounted, and ran across the field to where Margaret and her mount still lay. A doctor, summoned from the stands, examined the injured rider.

Tears of pain and disappointment streamed down Margaret's face. "She fouled us," she murmured as Fannie knelt over her. "You've got to beat her, Fannie."

The doctor announced a broken collarbone as a horse and surrey pulled onto the track and Margaret was lifted aboard.

Hester had left the track. She deliberately cut in front of me, Fannie thought. Poor Margaret will be out of the race now. It isn't fair.

At a pharmacy near the rooming house, Fannie bought a bottle of liniment and, after washing up at the washstand in her room, applied the stinging liquid to the abrasion on her knee. Then, more determined than ever to beat Hester McDonald, she slept soundly in the big brass bed.

Next morning, Fannie arrived at the track to learn that no replacement had been found for Margaret. Fannie was to continue the race against Hester by herself. Here was her chance. She wouldn't let Margaret down. She would prove that Hester's cheating was a poor way to win. She would beat this local favorite fair and square, leaving no doubt as to which girl was the better rider. Crowds packing into the big grandstand showed that the race had stirred up more than casual interest among Anaconda fans.

At the starting gun, Fannie was first away. Hester, leaning hard on the whip, caught her at the quarter and held the lead into the stalls. Fannie's second mount balked, allowing Hester to get out first for the second mile. Then, in the third heat Fannie's mount outdistanced Hester's for the first time since the race began. But she had bad luck remounting a nervous horse, and Hester, who had saved her fastest mount for last, finished about 3 lengths in the lead. Hester had won each of the first three races.

Fannie tried not to show her disappointment. "My horses are responding better every day," she told her mother. "I'm getting the feel of these Thoroughbreds, and they're getting to know me. With a little luck, I'm sure I can still beat her."

The next day, Fannie concentrated her whole being on the race as once again she waited for the starting gun, a knot tightening in the pit of her stomach. The pistol cracked. Fannie bounded onto her first horse, but Hester applied the whip, increasing her lead to nearly 10 lengths by the stretch. She held the lead, first in and first away again before Fannie could land on her second mount and get him started. Then Fannie gained in the stretch, hugging the rail and making up for lost time. Banty, her little black horse, usually the wildest of the string, was on good behavior, and she left Hester eating her dust around the third mile. Though Hester whipped all the way, she couldn't catch up.

Fannie hardly heard the screams of the crowd as she maintained her lead. In the last mile, she was first away by 5 lengths, but Hester, on the inside, running under the whip, pulled alongside. Fannie laid on her quirt, but her last horse tired in the stretch. Hester pounded past just at the finish line.

"The official time: McDonald, 8:25. Sperry, 8:25½."

When Fannie appeared at the 5:00 A.M. breakfast the next day, Johnson handed her the morning *Standard*, folded to the race report. Fannie read aloud.

The relay race promises to be more interesting and exciting today than at any time during the meet. Miss Sperry and Mrs. McDonald will contest, and, as Miss Sperry's horses are gradually getting better, there is no doubt about there being a close finish. Not only have Miss Sperry's horses improved since the first day, but Miss Sperry herself is changing much quicker. But for the fact that her last horse insisted on running next to the outside fence nearly all the way, she would have won yesterday's race.

"That's for darn sure." Fannie grinned.

The landlady plopped an extra helping of pancakes onto Fannie's plate. "We're all rooting for you."

The afternoon crowds grew restless as Fannie waited near the paddock. As usual, Hester strode onto the field with only a perfunctory nod to her opponent. Again, at the relay's starting signal, the two women sprang into action. But again, Hester won by a nose.

Fannie heard the announcement. "Once more, Mrs. McDonald beats Miss Sperry by one-half second. McDonald, 8:24. Sperry, 8:24½. That's the relay, folks. Official time for the four-day twenty-mile race is McDonald, 42:00½. Sperry, 42:05¼."

Cheers rocked the stands. Hester had won the race by less than five seconds. Fannie, concealing her disappointment, waved to the crowd, acknowledging her growing number of supporters, then watched glumly as Hester was carried away in triumph on the shoulders of her enthusiastic fans.

Will Johnson came running up. "Fannie, we've got another chance." He puffed from the exertion of pushing through the crowd. "They want you and Hester to ride an unscheduled exhibition race tomorrow, the last day of the meet."

Fannie felt her energy return. "One more race is all I need to beat her. I know it." She resisted an impulse to fling her arms around Johnson and instead clasped her hands together in delight.

"Not only that," Johnson continued. "Margaret wants you to ride Good Eye tomorrow. You've been struggling along on several half-broke mounts. Good Eye will give you a real chance."

Four races and one trotting event were on the card the following day before Fannie and Hester faced each other across the paddock for their final contest. The grandstand overflowed with screaming race fans eager to witness the final heat between the two outstanding women riders, and a hush of expectancy settled over the crowd as Fannie's green silk shirt and ribbons, contrasting with Hester's fawn outfit, identified the objects of many an impromptu bet.

The riding of both women proved superb, neck and neck for the first 3 miles. On the last mile, Fannie thundered around the track on Good Eye, bringing all her riding skills to bear, feeling one with the fine mount and steadily moving up in the stretch to cross the finish line 2 lengths ahead. A spectacular win. She dropped from Good Eye's back and leaned against his neck for a moment to blink her watering eyes into focus.

"Sperry, 8:11½. McDonald, 8:17½." Not only had she beaten Hester McDonald by six seconds, she had topped Margaret's 4-mile world record.

Fannie, suddenly weak in the knees, clung to her mount. "We did it, Good Eye." She choked back tears, wiping her cheeks against the horse's neck, then smiling, turned to face the stand. Spectators flowed across the track toward her. Fannie received warm waves of compliments and good wishes, but when she turned to congratulate her opponent, Hester had disappeared into the crowd.

"Good goin', Fannie," someone said. "We were with you all the way."

"What a race." Will Johnson accepted congratulations on behalf of the Capital Stock Food Company.

But one of the comments reddened Fannie's ears.

"If these women were men, they'd be the finest riders in racing."

Winter on the Homestead, Summer on the Track

6

New Year's Eve on the Beartooth found Fannie huddled in the shadow of the Sperry barn. Blinking away drowsiness that came with the dark cold, she crouched against the corral fence. Layers of woolen clothing and an old buffalo robe wrapped her against the frigid wind. As a thin trail of clouds wisped across the moon, an occasional glint from the barrel of her Winchester was all that distinguished her bulk from that of the calves in the corral.

A wolf's long mournful howl rose out of the stillness from over the Beartooth. Fannie hoped the Herrins had someone on watch. With the severe winter, wolf packs unable to find game in the heavy snow cover had come down from the north to invade local ranches. The Sperrys had lost a calf to the wolves, and Fannie and Walter volunteered to take turns standing guard through the siege.

Ranching is a hard living, she thought. So often, when a new year comes in, there's little to show for the last one. From the angle of the moon, she guessed it must be nearly midnight. It would soon be a brand-new year, 1905.

Christine had sashayed off to a house party with Will Craig. Lately, they seemed to be keeping steady company. Fannie had seen Chris's eyes when Will was around. He was stuck on her, too, that was sure. Will is nice enough, Fannie mused, but not much of a rider.

The whir of swift, padded feet through the crusted snow interrupted her thoughts. She scanned the broad expanse of white across the creek meadow and up the draw past the timberline, then down through the pines and out toward the flat. Nothing. The sound had stopped. She listened. Then she heard it again. Closer this time.

Suddenly, a gaunt gray form appeared around the corner of the barn not 20 feet away. The wolf crept under the fence, stalking the yearling calf that stood just beyond. Fannie slipped the mitten from her right hand and raised her rifle, sighting along the steely barrel. Just as the wolf crouched to spring for the calf, another shadowy form appeared behind the first.

Fannie squeezed the trigger. The first wolf dropped. With lightning speed, she chambered another shell and fired again. The second wolf slunk into the darkness. Throwing off the buffalo robe and running to the corner of the barn, she could barely make out the shadowy canine disappearing toward the trees. Again she jacked the rifle lever and scanned the area for signs of other pack members. The night was still except for the shifting of the nervous cattle.

Returning to the downed wolf, she held the Winchester at the ready. The animal lay lifeless on the frozen ground, a small, bleeding wound behind its left shoulder.

A light appeared in the kitchen door, and her father called out, "You all right, Fannie? Did you see something?"

"I got one, Pa. Maybe two. I'm going down to check." She trudged around the barn and along the pines, her pacs breaking through the snow with each step. A low growl ahead. She paused, raising her rifle toward the chilling sound. Just then, the wind stirred the clouds from the cold moon. There, not 3 yards before her, lay the injured wolf, its front left leg projecting awkwardly into a wash of bloody snow, its upper lip curled back.

Fannie quickly put a bullet through its head, then immediately reloaded, her eyes darting around her in all directions. She saw no others. Dragging the dead wolf by the tail, she retraced her steps. Her father came with a lantern to help stow the carcasses in the barn. "You get some sleep," he said. "I'll keep watch."

"There may be others. I heard howling from over toward the Herrin place." She handed the rifle to her father and picked up the buffalo hide and wrapped it around his shoulders.

"Happy New Year, Pa."

"Happy New Year, Fannie."

The threat of wolves continued through the winter months. Fannie and Walter caught five of the troublesome predators in their traps and bagged twenty-three coyotes. They pulled the carcasses back to the ranch on a wooden sled and skinned them out. By the end of March, when they observed Fannie's eighteenth birthday over another of Rachel's special dinners, a stack of pelts stood ready to sell in Helena. The milking and most of the other chores also fell on the two young Sperrys, as Bertha had said yes to N. D. Hilger's marriage proposal and was busy with plans for an April wedding.

One evening while sleet pelted against the windows and the family sat before the fire, Datus pored over a folder showing the prize Percherons exhibited at the 1904 World's Fair in St. Louis. He dreamed of owning a fine stallion and talked about someday buying one from the McLaughlin Brothers, breeders with stables in Columbus, Kansas City, and St. Paul.

"Yes sir, Arthur," he said to his oldest son, "someday we're going to get one of these champion stallions. Then we'll have us a real horse business."

Arthur glanced up uneasily from his book. Fannie, who sat surrounded by scraps of cloth, braiding a rag rug, could see it was a dream Arthur didn't share. But Walter dropped the leather punch he was using on a latigo and scrambled to his father's side to gaze fondly at the pictures of the prize horses in the folder.

"Yeah, Pa," Walter said. "Then we can print up one of these booklets, and the name of the owners will be D. E. Sperry and Sons, and we'll build us a . . ."

"Pa," Arthur interrupted. "I've been meaning to talk to you." His words came with difficulty. "Well . . . Edith and I have talked about this."

"Edith?" Datus seemed surprised. "What's she got to do with us owning some fine Percherons?" Edith Davis was the nineteen-year-old daughter of the man who operated the Beartooth ferry across the Missouri.

Arthur swallowed. "The only way I can get any money ahead is to hire out again this spring. If I go to smithing full time, I can soon save enough for Edith and me to . . . well . . . get married."

"Get married?" Rachel's mending fell to her lap. Fannie sensed her parents' reluctance to let their children drift away, one by one. First it was Carrie, who after three years of marriage already expected her third child. Bertha planned a spring wedding. And now Arthur.

Datus folded the brochure and placed it on the table beside him. "Well, I reckon if that's what you want, your ma and me won't stand in your way."

But Fannie knew that her father's calm response rested in his certainty that she and Walter would be on the ranch to take care of things.

Bertha and N. D., who wanted no part of a church wedding, were married in April by a justice of the peace and moved onto the Hilger ranch near the river. Carrie and Joe, who had been managing the place since their marriage, began homesteading their own place nearby.

Spring melted the snow still clinging to the mountains. Creeks ran full to overflowing, and mud clogged the roads. Then, as May sunshine dried the ranges, Fannie and Walter drove the calves to higher pasture and brought down three wild horses to begin breaking. Most of the Sperry string needed to be reshod, and Fannie undertook the task. Starting with Brownie, she backed up to the horse's belly and pulled the front-left hoof between her knees.

"Hello?" a voice called. "Miss Sperry?" A man wearing a derby hat rode toward the corral on a sleek Tennessee Walker. His voice was robust and cheerful. "Remember me? Walter Wilmot?" He dismounted and brushed the dust from the lapels of his gray suit. A heavy gold watch chain dangled across his portly middle. "I saw you ride in Anaconda against Hester McDonald last summer."

"Yes, you directed the cowboy tournament." They shook hands across the corral fence.

"I had business over this way so I took the opportunity to contact you. I'm representing the Black Rock Mining Company, who is sponsoring a women's relay team this summer. The Getts sisters have signed on. Margaret is fine now, anxious to ride again, and she suggested I talk to you. I'd also expect you to ride bucking horses."

"That'd suit me." Fannie ducked under the fence rail, hooked her hammer over a post, and stood facing Wilmot.

"We still have to find another rider, but we'll furnish and transport the stock. You girls will compete against each other in each race. But you'll be paid even if you don't win. We're offering each of you one hundred dollars each week that you ride, plus all traveling expenses."

"One hundred dollars a week?" She had never heard of so much money.

"You should get in a good six or eight weeks of pay, I'd say."

"Holy Moses, when do we start?" Fannie was too excited to try to hide her delight. Being paid to ride Thoroughbreds and bucking horses whether she won or not. This was a dream come true.

Datus, hearing the conversation, came from the barn. "Now, just a darn minute. This girl is only eighteen years old, and she's always been picketed pretty close to home."

Wilmot offered his hand to Datus. "I'm sure she has, Mr. Sperry. That's why we take great care in choosing where the girls will race and who they're with. I want you folks to feel entirely comfortable about your daughter riding with us. You and Mrs. Sperry can come along on the tour if you wish. At your own expense, of course."

"Pa, maybe Christine could come with me." Fannie brightened at the thought. "Mr. Wilmot, you say you need another rider. Christine Synness rides relay as good as me, and she'd be perfect for the fourth rider."

"That so?" Wilmot pulled on the gold chain and looked at his watch. "I'd be glad to talk to her if you'll tell me where I can find her."

The days dragged endlessly for Fannie before it was settled. Datus wrote to a law firm in Helena inquiring about the reputation of one Walter Wilmot, who dressed so fine in gray suits and twirled a gold watch chain. He received a prompt reply stating that members of the firm were acquainted with Mr. Wilmot and could vouch for his good character as well as that of his charming wife, Velma.

On June 6, 1905, Fannie and Christine signed contracts that spelled out their obligations and remuneration. Because she was still a minor, Fannie's contract had to be co-signed by her father. Andreas Synness, too, reluctantly signed for Christine. Neither parent could see how he would manage without his daughter at home during the busy season. Wilmot pocketed the signed contracts and promised to contact them as soon as the race schedule could be finalized.

"Gee, whiz!" Walter exclaimed when he heard the news. "You'll have a swell time, Fannie. Just think. You'll be going to big cities. Minneapolis. Des Moines."

"For two cents, I'd go with you," Rachel mused for the third time. "But your pa and Walter need me here, I'm afraid."

"I know, Ma. And don't worry. I'll be just fine. Besides, I'm not exactly a kid anymore." Fannie fitted the snakeskin belt she'd made to match the band around her hat.

The Helena and Butte newspapers carried prominent advance stories of the coming tour. *Wilmot has got women for jockeys*, the reports headlined. *Will conduct relay racing with Montana horses and riders at the fairs*. Rachel studied the items.

> *Walter Wilmot will shortly ship a carload of Montana horses and has secured contracts with several women riders who are already famous in this state for their horsemanship.*
>
> *Relay racing is a new sport in the East, especially where women riders are concerned. But it is safe to say the racing will prove the biggest kind of success, and with riders such as Fannie Sperry of Beartooth, a girl who has ridden every wild bronco on the ranch and is yet to be thrown; Katherine Synness, of McLeod's Basin, another daring rider; and the Getts sisters, the game will prove a money-making venture.*

"Hummph," Rachel grumbled. "They don't even have Christine's name right."

Fannie worked doubly hard during the next few weeks. Summer was the time when her father's asthma always acted up, and she worried about leaving everything to Walter and her mother while she went on tour. But they could certainly use the money she would earn. She and Christine stepped up their relay practice, mounting and dismounting ponies with Walter as their coach.

Late in June, when she rode the little buckskin mare to Mitchell to pick up the mail, she found a letter from Wilmot. Her eager eyes scanned the large handwriting under the Black Rock Mining Company letterhead. Then she mounted the buckskin as fast as she had ever mounted a relay pony in competition, gave the little mare full rein, and pounded across the flats toward the ranch. "Ma! Pa! Walter!" Her dismount would have gained her valuable seconds on the track. "Wilmot wants us in Butte on August twelfth to ride at Columbia Gardens! He's putting us in a Wild West show." She waved the letter as she ran into the kitchen.

The family, about to sit down to their noon meal of fresh garden vegetables and home-canned pork, gathered around to look at the letter.

"He says he'll furnish the horses, and we'll ride the same ones in Des Moines and Minneapolis later in the tour."

Walter took the letter. "Columbia Gardens! That's just about the best racetrack in the world."

"It's more than that," Datus said. "It's a showplace resort. They've added all kinds of facilities for family entertainment since it opened last year."

"He's calling us the Montana Girls." Fannie beamed at the three people who meant so much to her.

Datus gestured toward the letter. "You know, Fannie. This sounds like a big operation. I just read where Butte has the biggest payroll in the world in proportion to its population. They've got twelve thousand men in the mines with a payroll of a million-and-a-half dollars a month. Imagine that."

Walter dropped into the chair next to his father. "And the miners only have to work eight hours a day for it, too. That's the part that's hard to believe. Only eight hours a day for darn good money."

"Well, I'm only going to have to ride eight miles a day to earn a hundred dollars a week," Fannie said. "That's even better."

"Gosh, Fannie, you're right." Walter seemed genuinely impressed.

Rachel proceeded to dish up the boiled pork. "Those short hours just give the miners more time in the saloons," she said. "Just be sure you don't take up with any of those hooligans." Though her mother tried to joke, Fannie sensed the genuine concern behind the remark. Her father winked at her, and they all laughed. But she suddenly wanted to go to her mother, put her arms around the wiry little woman, and reassure her that her youngest daughter intended to do them all proud. That she would make up for being away when they needed her by becoming the finest, most principled rider who ever pounded turf at Columbia Gardens.

Fannie and Christine arrived by train in Butte a day early as planned, then boarded the Butte Street Railway that would take them from the station to the hotel accommodations Wilmot had arranged. The city sprawled over a

Fannie and Christine tour the city of Butte prior to riding with the Montana Girls relay racing team.

mountain, terraced with narrow thoroughfares, and the girls craned their necks to glimpse the mine scaffolds scattered across the upper slope. Smoke spewed from tall stacks, and clouds of smelly fumes belched forth from the smelters. Clusters of small cottages spilling topsy-turvy down from the diggings teemed with noisy children, barking dogs, and women hanging wash.

As the streetcar rumbled on toward the center of town, they saw people of every description hurrying along the sidewalks, each seemingly bent on an urgent errand. Fine horses pulled fancy carriages and broken-down plugs plodded along between the shafts of shabby drays. They passed stone mansions towering above them on the hillside, some with ornate wrought-iron gates and marble stepping-blocks or polished-brass hitching rails at the curb. "No wonder they call it the richest hill on earth," Fannie murmured.

The conductor signaled their stop and pointed out the wide, four-story brick facade of their hotel. Hesitantly, they carried their grips into a lobby hung with velvet draperies. There Fannie recognized Walter Wilmot and Margaret Getts, conversing with two other women near the center of the lavish, patterned carpet.

"Fannie, you're here!" Margaret ran to embrace her. "And you must be Christine." She hugged Christine, too. "And this is my sister, Dorothy."

Dorothy's happy smile somehow made right the reddish-brown hair that defied the plan she had for it. "I feel like I know you already, Fannie," she said. "Margaret has talked so much about you."

"Girls, this is my wife, Velma." Wilmot took the arm of a plump lady, who wore a lavender-flowered dress that covered her from her double chin to her pudgy ankles.

"Pleased to meet you." Velma's eyes twinkled with good humor as she offered a warm handshake, her large, corseted breasts heaving as she chuckled.

"Pleased to meet *you*, ma'am," they unisoned.

"Have you seen anything of the town?" Wilmot asked.

"Only from the streetcar." Fannie glanced around the lobby at the well-dressed men and women moving about. "I can't wait to see Columbia Gardens."

Margaret giggled. "We were just saying that we should show you two around the city."

"You girls go along. We'll see that your things get up to your rooms." Velma picked up two heavy grips and started toward the staircase.

Margaret donned her white sombrero. "Then what are we waiting for?" She looped her arm through Fannie's, then Christine's, and the four Montana Girls marched gaily across the lobby and out the door to the streetcar stop.

"Sutton's Opera House is brand-new." Margaret pointed out the grand facade so Fannie could get a look. "And we have seven theaters."

"Oh, I wish we could see a melodrama while we're here." Christine's blond curls bobbed about her shoulders as she turned from side to side to take in the wonders of Butte.

Margaret, continuing her tour commentary, indicated an inspiring church steeple. "They say the town has forty-two churches now. With sixty-four thousand people here, they need that many."

Dorothy laughed. "And more than two hundred saloons."

"Ma warned me about *them*," Fannie joked.

A short distance outside the city, as the car moved along the base of the great hill, they noticed an expanse of red-tiled roofs surrounded by a high wall. The cool green of young cottonwoods outlined a magnificent grand-stand that looked to Fannie like a storybook place, contrasting sharply with the barren, soot-blackened, rocky terrain outside the wall. "Don't tell me that's Columbia Gardens!"

"That's it, a regular paradise," Margaret said. "There wasn't a tree in Summit Valley—the mine companies had cut them all for timbering the mines—till the Anaconda Company hauled in dirt and planted those cottonwoods. Tomorrow you'll see the beautiful flowers and landscaping inside." The conductor announced the end of the line, and Margaret took another nickel from her pocket, indicating the return fare. "We better get back now so the Wilmots won't worry."

They arrived at the hotel in time for supper, and Wilmot ordered a bottle of sherry to celebrate the beginning of the tour. "Here's to the Montana Girls." He raised his glass. "And to great riding."

Fannie felt on top of the world. Being a professional relay racer was even more exciting and wonderful than she had imagined. If Ma and Pa could see me now, she thought as she sipped from her tiny glass, they'd think I'd gone to the devil for sure.

The Montana Girls

7

W hat! They're putting Fannie on that outlaw?" Velma Wilmot, standing with the others near the stands, heard the announcement that
Fannie would ride the vicious bronc Tracy in the first bucking event.

"That's the horse she drew." Wilmot toyed nervously with his watch
chain.

"But men have been hurt trying to ride that killer."

"Don't worry," Fannie reassured them. "I'll be all right."

Velma's worried look persisted as she adjusted the elastic garters that
held Fannie's sleeves in place. The red-silk shirt, a black high-crowned hat,
and a black-twill skirt newly purchased in a Butte emporium, plus snakeskin
belt and hatband, comprised the most handsome outfit Fannie had ever
owned. Her confidence soared as she headed for the arena, where two handlers were bringing out a balky bucking horse. Cheers drowned out the
announcer's voice when the crowd caught sight of her.

". . . and Miss Sperry is the first of three women who will compete on
the bucking horses this afternoon. She is the *only* woman riding slick saddle. That's right, ladies and gentlemen. Miss Sperry's stirrups will not be
hobbled or tied down to assist in her ride. The required strength must all
be hers. I'd say she's a brave little lady."

One of the handlers struggled to hold the lead rope, while the gray roan
strained against a second wrangler's grip on his ears. "Get a move on," he

muttered, throwing his strength against the horse's powerful neck. "We can't hold him." Fannie swung onto the saddled bronc, with barely time to adjust her grip before the handlers released him. Tracy careened away in a fast bucking stampede down the field with Fannie tugging the lead, her right arm flying.

"Look at that horse go!" Spectators strained forward.

Tracy's explosive charge carried Fannie to the far end in record time. Then the roan stopped cold. Fannie did not. She soared directly over the horse's head, made one undignified revolution in the air, and hit the ground with a thud. Gasps came from the crowd.

"She's hurt. Someone help her."

Stunned for a moment, Fannie lay crumpled on her side. Then she regained her senses and scrambled to her feet. She saw the demon roan a few yards away, head low, eyeing her, the lead tangled around his front leg. She ran forward and pulled the rope free. The horse shied back, but Fannie grabbed the saddle horn and was about to leap aboard when the hazer pulled her away. "Let me on," she cried. "I can ride him."

She felt Wilmot's firm grip on her arm. "No, Fannie, you know you can't get back on. When you're thrown, you're thrown. What's the matter with you?"

Fannie knew she was out of line. Biting her lip, she limped from the field as 2,000 voices in the stands howled with enthusiasm.

"Folks, Miss Sperry is all right, just a little shaken." The announcement brought more applause. "But you'll see this outlaw bronc ridden yet. Luke Redford has volunteered to ride him. As you know, Red is one of our top bronc twisters. If he can't ride him, nobody can."

Fannie's distress heightened as another roar went up from the crowd, and Tracy and his second rider shot across the arena. More determined than ever to be rid of his aggravation, the roan spun crazily, coming down hard and off balance. He threw back his head to right himself, then began another blind-bucking stampede, bellowing with each plunge. Redford wisely bounded off under his own steam.

But Tracy continued his frenzied gyrations, stomped the lead, broke the halter, and finally bucked the saddle loose. Cheers turned to screams as the ferocious horse, fighting the flopping saddle, crashed through the board fence, knocking a young boy to the ground. The hazers hurried to the boy lying beside the splintered fence.

"It's young Tim Sullivan," someone said. "Is he hurt?"

"Looks like his leg is broke. Stand back now. Let's get him to a doctor." Several cowboys carefully lifted the boy and carried him to a waiting wagon.

"Bad business that Tracy." Wilmot turned to Fannie. "No more broncs for you today, Fannie. You look a little shook. Go on over to the cookhouse and take a rest. You've got the relay tomorrow."

Fannie nodded. Her bruised arm and leg protested, but instead of heading for the cookhouse, she went to the stock barn to check her mounts.

"Are you sure you're up to the relay?" Velma Wilmot asked, inspecting the abrasion on Fannie's arm the next morning at breakfast.

"Just a little stiff, that's all. I'll be fine once I get limbered up."

Wilmot handed her a newspaper and pointed to the sports headline. *Record crowd attends meet at Gardens.* The third paragraph caught her eye. *Tracy was the feature of the wild-west conclave at Columbia Gardens yesterday. There were other founchin cayuses and some fractious steers, but compared with Tracy they were docile.* "Listen to this." Fannie glanced around the table at the others, then read aloud. "*'If there ever was an imp of his satanic majesty incarnated in the disguise of a horse, Tracy is one.'*"

"You can say that again." Margaret passed the platter of eggs and ham.

"Meanest bronc I ever saw," Wilmot agreed.

"What does the paper say about your ride?" Christine spooned eggs onto her plate and filled a plate for Fannie as she read.

"*'Tracy bounded into the limelight carrying Miss Sperry. Miss Sperry may be a bronco buster, and she proved she is game to the core, and can ride some. But she had about as much chance to ride Tracy as Jim Jeffries would have of earning a decision in a bout with a circular saw.'*" Fannie folded the paper. "Well, I can vouch for that." She laughed with the others.

Wilmot interrupted the merry mood. "Fannie, the girls and I were talking. We've decided to put you on Good Eye today in the final heat. That'll give you a bit more time to make your changes."

"But I can't take Margaret's best mount."

"We have to put on a show here." Wilmot glowered at Fannie. "You won't be able to make your usual time, stove up like you are, but the audience expects a close race."

The Montana Girls set new records in relay racing.

"Please ride Good Eye," Margaret said, and Fannie could see she meant it. "It's fun to change around once in a while anyway."

"All right, I will," Fannie agreed. "And I'll do my darnedest to be so far ahead by the time I get to him that you'll know it was my fast changes that beat you and not just Good Eye's speed."

"I can hold back a little if I see Fannie's having trouble," Christine offered.

"No, we won't have any holding back," Wilmot said. "These races have got to be on the level. If Fannie's a little slower at the change points, she'll make up for it on the track."

His prediction proved accurate. In the final race, after a tussle with balky Montana Mike in the third mile, Fannie came in third riding Good Eye, with Dorothy first, Christine second, and Margaret trailing by 4 lengths.

The following day, August 16, the Montana Girls, the Wilmots, and the string of Thoroughbreds boarded a train for Iowa. Wilmot enlisted the help of the girls to trail the horses from the Des Moines station to the fairgrounds. Eager Iowans gathered along the way to gape at the four Montana Girls and their sixteen Thoroughbred racers. After tending the stock, Fannie and Christine went directly to their small second-floor room.

"It's hot as a bake oven in here." Fannie fanned her throat with her hat, then crossed to the window and flung it open. "There's not a breath of a breeze." Looking out across an expanse of businesses and frame houses toward the capitol, she could see waves of heat rising from the brick street.

"So this is the East." She felt glum. Her mind's eye gazed past the prairie city to her home beneath the Beartooth. The cool, piney mountain above the sage-covered flats seemed far away. "I don't know which is worse," she said as they began unpacking their grips and putting their extra clothing into the chifforobe, "being thrown from an ornery bronc or spending eighteen hours of torture on that train." She stretched her arms to ease her aching body.

"Well, that's racing." Christine shrugged. "Why don't you get into the bathtub down the hall for a good soak? It'll do you good."

"Bathtub?"

"Didn't you notice when we came in? This is a high-class place with a real bathtub and running water, too. Come on, I'll show you."

Following Christine three doors down the hall, Fannie peeked into the wainscotted room. A former bedroom, with two windows that had been painted over halfway up, the room boasted a chain-pull water closet, a pedestal lavatory, and a huge iron bathtub.

"Come on, I'll run some hot water for you, and you can hop in."

"You mean take off my clothes?" Fannie remained near the door, clutching the placket on her shirtwaist. The room smelled of tar soap.

"It'll be good for your stiffness." Christine leaned over the tub to reach the faucets.

"I'll just sponge off in our room." Fannie intended to avoid any awkward encounter with modern plumbing.

"Don't be silly. A good, hot soak will do you good."

"I . . . I'd rather not."

"Why not?" Christine glanced at her incredulously. "Haven't you ever had a bath in a real bathtub before?"

"When I was a kid, Ma put me in the washtub." Fannie hesitated. "But now, we kind of . . . well, you know . . . in our camisoles in front of the sink after the boys have gone to bed."

"Oh, for Pete's sake. You don't know what you're missing."

"Where did *you* ever have a bath in a tub?" She stared at Christine as if seeing her for the first time.

"At my aunt's house in Helena. This handle is for hot water and this one for cold." Christine demonstrated. "And here are the towels." She indicated the fresh linens hanging on a rack at the foot of the tub. "Take as long as you want, but then it's my turn," Christine called as she closed the door behind her. "Hook the latch on the door and no one will bother you."

Nearly an hour later, Fannie emerged from the bathroom swathed in towels above her boots, her face glowing.

"Well, how did you like it?" Christine asked.

"All I can say is, I feel so good I could tackle that Tracy again right now."

The three-week tour of state fairs drew rave notices in local papers wherever the Montana Girls raced. Fannie clipped articles to be sent home to her mother, then read them aloud during supper in the boardinghouse.

> *The lightness, ease and grace with which the girls vaulted into their saddles, plus their confidence and control of their mounts, won them enthusiastic admiration among those familiar with the feat of controlling a running horse.*
>
> *Yesterday, while the Montana Girls were engaged in teaching their horses to quickly enter the stalls into which they are run at the end of each mile, 2,000 people watched them exercise their mounts.*

Some items, Fannie thought, were poorly reported and uninformed.

> *The girls wear divided skirts which do not seem to interfere with their movements, but the costumes are decidedly out of fashion. These cowgirls could hardly be called ladies.*

Margaret took the paper. "They're calling us cowgirls now, since that New York reporter at Madison Square Garden called Lucille Mulhall a cowgirl a few months ago."

"Yes, but she *is* a cowgirl. She ropes steers in her act. We're horsewomen."

"That makes no difference. They call horsemen cowboys, don't they? I think it's a compliment." Christine always looked at the bright side of things.

"Cowgirls or horsewomen," Fannie said, "here's someone who doesn't think we should even be on a horse. She read, "'*Horseback riding is physically unhygienic for women, except when the sidesaddle is employed.*'" The girls broke into giggles.

The Montana Girls event at the State Fair in Helena attracted record crowds. According to the *Daily Independent* report:

> *More than 5,000 visitors passed through the gates yesterday while the exhibits were being placed. Today, when the famous Professor Liverati's military band officially opens the fair with a four-o'clock concert, they estimate there'll be 10,000 people within the grounds.*

Fannie's injury had been forgotten, and she brought home three wins to Margaret's one during the four days of the fair.

Her luck continued in September at the Minnesota State Fair in Hamlin. Winning a 24-mile race over three days, she was awarded a stick-pin engraved FOR MERITORIOUS RIDING.

"I don't know what happened," she told the others as they gathered in the cook tent. "Even Montana Mike was on his best behavior."

"You showed him who's boss, that's what." At the interjection of a strange voice, Fannie turned to see a stocky, round-faced girl with a wayward mane of dark hair at the tent entrance. "I'm Anna Pauls." She walked confidently toward their table. "I ride, too."

"Well, have a seat." Dorothy got up to get an extra chair. "How long you been riding?" The girl looked no older than fifteen.

"Ever since I can remember." She spun the chair around and plopped into it backward, her leather riding skirt straining at the knees with the unseemly posture. "I ride on our ranch. I'm from out near Spokane."

"You ride broncs?" Fannie asked.

"Not so much. I'm more relay." Anna's bright smile and sparkling, dark eyes reflected her youthful vitality. "I'm just here with my dad, but I wanted to come and meet all of you. And to say I'm glad about your award, Fannie. You're really something."

"Come and work with us in the morning," Fannie invited. "Maybe you can help me talk some sense into Montana Mike."

"Gee, that'd be swell." And from that moment until the Minnesota fair ended, Anna Pauls spent every waking moment in the company of her idols, the Montana Girls.

The closing of the fair marked the last day of their tour, and the Wilmots invited everyone to a special farewell supper, topped off with a decorated cake provided by Velma. Wilmot stood at the head of the table, his thumbs resting in his vest pockets, smiling at the happy faces before him. "Well, girls, I have your pay all sorted out here in these envelopes. The tour amounts to seven hundred and fifty dollars for each of you."

"Seven hundred and . . ." The girls looked at each other in amazement.

"And I'm counting on each of you for the team next year." Wilmot handed the cash-filled envelopes to the four girls. "I've booked a tour with J. Ellison Carroll's Wild West show."

"Holy Moses." The evening was full of wonderful surprises. Fannie had heard of J. Ellison Carroll, a Texas cowboy who had parlayed his reputation as a steer roper into a successful touring show.

"Carroll's the roper who won a five-thousand-dollar purse by beating Clay McGonagill at the big roping in San Antonio last year," Wilmot explained. "He's doing real good with his show, too."

"I'm afraid I won't be going with you." All turned at Margaret's startling announcement.

"But why not, my dear?" The familiar furrow creased Velma's brow.

"Well, don't look so serious." Margaret broke into a mischievous grin. "I guess I can tell now. I'm getting married. I'm going to be a rancher's wife."

Christine managed a smile. "Why, that's wonderful, Margaret." The Wilmots offered reserved congratulations. Fannie sat stunned. Margaret not riding? The team wouldn't be anything without her.

Dorothy spoke then. "So, of course I won't be coming back, either." Her words came as an added shock to the others.

"Don't tell us you're getting married, too."

"Don't I wish," Dorothy said wistfully. Then she added, "The folks don't want me to travel without Margaret, and it just wouldn't be the same without her."

Wilmot looked flustered. "Well, now, I hadn't expected this." He gazed across the table at Anna. "I suppose we could give this little girl a chance. I've watched her ride during the workouts. She might make a fine replacement."

Anna gasped her delight, as the others voiced their approval.

"We'd be glad to have you," Fannie said. Glancing at Christine, she added, "And there's two more of us here who can't wait to get started on that Kansas tour with Ellison Carroll."

"We wish you all the best." Margaret stood to leave, her eyes suddenly glistening with tears. "We'll keep in touch." The Montana Girls hugged all around.

"We will. We'll keep in touch," they chorused.

When the others had gone, Fannie and Christine strolled out through the crisp Minnesota autumn. Leaves crunched under their boots and drifted down around them as they moved along a pleasant, residential street. The smell of bonfires hung on the early evening air.

"How can they just up and leave?" Fannie felt both sadness and disbelief. "Don't they see they represent the best in racing?"

"Seven hundred fifty dollars." Christine repeated the number slowly, savoring the sound. Fannie could see that Chris was trying to cheer her up. "Imagine getting that much money for doing what you love to do. I can tell you one thing. I'll sure be on hand for the Kansas tour next summer."

"You bet." Fannie smiled. "We're not quitting. Ever."

Boarding the Northern Pacific in Minneapolis for the long trip home, Fannie touched the envelope to make sure it was still pinned to her camisole. "This money will help Pa get that Percheron stallion he's been wanting for so long."

"Mine is going into my hope chest."

"Hope chest? Now don't you go and get married on me."

"No, no, nothing like that," Christine said.

But Will Craig was waiting at the station to meet her when they arrived in Mitchell, and he drove the two returning Montana Girls up Prickly Pear Valley to their homes.

"Fannie, they're saying you're the best in the West," Walter shouted as he came running to take her grip.

"Who's saying that?" She drank in the natural beauty of the mountain as they walked toward the house. The creek and the meadow were lovely as ever, and a few apples hung on the apple tree. Wooden apples, her mother called them, because they never quite ripened before the frost.

Her mother hurried from the kitchen. "Walter's right," she said. "The paper says you're leading the bunch." And almost before they could get into the house, she brought the scrapbook and opened it to a news item from the July 10, 1905, *Independent*. She had underlined the final paragraph, and now she read it aloud.

The sport these races furnish is thrilling to say the least. These girls are known to be the greatest horsewomen in the West. In fact, there is not anything a cowboy has to do in the rough-and-ready life of a big western ranch that these girls cannot do.

Rachel snapped the book shut. "Yes, siree," she said with a satisfied nod. "And they finally put the write-up on page one where it belongs."

Touring the Midwest  8

The wet spring of 1906 had turned the countryside a luminous green, and the continuing rain beat against the top of the Sperrys' new surrey as Walter drove Fannie and Christine to the train on June 9. The downpour did little to dampen the excitement of finally getting away on the new season's tour. Twice they mired down on the muddy road, and Fannie had to take the lines while Walter got out and pushed, and Christine held a black umbrella to shield their skirts and boots against splatters from the wheels. They made the Mitchell depot just minutes ahead of the train.

"I'll send you a postcard from Kansas City." Fannie's farewell shout to Walter was lost in the din of the rain and the hiss of the locomotive.

Once seated in the plush car, the girls gazed fondly at the muted green of the undulating rangeland and the misty mountains as the train picked up speed, heading south toward Helena and points beyond. They would join the Wilmots and Anna Pauls in Cheyenne before traveling on to Kansas for two weeks with J. Ellison Carroll's Wild West show.

"Carroll's show last year in Kansas City sold out." Fannie opened the small valise at her feet and produced a half-finished crocheted doily.

Christine took her embroidery from her handbag. "Can't do us any harm to ride with a champion like him. Imagine roping and tying twenty-eight steers in succession—with an average time of thirty-two seconds." She picked at a snag in her embroidery floss.

"I read that his top time was eighteen seconds." An image of Walter roping a calf came to Fannie's mind. She could still see her brother waving from the surrey as they boarded the train. He seemed always to be waving good-bye to her when, if truth be known, he should be riding at exhibitions, too.

They met the Wilmots and Anna in Cheyenne, where they were to change trains to continue on to Denver. A three-hour layover gave them time to help Wilmot transfer his horses into the Denver-bound stockcars. Fannie was happy to see Lucky Girl and Baby Face. Two new mounts, Kentucky Prince and Songbird, replaced the troublesome Montana Mike and the slower Sesame.

Wilmot had booked the Montana Girls beginning June 14 for appearances in Junction City, Salina, Hutchenson, and Coffeeville, winding up in Kansas City, Missouri, on July 4. The girls would then leave Carroll's show and proceed on their own to fairs in Sedalia and Grand Rapids, Michigan.

"You'll be riding bucking horses, too, Fannie," Wilmot said. "I've signed you up to ride whatever you draw, right along with the men."

Anna Pauls, the same exuberant, round-faced, tough-as-nails teenager they remembered from Minnesota the year before, proved to be an expert hand with the traveling stock.

"Anna's a little rough around the edges," Christine said as they took up their needlework for the Denver leg, "but she's a hard worker . . . and good-hearted."

"Good women riders are few and far between." Fannie's nimble fingers, coarsened by her years of rough ranch work, manipulated the crochet hook in and out of the lacy doily pattern. "Most of the best ones—unless they're married to bronc busters—their folks won't let them travel."

Christine paused in her needlework to look earnestly at Fannie. "I wonder how we ever managed it?"

Rain pelted the train all along the eastern slopes of the Rockies, and the deluge continued in Denver while they transferred the stock to the Kansas-Pacific rail line and headed east across Kansas.

By now the girls knew the routine. They trailed the horses from depot to fairgrounds, settled into lodgings nearby, grabbed a bite of supper, and, after their grueling 1,500-mile journey, each had a glorious hot bath before drifting into sleep to the faraway sound of crickets chirping on the Kansas prairie.

Fannie awoke and dressed before Wilmot's rap on the door told her it was five o'clock. She shook Christine, who tumbled out of bed and sleepily splashed cold water on her face. "Hurry," Fannie urged, braiding her hair into one long braid down her back, "or we'll miss breakfast."

Joining Anna and the Wilmots in the cook tent, Fannie gasped when she saw the outfit Anna wore. Full calf-length black bloomers, gathered above her boots and topped with a matching middy. "Anna, where's your skirt?" she whispered.

"What skirt? This is my new outfit. It's all the rage now for sports."

"They're very nice, dear," Velma said. "And so practical."

Christine, inspecting the cut of the bloomers, winked at Fannie. "I like them."

But on the brief walk to the fairgrounds, Anna's outfit caused many a head to turn, including a tall cowboy practicing rope tricks near the cook tent. His sleeves were rolled, and Fannie noted his powerful shoulders and arms.

"Hold it a minute, girls," Wilmot said, waving to the cowboy. "I want you to meet Ellison Carroll." The muscled cowboy was their new boss.

"So these are the famous Montana Girls." Carroll shook hands all around. Handsome, with brown hair and eyes, he appeared to be in his thirties. "Montana is one of my favorite places. I spent some time trailing longhorns up there in the eighties."

"Way back then?" Anna stared openly at Carroll's strong chin and sharp nose. "My grandpa was on those drives."

Fannie shot a disapproving glance at the teen. She didn't want him getting the impression that she, too, thought he was an old man. "You must have been just a kid then, Mr. Carroll."

"Sure was. Guess you might say I cut my molars on chuckwagon biscuits. You girls do any roping?" Carroll asked. "I could sure use some ropers."

"Fannie can rope," Christine said.

"Oh, no," Fannie protested. "I can get a loop around a horse's neck, but I've never done any fancy roping." Then she added, "But I sure am anxious to see you handle a lariat, Mr. Carroll."

"Well, if you're all as fast in relay as they say, you don't need to worry about being ropers, too. How about sharpshooting?"

The girls shook their heads. Sharpshooting. Fannie had never seen a real Wild West show that featured sharpshooting, but she *was* pretty handy with a rifle. That might be something to think about.

The Montana Girls headed the afternoon performance before a full grandstand. Anna's bloomer outfit proved a special attraction and, for the first time, she came in first in the relay.

"There's something to be said for those britches," Fannie commented.

Fannie made a good showing in the bucking events. Then the steer roping was called, and the girls sat spellbound as Ellison Carroll showed his expertise with a lariat.

"I wonder if he's married." Anna sighed, watching Carroll's back muscles ripple under his shirt as he circled a wide loop above his head, then tossed it over the horns of a stampeding steer.

"Of course he's married." Fannie laughed, then added, "He must be."

Christine giggled. "Isn't everybody?"

Carroll set a new world's record in Junction City. Giving a 1,000-pound steer a 90-foot start, he roped the animal in seventeen seconds flat. Though rain fell throughout the week, and the show took place on muddy ground every day, crowds packed the stands to see the famous roper, then stayed to cheer the plucky Montana Girls. Each morning the girls exercised their mounts, and Fannie, mindful of Anna's growing skill, worked on improving her own quick mounts and dismounts on Kentucky Prince and Songbird, accustoming them to the relay procedure.

"You're some rider, Fannie," Carroll told her after her exhibition bronc ride in Salina.

She had felt the outpouring of warmth from the spectators in the relays, and when they saw her perform on a bucking horse, their cheering told her she had become an audience favorite. "I've been lucky."

"It's more than luck." Carroll held the gate for her when they left the arena. "You have something special."

Fannie returned his grin. And, as they went separate ways, she turned to watch his tall form turn the corner around the steer barn.

Fannie and Christine had given considerable thought to Anna's deft performance in her riding bloomers. At a Salina emporium they bought 12 yards of sturdy black twill, and Velma Wilmot borrowed a sewing machine and made riding bloomers for them. To complete the Montana Girls' daring new costumes, Velma sewed bright-colored silk shirts to distinguish one from the other on the track. Anna chose flaming red, Christine yellow, and Fannie royal blue.

The J. Ellison Carroll Wild West Show arrived in Kansas City during another downpour, and at race time the next day, the paddock was under 2 inches of water. In the grandstand, scattered clusters of spectators huddled under umbrellas and dusters, some holding drenched newspapers over their heads. The Montana Girls decided not to debut their new bloomer costumes in the dismal weather, and Carroll cut short the steer roping and bucking events.

"Be careful, that track is slippery as hell," he warned. "You'll have to change mounts in that grassy area across from the paddock." Fannie's inspection found the grass concealing an inch of muddy runoff.

At the relay's starting gun, the Thoroughbreds slogged gamely around the heavy track, but the going was slow and, except for the slipping and sliding, the first three heats proved unexciting. In the last mile, Fannie, on Baby Face, made an outstanding run to cross the finish line several lengths ahead. But she heard only scattered applause.

Dismounting, she turned to watch Christine and Anna, spattered with mud, come in and swing from their horses. "Thank goodness this is the last day." Christine wiped her hand across her streaked face. "Riding in this swamp is more than I bargained for."

They trudged back to the barn to put up the horses. Fannie finished her chores first and headed for the cook tent for a cup of reviving hot coffee. The drizzle had ended, and the sky showed patches of blue as she picked her way through the standing puddles. Ellison Carroll appeared from the direction of the steer barn. "Congratulations, Fannie."

"Are you talking about the race or the amount of mud I've collected?" She rubbed her cheek with a corner of her neckerchief.

"You're doing fine in both areas." He took the handkerchief and dabbed at a splatter above her eyebrow. "Shall we dry out with a cup of coffee?"

A two-gallon pot on the huge iron cookstove sent the aroma of strong coffee about the tent. Carroll poured two cups and carried them to one end

Fannie practices for her relay racing in her new bloomer costume.

of the plank table where Fannie sat waiting. His brown eyes watched her over the rim of his cup as they sipped the hot liquid. "The thing about you, Fannie, is that you never give up."

"'Course not. Neither do you. None of us do, do we?"

"Not usually. But you give all you've got every time. And you do it with style. That kind of effort . . . well . . . it's called professionalism."

Fannie blushed. She had never had a nicer compliment.

"Sorry I can't go on to ride at the fairs with you girls. Maybe we can work together again next summer." He drained his cup, then stood and pushed his chair under the table. "Gotta hurry. We're loading the stock."

They shook hands and Carroll tipped his hat. "So long, Fannie." He stepped outside the tent flap and was gone.

A few pale rays of late-afternoon sun slanted across the empty fair-grounds as she left through the main gate and walked along the road toward the rooming house. Everything smelled wonderfully fresh, and a chorus of birds sang their after-rain song from the roadside trees.

Sharpshooting. Carroll had said he could use a sharpshooter. She would begin target practice as soon as she got back to the Beartooth.

The Montana Girls and the Wilmots moved on to the Missouri State Fair at Sedalia for three days, then loaded the horses for a long train trip to Grand Rapids, Michigan, where the girls had decided to debut their new bloomer outfits. After all, they reasoned, Grand Rapids was farther east, where folks were more up to date and the costumes would not attract unwanted attention.

But when the three girls ran out onto the Grand Rapids track, gasps and tittering rose among the spectators, then whistles and hoots. Ignoring the uproar, the girls, with their new black bloomers tucked into their boot tops, felt ready for action.

Though her teammates rode a challenging race, again Fannie surged across the finish line ahead by several lengths. She had pushed her mounts in a 4-mile run to a remarkable 8:17¾ to set a new women's record in professional relay racing. Her 8:13½ exhibition ride against Hester McDonald hadn't counted for the record, but now she would be credited with the best time ever achieved by a woman in a professional race.

Setting the new record topped off the tour for Fannie. Riding relay and broncs before enthusiastic crowds satisfied her competitive spirit, but to earn a world record, that was special. The thrill of this honor banished her fatigue from the long hard days of riding and moving from town to town. While Christine and Anna packed their things for the trip home, Fannie sat by the window of their room, scissors in hand, perusing newspaper accounts of her triumph. "Here's a good one." She held a clipping nearer the light and read aloud.

The girls are fearless and have had several narrow escapes from serious accidents. Sometimes their horses jump the fence, carrying rider with them, and the young ladies make it a rule to force the horse to jump over the fence onto the track again and continue the race. Miss Sperry, in addition to riding in the relay races, rides the bucking bronco Jim Noonon in front of the grandstand each day. She is the girl who breaks her own horses at her ranch at Beartooth, Montana. When a rancher in that country gets an "outlaw" he can't handle, he sends for Miss Sperry, and she rides and breaks him thoroughly. She is known as the best handler of rough horses in the entire state.

Fannie smiled. "They exaggerate a good bit here."

"They do not." Christine sat on the lid of her battered trunk to snap the latches. "You *are* the best bronc buster in the state."

"They mention you, too, Chris. '*Miss Synness lives at McLeod Basin, Montana, and breaks her own horses. Last year, with her brothers, she rode 45 days in the roundup of their cattle, then assisted in branding and corralling them.*'"

Christine shrugged. "What's so unusual about that?"

"Don't they say anything about me?" Anna hurried to Fannie's side, pulling on her camisole and tying the ribbons at the waist.

"Yes, you're in here, too. Listen to this. '*Miss Anna Pauls is the youngest rider, but is absolutely fearless and has ridden with her father for years on their ranch in the state of Washington.*'"

"Does it really say I'm fearless?" Anna craned her neck to see the words Fannie pointed out. "Gosh, I'm scared to death every time one of the horses crashes the fence. Sometimes I think I'm not cut out to drive critters around a racetrack."

"Don't be silly," Christine said. "We all have our moments of being scared."

Fannie's scissors snipped expertly along the newspaper border and around a headline. "Not me. Worried, maybe, about whether I'll make a good showing, but never scared. Even on a bucking horse, I'm concentrating too hard to be scared."

News of Fannie's record-breaking ride preceded her to the Beartooth. As she and Christine stepped from the train in Mitchell, Walter waved his shabby hat, his face breaking into a wide grin. She saw with some surprise that he was more than 6-feet tall and, though she had been away less than three months, he seemed somehow more mature than she remembered. He'd dressed for the homecoming in his best jacket and trousers, hand-me-downs their mother had remade. Now the jacket was too short in the sleeves and too tight to button over his freshly ironed shirt and snakeskin belt.

"Are you the famous Montana Girls?" He swept his hat from his head and bowed a courtly welcome. "How was the tour?"

"Sensational." Fannie looped her arm through his as they moved along the platform. "Oh, I've so much to tell you."

He grinned. "I want to hear it all." His gaze lingered on her face, and Fannie wondered if *she* had changed. Was she as much a stranger to him as he was to her?

Walter, helping with the luggage, steered them toward the hitching post at the end of the platform where the team and surrey stood waiting. Fannie greeted the team with affection, allowing them to nuzzle her hands and face. Then she noticed a young boy of about ten seated in the surrey, holding the lines.

"We have a new neighbor," Walter explained. "Brian O'Connell. Lost his ma, so he's come to live with Harley and Mame Herrins. Mame is his sister. Brian, here's Fannie and Christine."

Beneath a frazzled straw hat, a pair of bright blue eyes peered at Fannie through a fine crop of freckles. "Pleased to meet 'cha." The boy snatched the hat from his mop of orange-red hair. "I'm gonna ride at roundups, too, when I get older."

"I bet you will." Fannie climbed onto the front seat. The boy handed the lines to Walter and scrambled onto the back seat with Christine as the team, eager to be off, pulled away from the station hitching post.

"Brian's been helping me out while you've been gone," Walter said. "I've been letting him try some broncs, and he sticks on those cayuses like a cockleburr."

"Walter helped me drive a wild pinto down from the mountain," Brian said.

"A pinto?" Fannie thought of her first pony, Rainbow. It seemed a long time since she had ridden one of her wild favorites.

"Harley says he ain't good for much. Just a dumb Injun pony."

Fannie turned to the boy. "I'll tell you what. If Harley don't want you to keep him, I'll trade you a good saddle horse for him."

"Gosh." The boy hesitated. "That wouldn't be fair to you, would it?"

"It's fair. Those pinto ponies are mighty pretty."

Lamps glowed in the windows of the log house by the time they had dropped Christine at the Synness ranch and Brian had picked up his horse and started home. Rounding the bend in the Sperry lane, Fannie realized how much she had missed the warmth of those lamps.

"Oh, Fannie, it's good to have you home." Her mother, excited as a child, chattered nonstop. "Got a good supper waiting for you. Is that a new shirt?"

"We missed you," her father said. "More than ever this time."

The fire in the fireplace cast a cheerful glow that took the September chill off the front room, but everything seemed different somehow, smaller than she remembered. Through the kitchen door, she glimpsed the big table laden with roast beef, potatoes, and fresh tomatoes. From the delicious smells, she guessed there would be corn pudding, too, and baked apples. Tears welled up in her eyes. No matter how far she traveled, here was where her heart would remain. During the happy homecoming supper, she told them about the Kansas tour, about Ellison Carroll, the muddy racetracks, and her record time in Grand Rapids.

Her mother sat spellbound. "Fannie, it's no fun just sitting here waiting for you to come home with the news. I want to see you ride. See you win." She turned to Datus, her eyes bright with eagerness. "Here we have a daughter who's a champion, and we sit at home like bumps on a log. Let's go with her next summer."

The lines around Datus's eyes crinkled into a wistful smile. "Sure wish we could." He spoke slowly, his breathing labored. "But I'm afraid I couldn't take it, the dust and all." Then he brightened. "But no reason you shouldn't go if you want to, Rachel. You could bunk in with the girls without much extra cost. Walter and me can handle the milking and haying here at home."

"Can't we work out something so you can all come?" Fannie said.

"It's all right, Sis." Unsmiling, Walter got up to leave the table. "We all do what we have to do."

Fannie rose at dawn to help with the milking. After chores, she saddled Toots, a gray mare she rarely found time to ride, and took the 8-mile short-cut over the Beartooth to the Herrin ranch, where she planned to trade Toots for young Brian O'Connell's pinto. As she guided the horse up the steep incline, picking her way among the rocks, the mare began to favor her right hind foot. By the time she reached the crest and started down the other side, the limp grew worse, and Fannie got off to inspect the lame foot. She could see nothing wrong. Fine thing, she mused. How can I trade off a horse that's gone lame?

At the Herrin ranch, Brian ran to meet her from the corral where Harley and a hired hand had just succeeded in bridling a sleek black-and-white piebald. He looped the reins to a post as his wife, Mame, came from the ranch house. "Hello, Fannie." Mame was a sweet-faced young woman with tendrils of orange-red hair curled around her face. The men turned to see Fannie approach leading the lame mare. "What happened to her leg?"

"Just went lame on me coming over the mountain." Fannie again picked up Toots's foot to inspect the frog and feel along the shank.

"Got a stone under the shoe?" Harley, too, inspected the raised hoof, then said, "Don't see anything."

"How's the family, Fannie," Mame asked. "We never see you folks. I hear Carrie and Bertha are both . . ." She lowered her voice to a whisper. ". . . in the family way again."

"Yes, they're busy as beavers. But it's fun being an aunt. I like the kids."

"Brian came home so excited about your tour. We sure were pleased to hear about you settin' a record."

"You betcha," Harley said. "Nice goin', Fannie."

"Thanks. But here at home, I can't seem to get a pony across a little old mountain without her going lame." Fannie turned her attention to the lame mare.

Harley opened the mare's mouth to look at her teeth. "Brian said you might be interested in tradin' for this piebald." The large, white-faced horse had white patches spread over his gleaming black withers and flanks. "We named him Napoleon. He's pretty strong willed."

"*That's* the horse he wants to trade? Not a bad-looking animal. But now that my mare's got a bad foot . . ."

"Could be she just sprained it comin' over the hill."

"She'll be okay, won't she?" Brian pressed Toots's reins between his palms. "Harley says Napoleon's too wild for a kid my age."

"I'm willin' to take a chance on her if Brian is," Harley said. "But, Brian, you'll have to stay off her till her foot heals."

"Gosh!" Brian's freckled cheeks glowed like two red apples as he patted the mare's nose. "This is the first horse I ever had for my own self."

Fannie walked over to the piebald. His ears flattened as she approached, and he sidled against the fence, jerking his head against the tethered rein.

"Whoa, Napoleon. Easy now. We're just going for a little ride." She stepped up onto the corral rail next to the wary-eyed horse, speaking softly to him while loosening the reins from the post. "I'll be back for my saddle later."

"But he ain't broke yet," Brian cautioned.

"He will be by the time I get there." After a few more encouraging words to the big horse, she eased herself onto his bare back. The uneasy onlookers instinctively stepped back. Napoleon stiffened and began to crowhop along the fence. Fannie sat lightly, moving easily with the horse's skittering. "I think he's going to see things my way," she called to them as she urged the jumpy black-and-white horse toward the meadow sloping up to the mountain.

"Well, I'll be a lop-eared jackass," Harley mumbled. "Don't that beat anything." Harley and the hired hand looked at each other in amazement.

"How'd she tame him down so quick. It was all we could do to get the dang bridle on him."

"Walter says she talks to horses," Brian said. "They talk to her, too." Beaming with admiration, he stood beside his new gray mare and watched the figure of the young woman on the unbroke piebald disappear among the pines above the meadow.

Montana's Lady Bucking-Horse Champion  9

L adies and gentlemen. The Lady Bucking-Horse Champion of Montana! Fannieeee . . . Sperry!"

The roar of Helena's Fourth of July crowd accompanied Fannie to the platform in front of the Central Park grandstand at the Lewis and Clark Anniversary Celebration. Clasping both arms above her head in a victory salute, she looked out over the faces of her fellow Montanans. Those who had cheered her for years now applauded their new state champion. A judge pinned a small gold medal to the knot of her neckerchief and shook her hand earnestly. "I've known a lot of fine bronc riders, Fannie, but you're the best." The other judges, too, stepped forward and clasped her hand. "Congratulations, Fannie."

Fannie felt a lump rising in her throat. No use pretending this was just another exhibition. These were *her* people, Montanans, declaring *her* their state champion. Walter and Christine broke through the crowd around the platform, followed by Rachel and Datus. When she saw her mother's misty eyes, she had to blink back her own tears. "Ma, I want you to have this." She took the medal from her scarf and pinned it on the collar of Rachel's dress. "You're the real champion of Montana."

Spectators surged onto the field, many pushing close. "Fine ride, Fannie."

"Puts me in mind of Lucille Mulhall the year she rode that outlaw bronc in Oklahoma City."

A few of the women passed by haughtily with disdainful looks and loud whispers. "What kind of lady would make such a spectacle of herself?"

"Such a nice-looking girl, too."

Datus guided his wife and daughter, an arm around each, toward the gate. "Yes, siree," he said. "I have me two champions here." And he bestowed a rare kiss on the cheek of each.

That auspicious beginning of the 1907 season proved to be merely a teaser for Rachel. Five days later, on July 9, she boarded the train with Fannie and Christine bound for the Winnipeg Stampede in Manitoba, Canada. Joining them at the Helena station was Violet Keigel, daughter of bronc rider Wes Keigel. Wilmot had contracted Violet, well-known locally as an extraordinary horsewoman, to ride with the Montana Girls for the season. Anna Pauls would join them in Winnipeg.

The *Independent* carried a small notice of their departure.

Three of Montana's best-known and most competent horse-women left last night for Canada, where they have been engaged to ride in relay races at the Winnipeg Stampede for W. R. Wilmot, one of the most prominent horse owners on the American turf.

In Winnipeg the girls enjoyed a reunion with Anna Pauls and the Thoroughbreds. Kentucky Prince and Songbird were now well-seasoned and fast, along with Fannie's other regulars, Lucky Girl and Baby Face. One of Christine's mounts, Minnie Blue, still needed some prodding.

Responding to her mother's need to keep busy, Fannie invited sixty-four-year-old Rachel to ride during the first morning's workout at the track. "Ma, why don't you try Baby Face?"

"I've never tried a racing saddle," Rachel said meekly. But sitting the sleek animal as if she had grown up on a racing saddle, she spent the morning putting Baby Face through his paces.

Christine expressed her admiration. "You should be riding as the fifth Montana Girl."

"We could get Velma to make another pair of bloomers," Fannie teased. Rachel laughed with the others. Violet, a plain young woman, whose ruddy face showed its exposure to Montana wind and sun, remained reserved amid the spontaneous banter. She rode well, bucking horses as well as relay, but she, too, hobbled her stirrups.

"My dad won't let me near a bronc unless the stirrups are tied," she confided. "Anyway, it's easier to stay glued when they're hobbled. If the horse falls, I can kick loose."

Fannie remained unconvinced.

The Winnipeg fair proved that western riding events were as popular above the international border as below, with riders arriving from all the western states and Canada. The women's relay race featured a new wrinkle. Instead of merely changing from one saddled mount to another, the contestants also would be required to unsaddle the horse and saddle the next mount before each round.

"They can't make us do that," Violet protested.

"Those are the rules this year," Wilmot said. "And they aren't allowing anyone to hold the mounts while you're saddling or to help you in any way. You can blindfold the horse if it seems necessary."

Fannie used her energy well in the Winnipeg relays. And that of her mounts. Riding a 4-mile heat each day on a half-mile track, changing horses and saddles each mile, she made the top 4-mile time of 9:42.

On the trip back to the Beartooth, Rachel sat proud as a queen returning from a triumphal tour of the provinces—and fully determined to accompany Fannie for the rest of the season. In August, as soon as they finished haying, she and Fannie left with Christine for the state fair in Grand Forks, North Dakota, to be followed by the Minnesota State Fair over Labor Day. Violet Keigel was unable to accompany them on this last leg of the tour. Her father needed her help with haying on their ranch, so there would be only three Montana Girls.

Rachel sat gripping the edge of her seat on one of the Minneapolis street-railway electric cars that carried passengers from the city to the fairgrounds in suburban Hamlin. "People weren't meant to go this fast," she said, "unless it's on horseback."

They alighted from the car with other fairgoers eager to see this biggest of all the grand fairs. Miles of concrete walks led to all parts of the 200-acre grounds. A band, uniformed in red and white, played marches on one of the well-manicured lawns. Fannie, checking the fairground map in the souvenir program, pointed out the locations of the horse barns and the huge, two-tier grandstand among the many exposition buildings. The program stated that 295,000 visitors had attended during the four days of the fair the previous year.

"Everything is so beautiful." Velma Wilmot gazed at the landscaped gardens around the horticultural building. Her husband had gone to see about getting some men to trail the horses to the fairground.

"I want to see the dairy building," Rachel said.

"First I'm treating you to a fine dinner, Ma. We could all use some food." Fannie guided her toward one of the pavilions where, through awninged windows, they saw diners seated at well-appointed tables.

Rachel protested such extravagance. "We should have brought sandwiches."

"Not this time. You're our guest." Christine, looking lovely in a summery white shirtwaist, took her arm. After a sumptuous meal that included catfish and strawberry ice cream, they toured the exhibitions. Rachel studied production innovations in the cattle, horse, and poultry pavilions, including a 90-foot refrigerator in the dairy barn. But she was most impressed with the elaborate public-comfort stations about the grounds and the telephones in the exposition building. Afternoon amusements in front of the grandstand attracted them to the upper tier, where they applauded Fink's Trained Mule and Dog Act, the Jackson Family Bicycle Act, and a troupe of Arabian acrobats.

It was growing dark when the performance ended and, just as they emerged from the grandstand, the electricity switch was thrown, illuminating the entire fairgrounds. The Montana Girls and their party gasped along with the rest of the crowd at the dazzling spectacle of incandescent lamps outlining the buildings with fire-like light. Everyone paused on the walks to enjoy the unusual brilliance. Touring the women's building, Rachel was more impressed by the dozens of lighted bulbs hanging from the ceiling than by the displays. "Why, it's bright as day in here."

"Wait till you see the automobiles." Christine had heard the Wilmots talk of buying one. "Auto clubs from all over are showing their machines. Supposed to be the biggest automobile meet ever seen in the West."

"Cars ain't so unusual these days," Anna said. "But airships are. There's going to be an airship flight twice every day from the hill over there."

"My word!" Rachel exclaimed.

"I heard it might fly over the grandstand during the racing." Velma turned to Rachel. "I hope all this excitement won't be too much for you, Mrs. Sperry."

"Heavens to Betsy, you talk like I'm an old lady." Rachel led the way down the walk. "Let's go have a look at that airship. And I want to see Dan Patch. He's the world's fastest harness horse, you know." She turned to Fannie. "Wish your pa was here to see him."

Wilmot, carrying the race schedule, joined the ladies. "Women's relay will head the afternoon events tomorrow," he said, "following Dan Patch's exhibition run."

"He's running to break the record, you know," Rachel informed them. "Datus told me some fella here in Minnesota owns him now." And she and Wilmot launched into a discussion of harness horses. When the girls began to stifle yawns, Wilmot drove the exhausted troupe in a hired buggy to their lodgings.

Fannie rubbed her aching feet as they prepared for bed. "Well, Ma, I'm glad we had time to see the fair before the races start. Did you like it?"

"Like it?" The little woman grinned. "I thought I'd died and gone to heaven."

Labor Day crowds on Monday, September 2, 1907, topped even the previous year's record attendance. Thousands of visitors joined Minnesotans milling about the grounds, and they thronged into the grandstand for the afternoon races. With Rachel and the Wilmots watching from the upper tier, the three Montana Girls strode onto the track for the opening event.

Murmurs turned to cheers as the spectators caught sight of the girls in their brightly colored shirts. Then the cheering soared into whistles and hollers for the black bloomers. The roar of the thousands of voices reminded Fannie of Montana's winter wind, swelling and modulating in great howling waves.

At the starting signal, each girl ran forward to flip a saddle onto her first mount, cinch up, then yank the horse's blindfold as she swung aboard. Christine held the lead for two changes, but heading down the track for the third round on balky Millie Blue, she dropped her quirt. Fannie, pulling alongside, reached over and handed her quirt to Christine. "Take it," she shouted over the pounding hoofs.

Christine's fingers closed around the leather and she applied it at once to drive her temperamental mount into the last change. She saddled quickly but, eager to regain her lead, she neglected to remove the blindfold. The confused horse plunged through a wooden fence on the inside track, throwing Christine through the splintered boards.

As Fannie crossed the finish line, she saw Christine, still clutching one rein, being helped to her feet. She dismounted and ran to the accident scene, oblivious of the announcement of her winning time.

"Are you hurt?" Fannie gripped the horse's bridle, patting his neck to calm him.

"Just scratched up a little." Christine held her left shoulder, where blood from a deep abrasion soaked through her sleeve. "Thanks for the quirt, Fannie. That was good of you."

"I didn't mean for you to whip him into the fence," Fannie teased. Christine, trying to smile, winced as Fannie pressed a handkerchief to her bleeding arm.

The Montana Girls continued on by train to county fairs in Stevens Point and Chippawa Falls, Wisconsin, before heading home. The tour had been grueling. Christine, sore from her accident, settled back in the seat and closed her eyes. Fannie felt worn out, too. But her mother's energy seemed inexhaustible. "I hate to see it end," Rachel said as the locomotive chugged into the Helena station.

"It was splendid!" she announced to the waiting Datus and Walter. "I'm going with Fannie every year till I'm too old to walk . . . or crawl."

But Rachel didn't go on tour the following season. Nor did Fannie. Shortly after the new year, Wilmot wrote saying he had a business opportunity in Ogden and had decided to get out of racing.

Fannie was stunned by the news that she wouldn't be riding with the

Montana Girls that summer. That, in fact, there were no more Montana Girls.

Her father tried to cheer her up. "Why don't you go down to the fair in Helena and ride bucking horses. Maybe they'll even get up a relay."

"It wouldn't be the same, Pa."

"No," her mother echoed, "it wouldn't be the same."

In the frigid March weather of 1909, Fannie lugged a pail of milk to the barn to feed a bucket calf. Rejected by its mother, the week-old Holstein was now taking milk from a teat Fannie had rigged at the bottom of a milk pail. She rubbed the calf's ears as it drank. Small satisfactions sparked Fannie's life on the homestead.

"Your calf looks good," Walter called. Having spread a load of hay in the meadow for the cattle, he drove the team of mules hitched to the hayrack into the semifrozen ooze of the corral. "I think you've pulled him through." Leaving the hayrack on frozen ground next to the fence, he climbed down and took off his gloves to unhook the doubletrees. When he finished, he leaned against the rack and pushed back his hat with his thumb.

"Fannie, I been thinkin'. . . ." He had a mischievous look in his eyes. "Why don't you and me take in the dance over at Craig tonight? It's time a pretty girl like you got waltzed around the dance floor. A whole herd of young swains are just waiting to get the chance."

"What swains are those?" Fannie poked her fingers into each cheek to make a dimple, then pretended to be knock-kneed.

Walter chuckled. "Fannie, you take the cake. Here you are, hiding yourself away on this ranch, working all the time."

"What about yourself? I don't see you sparkin' anybody."

"That's what I mean. We're both a couple of stick-in-the-muds. How about it? Why don't you get all gussied up, and we'll go out steppin'?"

"But I hoped you'd toss some targets for me."

"We can do that, too."

His enthusiasm changed her mind. He needs to have some fun, too, she thought. He was becoming more like their father every day.

"All right, I'll go . . . if you can outshoot me hitting these stones." She showed him a handful of pebbles she'd collected in her pocket. "I'll get the rifle while you put up the mules."

When Fannie returned with the .22 Winchester, Walter tossed the pebbles, one by one, high into the air, and she picked off nine out of ten in rapid succession, pumping the Winchester between each shot to chamber another round. Walter hit only four out of ten.

"But I thought you were going to let me win so you wouldn't have to go to the dance," he said.

"Now, that wouldn't be right, would it? I want to go to the dance. I just wanted to get in my practice first."

"You're a crack shot, Fannie," he said. "In fact, you're so doggone good, you scare me—and probably half the eligible bachelors in the county, too."

"Why? They haven't seen me shoot."

"No, but they've seen you ride. That's enough to make 'em stand back a few paces."

She sighted along the empty rifle barrel. "I'll tell you one thing. I'm not sashaying around for nobody. They either like me like I am or to heck with 'em."

"I was just teasing, Fannie. You know how they hang around you at dances. With your looks, any one of them would give his right arm to come callin' on you."

"Fiddlesticks. Just because I'm practically an old maid doesn't mean you have to lard it on so thick."

Rachel seemed glad when Fannie told her about the dance. "You and Walter should go more often."

Datus, wheezing from an asthma attack, agreed. "Your ma and me can do the milking. You get on your best duds and get going."

Fannie carried hot water in the teakettle to her bedroom washstand. After bathing, she dressed in her red-silk shirt with her best riding skirt and boots, combed her hair into one glossy braid and coiled it at the nape of her neck, then—as an afterthought—dabbed her earlobes with a few drops of the rose water Bertha had given her for Christmas.

Walter pursed his lips in a low whistle as she joined the family in the front room. He wore a fresh shirt and his best trousers. His hair, parted in the middle, was slicked down in a wide wave on each side.

"Land sakes, if you both ain't real pretty," Rachel said.

"Makes me wish I was young enough to go with you." Their father's watery eyes crinkled with affection. "You bundle up warm now."

Wrapped in heavy coats with woolen mufflers tied over their hats,

Fannie and Walter climbed into the buggy behind the team of Morgans and drove down the road into the wintry dusk.

Their arrival spread a flurry of greetings through the upstairs lodge hall where the dance was in progress. At the far end of the room, the Synness brothers sawed away on their fiddles, while the plank floor, crowded with dancers of all ages, throbbed to the beat of a lively, foot-stomping tune. Fannie and Walter nodded or waved to various dancers as they held their cold hands close to the potbellied stove. Friendly voices called to them.

"Hey, Fannie."

"Why, it's Fannie Sperry. Save a dance for me, Fannie."

She waved and returned the greetings. I haven't seen some of these folks for a month of Sundays, she thought. I'm glad I came. Walter's right. I have been keeping too much to home.

"Fannie, you're here!" Christine, towing Will Craig by the hand, appeared from among the dancers. "Oh, it's good to see you." Then she whirled away in Will's arms, her long dress billowing over trim high-buttoned shoes.

"I'll hang up our coats," Walter said, helping Fannie with hers. "It's hot enough in here to roast a hog." Fannie smoothed back her hair, her face still tingling from the frosty ride.

"Miss Fannie, could I please have this dance?" A soft throaty voice at her elbow gained her attention. She saw Jonah Stokes, a ranch hand from Wolf Creek adjusting the string tie that anchored his stiff collar.

"Hello, Jonah." Dull-witted Jonah Stokes had been rejected by nearly every girl in the county. "I . . . uh . . ." She tried to keep her disinterest from showing. "I just got here, Jonah."

"Movin' around'll warm you up." He gripped her around the waist and shuffled clumsily onto the dance floor. She had to do some fancy footwork just to keep her toes from ending up under his. Mercifully, the music soon ended and she moved away from her oafish partner to chat with some schoolboys, who wanted to know if she would be riding at the fair again next summer.

"Well, if it ain't the bucking-horse champion of Montana." A tall, lanky cowboy wearing a ten-gallon hat leaned against the wall to block her path. "Where's your horse, Fannie?" His comment brought snickers from his stocky companion. Fannie recognized the cowboy from last summer's buck-ing events in Helena. His good looks were spoiled, she remembered, by his arrogant manner. "How about you and me doin' a little dancin'? Or are you and Jonah keeping company?"

His short, stocky pal chuckled, blowing a stream of cigarette smoke toward the ceiling. "Watch out there, George. You wouldn't want her to get a hold on *your* hackamore." His laugh revealed a row of tobacco-stained teeth.

"I'll take my chances." The cowboy's dark eyes swept over her. "I'm George Archer. Hazed for you down at the fair. Remember?"

"Well, yes. I guess I do." Fannie could feel her face flush.

"Shorty and me were bettin' you'd quit that bronc in two seconds flat. But you fooled us. You rode that bugger to a standstill."

"He wasn't that tough." Fannie looked around for Walter.

"You women got guts, I'll give you that much." His gaze dropped to her slim waist as he teased, "But those broncs they put you women on are about wore out."

"Wore out? They are not. I draw for my broncs from the same hat you men do." Her anger flashed.

Shorty's grin widened. "What'd I tell you, George. These lady bronc-stompers are a pretty feisty bunch."

"This one's just plain pretty." George grabbed her hand. "Let's you and me dance." As he pulled her to him and moved among the dancers, Fannie caught sight of Walter returning from the coatroom. When he saw her, he smiled warmly. Good Lord, she thought, Walter's *pleased* to see me dancing with this galoot.

When the music ended, George maneuvered her toward the spot where Shorty leaned against the wall. Shorty nudged another cowhand, who stood staring as George introduced her. "Boys, this here's our lady bucking-horse champeen."

"You don't say." The cowhand reeked of whiskey. "Most ladies I know wear dresses." Deadpan, he raised one eyebrow at her riding skirt and boots, then laughed raucously with the others.

"If you'll excuse me. . . ." Fannie edged away.

"Well, I'll be. . . ." she heard George say. "She's sure got her nose in the air." More laughter floated after her as she made her way toward two young women, former classmates at the Mitchell school.

"Hello, Clara. Hazel." She managed a smile and held out her hand. Clara, prim in a high-lace collar and small round eyeglasses, clasped Fannie's hand, looking at her with affection. "It's nice to see you, Fannie."

Hazel's icy gaze swept past her toward George Archer. "You hanging out with cowboys now?"

"No, not really."

"I heard you were traveling all over to roundups and races . . . without your mother." Hazel plumped her sausage curls. She had rouged her cheeks and looked like a regular hussy, Fannie thought.

"Ma went with me to Winnipeg and Minneapolis."

"That sounds exciting, Fannie," Clara said.

"I wouldn't be caught dead on a bucking horse." Hazel swished her taffeta petticoat as she turned away, parading toward Archer and his pals.

"Don't mind her," Clara said. "She's jealous. I'm proud you're the Montana champion. I only wish I could do something that well."

"But, you can," Fannie assured her. "You're the best quilt maker in six counties. I love your beautiful comforters."

Clara smiled. "I'll make one for you."

"Would you, Clara? I have some money saved."

"I couldn't let you pay me." Clara's earnest gaze enhanced her plain features. "It'd be an honor to make one for you."

Before she could protest Clara's generosity, a voice sounded behind her and two hands covered her eyes. "Guess who!" She turned to see John Synness, his violin tucked under his arm. Christine's brother was blond and rosy-cheeked, like Christine. He also had his sister's sensitivity, and Fannie liked him.

"John, your music gets better every time I hear you play."

"Wish we could see you around more often, Fannie. Christine has missed you this winter."

"I know. And I've missed her."

"Can we play a tune for you, Fannie?"

"My favorite is a new song called 'Springtime in the Rockies.' Do you know it?"

"You bet! It's real pretty. We'll play it for you." When John rejoined Albert, they shouldered their instruments and began the tune. Walter reappeared, took Fannie's hand, and waltzed her around the room.

"I'm glad you're here," she whispered. "Those rubes over there were pestering me." She glanced toward Archer and Shorty, who were getting boisterous with Hazel.

"Pay no attention to them. They don't have the sense they were born with."

"May I cut in?" Will Craig tapped Walter on the shoulder and took Fannie's hand.

"No one should waltz with her own brother," Christine said gaily as she danced off with Walter. Will and Fannie exchanged pleasantries until the music ended and he thanked her for the dance. Fannie nodded cordially. Will was kind to dance with me, she mused, but I'm sure Christine put him up to it.

After his dance with Christine, Walter partnered with several of the unattached young women, while Fannie smiled through dances with neighboring ranchers, itinerant hired hands, and an older widower with eight half-grown children.

The evening wore on. At midnight Christine and Will joined them for sandwiches and coffee served by the ladies' auxiliary. "No sense in you two tryin' to drive home tonight," Will said. "Why don't you stay over at my place?"

"Oh, please do," Christine urged. "I'm staying, and Will's mother insisted we ask you two."

"That's nice of you, Will." Fannie put down her cup. "And I'm much obliged to your mother. But we have to get back. I'm hand-feeding a new calf."

"You don't have to mother it personally, do you?" Christine giggled and offered another sandwich to Will.

"No, but we can't leave all the chores to Ma and Pa." She smiled warmly at Christine. "We'll get together real soon. I promise."

Walter stood, saying, "I'll get the team. We've a ride ahead of us."

After appropriate good-byes, Fannie and Walter headed back toward the Beartooth huddled in the buggy beneath the old buffalo robe. For a time they rode in silence, enjoying the cold air against their faces after the overheated hall. The night was clear, and Fannie studied the stars in the deep hollow of the sky.

"Did you have a good time, Walter?" she asked. "You must have danced every dance."

He nodded reflectively. "I don't know, Fannie, all the girls seem so empty-headed. They don't have anything on their minds. They don't even like ranching. They all want to move to town."

Fannie turned to study his expression. Usually Walter didn't talk about his feelings. "Walter, you're barely twenty years old. You have plenty of time to meet the right girl."

He looked at her earnestly through the darkness. "What about you? You didn't seem to have a very good time tonight."

"Yes I did. It was nice. It's just that I . . . I don't seem to fit in anymore."

"Fit in? You're popular, Fannie."

"Yes. With rude cowpokes. Or tottering old ranchers. Or kids."

"Now wait a minute," he teased. "How about me? I don't fit any of those categories."

"No." She grinned. "You're more in the brother category."

"True," he mused. "But you'll have to admit . . . a hell of a waltzer."

"Yes." Fannie patted his arm affectionately. "A hell of a waltzer."

A Peer among the Best  10

More than a year later, on a June day in 1910, Datus returned from his Helena deliveries with a broader grin than usual. "Fannie, they're getting up a relay race for the Fourth again this year. Folks are wondering if you'll be riding."

Fannie shrugged. "I think I'm a little out of practice."

"Hogwash. You don't need any practice. Why don't you go down there and show them what relay is all about?"

"Maybe Christine would like to ride, too," her mother suggested eagerly. Both the elder Sperrys had felt a growing concern for Fannie's lack of enthusiasm for her daily ranch chores. "Why don't you take some of that nice apple butter over to her?" Rachel went out to the old dugout where she kept her canned goods and returned with one of the few remaining jars from last fall's preserves. "It's a beautiful day for a ride."

Fannie pondered entering the relay race as she rode to the Synness ranch. She found Christine preparing food for a branding crew and explained her mission. "How about it, Chris? We haven't ridden together lately, not even around the ranch. It'd be fun."

"Fannie," Christine interrupted, "don't you think we're getting a little long in the tooth for that sort of thing?"

"What's age got to do with it?"

Fannie on one of her pintos at the Beartooth homestead, about 1910.

"We're twenty-three years old." Christine dropped the last dumpling into the chicken broth. "I'm not as quick as I used to be. See this?" She patted her nicely rounded hips through the homespun apron. "I'm getting fat."

Fannie scoffed. "If you're fat, I'm Sitting Bull." She spooned sugar into the coffee Christine placed in front of her.

"It *would* be fun, wouldn't it?" Christine rinsed her hands at the sink and sat down at the table, which was already set with freshly baked bread and homemade jam and relishes. Two raisin pies stood steaming on the sideboard.

"Then you'll do it?" Fannie felt some of the old excitement.

Christine paused. "Only if you'll stay for dinner. All I see are my brothers' beards over my cooking." Then, jumping up to check the dumplings, she grinned. "I may have to get married just for a change of scenery."

Bleachers in front of the dirt track around the Central Park ball diamond were a far cry from the double-decked grandstand at the Minnesota State Fair, but Fannie and Christine were happy to be back in the saddle with their former teammate Violet Keigel. The race, for cowponies only, also was a change from the Thoroughbreds the girls had ridden for Walter Wilmot.

Fannie's divided riding skirt of blue serge was more cumbersome than the black riding bloomers the Montana Girls had worn, but nothing could inhibit her eagerness to get on with the race. Christine's cheeks flushed almost as pink as her shirt, and Fannie could see she was nervous. Violet, always more confident on cowponies than Thoroughbreds, stood ready to go.

The starting flag fell. When Fannie sprang forward, squeezing between the stall and her mount, the startled horse kicked, catching the pocket of her skirt with his hoof. Buttons popped in every direction, and the heavy skirt fell to the ground.

Gasps, then laughter rose from the spectators as they caught sight of her knee-length muslin knickers. But Fannie swung into the saddle and spurred the horse onto the track. Whistles and hoots followed her around the course and across the finish line, two lengths ahead of Christine and Violet. She dismounted and ran into the stall where her skirt still lay in a heap. She picked it up and stepped into it, clutching the placket with one hand and waving to the crowd with the other. The crowd applauded.

"Miss Sperry, I'm a reporter for the *Independent*." A bookish-looking young man approached, balancing a notebook. "Could I talk with you?"

"You bet." Fannie adjusted her grip on her skirt while Rachel looked for the missing buttons.

"Do you plan to ride at the new Pendleton Roundup?" the reporter asked. "I understand the Millers' 101 Wild West Show will be featured and all the top cowboys will ride." Fannie hadn't heard about the new Pendleton Roundup.

"Of course, she's riding at Pendleton," Rachel said, eager to sustain the rekindled sparkle in Fannie's eyes.

Fannie smiled. "I guess I am," she told the reporter. "I think we can make it as far as Pendleton, huh, Chris?"

"Fannie, I have to tell you." Christine led her away from the group, her eyes shining mischievously. "Will asked me last night. We're getting married."

Fannie could only stare at her friend's radiant face.

Christine seemed puzzled by Fannie's reaction. "Aren't you happy for me?"

"Sure, I am." Fannie managed a smile. "But you can still ride at Pendleton, can't you? You and Will could both come."

"Not this year. We'll be working for his pa. They're shorthanded."

Fannie suddenly felt abandoned. Was she the only one who cared, really cared, about riding?

"I hope you'll be around for the wedding."

"Sure, Chris. Of course, I will."

Three days after the church ceremony uniting Christine and Will Craig in marriage, Fannie arrived in Pendleton and made her way among the assembled riders to the check-in booth behind the grandstand. As she studied the lineup sheet, two cowboys stepped up to check the events.

"If you ask me, they ought'a keep those fool women out of exhibition," one grumbled. "A female ain't got no business on a bucking horse." His weathered face and neck emphasized his rough demeanor.

His companion agreed. "Ruins the event for us men."

The rough cowboy snickered. "Women are built for havin' babies, not ridin' broncs."

Her cheeks burning, Fannie turned to the men and blurted in a joking tone, "Listen, we can give you boys a run for your money any day of the week and twice on Sunday."

"So, you're one of 'em." The snickering stopped, and the cowboy's snide smile faded. "The sheriff should run you cheeky squaws out of town."

Fannie, startled by the real anger in his remark, tried to smooth over his angry words. "Now, wait a minute. No need to get all steamed up. What's wrong with good riders competing, even if they are women?"

"I'll tell you what's wrong with it." The cowboy glowered. "You girls can't ride worth a damn. You spoil the horses. And you water down the events till there's no challenge in 'em."

Fannie stood her ground. "You're wrong, mister. Just watch us today."

"I'm getting up a petition to have all of you thrown out of the roundup."

Suddenly aware that he was serious and that the confrontation was attracting attention, Fannie turned and walked away.

A stout, dark-complexioned woman in a leather vest and skirt stepped up beside her. "You from around here?" The woman's straight, black hair was tied back with a beaded thong, and her broad grin revealed a chipped front tooth.

"Montana." Shrugging off the unpleasant encounter with the cowboys, Fannie offered her hand. "I'm Fannie Sperry."

"The bronc rider?" She gripped Fannie's hand in both of hers. "I've been hearing about you. Riding slick, I mean. I'm Bertha Blancett. I ride slick, too."

"So, you're Bertha." The friendly woman's reputation as a bronc rider was well known.

"I'm hazing for my husband, Del, he's a bulldogger, and doing a little Roman riding. Will you be taking on an exhibition bronc this afternoon?"

Fannie nodded. "And riding relay. But I wish someone would tell me why we can't ride bucking horses with the men. Did you hear those two cowboys just now? They don't want us to ride at all."

Bertha's grin faded. "I know. They say we're spoilin' the events. But you and me don't ask no favors. We take 'em like we draw 'em and ride 'em slick."

"Some seem to think it's just luck when we beat them."

Bertha snorted. "Luck don't interest me. I'm here for the purse." She laughed then and, taking Fannie's elbow, guided her among the arriving riders. "Come on, I want you to meet some of the regulars. They're not all numskulls." They approached a tall cowboy in a black hat who stood talking with two others. "What say, Clay?" Bertha shook hands with the cowboy, whose dark eyes and square jaw dominated his rugged face. "Fannie, this here's Clay McGonagill." McGonagill was the roper Ellison Carroll had challenged at the Big Roping in San Antonio. "Boys, this is Fannie Sperry," Bertha continued. "She just won the Montana Bucking-Horse Championship."

"That so? Congratulations." McGonagill's handshake was firm and friendly. "Say hello to the ramrod of the Miller Brothers show, Guy Weadick." The handsome Weadick wore a ridiculously high-crowned white hat and a huge red neckerchief around his neck. His ready smile held her gaze.

"And this is Johnnie Mullens, our arena director and the best judge of outlaw horseflesh in the West. He's brought enough bad horses with him to stove us all up till Christmas."

Mullens, small and wiry, standing with his thumbs in his belt, extended his hand. "Howdy." His Texas accent hung thick as he said, "You rode relay for Wilmot." Fannie remembered that Mullens, a top horseman and trail boss turned bronc rider, had been at Winnipeg. She liked his slow manner, and her dismay at the hostility of the two rude cowboys began to fade.

"Fannie rides slick," Bertha said.

"No cheat straps, eh?" Clay looked more closely at Fannie. "Well, that's to your credit."

"I figure I should give the horse an even chance," Fannie quipped.

The men chuckled.

"You fellas better watch out for this little gal." Bertha flashed her chipped tooth in a broad grin. "I hear she's dynamite."

"They seem like a nice bunch," Fannie said as they walked on.

"They're tops. Some cowpokes make light of women riders. But not all." Then, shifting her gaze to Fannie, Bertha said, "Ever taken a bad spill?"

"I bit the dust once. In Anaconda. Ornery bronc named Tracy dumped me."

"Once? I've hit the dirt more times than I care to think about." She gestured toward a young cowboy. "See that good-looking kid over there. That's Lee Caldwell. Only eighteen, and one of the best bronc riders ever forked a bad horse." The slightly built youth wore leather chaps. "Raised near here on the Umatilla Indian Reservation," Bertha continued. "His dad's a wheat farmer, but he learned to ride on Injun ponies. Won the bronc stomping here last year."

"I guess you know just about everybody." Fannie had felt lonely traveling without her mother or Christine, but now she realized that it had its advantages, enabling her to mix more with other riders and get to know them.

"I've been around a bit. And Del's helped me get acquainted." Bertha put on the ten-gallon hat she'd been carrying. "Let's go round him up," she said, "so we can catch Lucille Mulhall's opener."

"She's here, too?" Lucille Mulhall had been Fannie's idol since she and Walter read about "The Girl Ranger" in a *Wild West* magazine. "I thought she must be old by now."

"She's a year younger than me," Bertha said. "Twenty-five. Will Rogers hung out at her dad's ranch and taught her to rope. When Colonel Mulhall started his Wild West show, they both performed in it. Trouble is, there's hardly any women steer ropers to compete against. She competes with men or, sometimes, does exhibitions. But she's known mostly now as a trick roper. No one can rope like Lucy Mulhall. Come on, let's hurry or we'll miss her. The deuce with Del. He can find *us*."

Bertha led the way toward the bleachers flanking the grandstand. All seats were filled, and the overflow of spectators formed a solid mass of eager faces crowded around the field. Bertha found a spot for them up front just as Lucille Mulhall galloped onto the field on a palomino gelding. An attractive blonde, wearing a fringed buckskin outfit, she rode with a commanding air, strong and confident, her silver-studded saddle and bridle glinting in the sun. Fannie watched in awe as the seasoned performer twirled her lasso around herself and her palomino while the horse stepped in and out of the huge loop. After a few fancy throws from horseback, she dismounted to continue her spectacular roping on foot, whirling the lariat across the track and dropping it neatly over the heads of five horses galloping abreast, a rider aboard each.

Bertha and Fannie added their enthusiastic applause to that of the other delighted spectators, then made their way toward the gate as Lucille left the arena. Lucille waved when she saw Bertha.

"How was I?" she called, reining the palomino to where they stood. Up close, her flaxen hair and creamy skin made her look more like a calendar girl than a roper, Fannie thought.

"First rate," Bertha said. "I got someone here who wants to meet you. This is Fannie Sperry."

"So, you're Fannie." The pretty roper smiled approval. "I hear you ride slick." Fannie, astonished that the headliner knew who she was, managed an assenting nod. "Believe me," the roper continued, "those of us who know the difference can sure appreciate what you do."

"Thanks, Miss Mulhall." Fannie had intended to compliment *her*, and here *she* was praising Fannie.

"Call me Lucy. Where you been riding, Fannie?"

"I rode relay with the Montana Girls, and lately I've just been riding broncs."

"Riding broncs?" Bertha scoffed at Fannie's modesty. "She's Lady Bucking-Horse Champion of Montana, is all."

"That's swell," Lucy said. "I guess you know Bertha rides slick, too. She's about the best all-round cowgirl ever seen, can throw a steer good as any man."

A weathered cowhand with a pale, sandy mustache overtook them and fell in with their stride. "You betcha, and she learned it all from Pawnee Bill."

Bertha grinned. "Fannie, this is Del, my husband."

"What's this about Pawnee Bill?" Lucy said.

"Bertha was ridin' for Pawnee Bill's show in Cheyenne when I met her. Ain't nothing she can't do in the saddle."

"Well, you won't see me in no *racing* saddle." Bertha grinned, patting her ample figure. "I'm better off with two mounts, standing with a foot on each one." They laughed with her, and Del gave his wife an affectionate squeeze.

The thrill of meeting the champions sparked Fannie's performance. Each day she made top time in the relay and basked in the adulation of thousands as she rode her exhibition broncs to a standstill.

On the last day she walked with Lucy into the cook tent, where a group of cowboys had gathered around a table. She recognized McGonagill, Mullens, and one or two others. A lanky, blue-eyed cowboy with a boyish, engaging smile was telling a story. When he saw Fannie, he stopped short. "Say, ain't you the girl who rode that Helena relay in her knickers?"

Fannie blushed as all turned to look at her. "If I am," she snapped, "it's none of *your* business." She turned and strode from the tent. Lucy followed. Outside, Fannie covered her burning cheeks with her hands. "Who is that rude cowpoke?"

Lucy smiled. "That's Bill Steele."

"Those saddle tramps are all alike," Fannie sputtered. "I wouldn't give you a plugged nickel for a carload."

Competing at the First Calgary Stampede, 1912

11

A familiar sense of freedom surged through Fannie as she spurred her big piebald, Napoleon, into a gallop. They moved across the valley, the horse's mane and tail whipping in the wind, the young woman's dark braid flying. Leaning into his long strides, she scanned the slope where the home-place nestled in its arc of meadow near the base of the Beartooth. She savored the aroma of late-summer sagebrush mixed with the fresh smell of approaching rain and the pungency of saddle leather and horse sweat. It felt good to be in the saddle again after two weeks of haying, and her thoughts raced with the rhythm of Napoleon's hoofbeats.

The letter that came early in June had surprised her.

Dear Miss Sperry. I'm impressed with your bronc riding. If you can come to the Stampede I'm putting on in Calgary in September, I'm sure you can win some big money. You'll be riding for the world's championship.

Fannie looked at the signature. Guy Weadick. Her heart quickened. Bertha Blancett had written her about his efforts to get backers for a big stam-pede in Calgary, one that promised to be the finest event of its kind ever produced. A real competition between the finest riders. Not just an exhibition. Now he was inviting her to be part of it. And for the world's title.

Her mother seemed hesitant. "Fannie, it's good that this Weadick invited you. But . . . well . . . it's a long way up there to Canada."

"Look at it this way," her father said. "Traipsing across the country was fine when you were younger, but it isn't proper for a twenty-five-year-old woman to be parading herself like that."

"Pa! I'm going up there to ride, not to parade myself."

"I don't mean it that way," Datus said. "What your ma means is . . . where is all this riding getting you? You should be thinking about settling down. Your sister Carrie already has five kids. Bertha and Arthur each have two."

"I know that, Pa."

Rachel ignored her husband's remark. "It'd be hard for us without you, Fannie. That's about the size of it."

Fannie studied her mother's work-weathered face. Her father did his best, but with his asthma getting worse every year he could barely handle his routine chores.

"I hate to leave everything to you and Walter," Fannie said. "But don't you see, I have to go. Just this one more time."

Rachel sighed. "We know you do."

"All right, then," her father summed up. "Your ma will go with you. Walter and me will manage somehow."

Rachel launched into a whirlwind of activities in preparation, one of which was to design and sew a divided riding skirt for Fannie. Its trim line included a special panel in front, buttoned on either side from waist to hem. Unbuttoned it became roomy culottes, comfortable for riding astride; buttoned, it appeared to be a conventional ankle-length skirt. "You won't have a bulky skirt holding you back," she said. "And you'll still look like a lady between rides."

Buoyed by thoughts of her mother's spunky devotion, Fannie reined Napoleon into a wide turn, and he settled into an easy lope back toward the ranch. She had written Weadick asking if she could bring Napoleon for the relays. Weadick replied that he couldn't allow it because he didn't want anyone claiming he had in any way given preference to a contestant. Reading and rereading, Fannie had nearly memorized his enclosed flyer.

The Calgary Frontier Days Celebration and Stampede offers prizes totaling $25,000. First prize in the women's bucking-horse event is $1,000. And lady contestants will not be charged an entrance fee.

The rain began as she and Napoleon reached the barn but, still absorbed in thoughts of Weadick's letter and the Stampede, she hardly noticed.

There will be five lady bucking-horse riders entered. She hoped Bertha Blancett would be among the five. *The best in the country.* That meant Bertha. *It is needless for me to say that any lady riding slick and clean will certainly be considered by the judges much better than those who hobble their stirrups. Of course, lady contestants have the privilege of riding either way.*

"Weadick knows I only ride slick," she murmured aloud as she curried and grained Napoleon.

Next morning, September 1, 1912, the steady drizzle continued as Fannie and her mother hurried across the platform toward the train that would take them to Calgary, Alberta, 150 miles above the Canadian border. The Helena station bustled with ranchers and cowboys shaking raindrops from their hats before boarding. A few prosperous-looking businessmen struggled with suitcases, and women in ankle-length dusters held umbrellas above their ostrich-feathered hats.

"The Stampede's bringing out lots of folks." Rachel clutched their two small grips, while Fannie, balancing her saddle against her hip, maneuvered through the small groups of travelers. Departure from the Helena station always seemed more adventuresome than boarding the train at the lonely Mitchell stop. The huge locomotive snorted and hissed, its sinewy pistons and valves flexing with the hammer of the boiler.

Dodging a sudden spurt of steam, Fannie led the way along the platform beside the waiting train, past the tender piled high with wood and the open door of the baggage car, where she saw stacked crates of produce and freight, mail bags, and trunks. She was glad she hadn't let them take her saddle. They'd more than likely plop it down wrong and warp the stirrups.

"All aboard!" the conductor shouted above the squeal of the whistle. Several buckskin-clad Blackfeet clamored onto the train, the women carrying assorted bundles and herding lively children. Fannie hoisted her saddle onto the first of the two passenger cars, then turned to help her mother board.

The car's darkened interior smelled of damp woolens and horse hair as she carried the saddle down the crowded aisle. Finding an unoccupied row among the green-plush seats, she stowed the saddle upended on its pommel next to the window. She let her mother squeeze in beside it, then seated herself. The train chugged out of the station amid a confusion of whistles, bells, and hissing steam. As it picked up speed and headed north, Fannie tried to make out the gray outline of their familiar mountain 20 miles to the north, but it was obscured by clouds.

"The Sleeping Giant is all fogged over," she told her mother.

Rachel squinted in an attempt to glimpse the mountain's crest through the rain-splashed window. "You mean my lucky Beartooth?"

Fannie leaned her head back against the seat, anticipating the long journey. "I hope it's very, very lucky."

They arrived at their Calgary lodgings late at night, slept soundly to the patter of rain on the boardinghouse roof, and awakened to another day of mist and gray skies. Fannie, dressed in her riding clothes, watched her mother turn this way and that before the bureau mirror, fussing with her hair, which she wore in a knot at the back of her head.

"You look fine, Ma. Hurry or we'll miss breakfast."

Downstairs in the dining room, several men and women were gathered around the big table when Fannie and her mother entered the room. A hired girl hurried from the kitchen carrying a steaming tray of pancakes, sausages, fried potatoes, and eggs.

"Fannie!" Bertha Blancett got up from her seat and came to greet them. "It's good to see you."

"Golly, I'm glad you're here, Bertha. This is my ma." Fannie smiled across the table at Del Blancett and Clay McGonagill.

The lanky Clay, wearing his black hat, unfolded his legs from the chair and stood politely. "Mornin'."

Rachel looked pleased as Del, his pale mustache still looking out of place on his weathered face, stood to hold a chair for her. Fannie took the remaining chair beside a serious-looking cowboy in a faded denim shirt, a bandana around his neck.

"Howdy. I'm Bernie St. Clair." He motioned toward the young woman beside him. "This here's my wife, Goldie." He grinned, then added, "Canada's top horsewoman." Goldie's blond curls framed pale-blue eyes and a pretty mouth.

"And this little gal is Annie Shaffer from Texas." Annie, who appeared to be in her thirties, wore a thick braid of mousy hair hanging down her back. She held her calico sleeve up out of the plate of sausages as she reached across to shake Fannie's hand.

"I've been looking forward to meetin' you, Fannie. Bertha, here, says you don't hobble your stirrups." There were dark circles under Annie's eyes.

"That's right. Do you?"

Annie nodded.

"Not many female slick riders around." Clay McGonagill rewrapped himself around his chair and attacked his pancakes. "Tillie Baldwin, and maybe Nettie Hawn, are the only women I know that don't hobble—besides you two." He indicated Fannie and Bertha.

"I ride slick myself," Rachel said, puddling syrup around her pancakes.

Warmed by the hot breakfast and pleasant company, Fannie, Rachel, and the St. Clairs rode with the Blancetts in their rented surrey to Victoria Park, a quarter of a mile from the center of town.

Despite the drizzle, Victoria Park bustled with activity—cowboys on saddle horses, wagons delivering supplies, livestock being herded into the corrals. Fannie and her friends inspected the park's permanent stables, which accommodated 500 horses. Outside corrals had been built to hold an additional 300 horses and 300 head of cattle.

On the exhibition grounds, exact replicas of the original Hudson's Bay trading post and of Old Fort Whoop-up had been erected, along with the tepees of several Indian camps. Fannie noted the general admission price of one dollar for a seat in the new bleachers that completely encircled the half-mile track, plus fifty cents more for a reserved seat in the covered grandstand. A row of shotgun chutes lined one edge of the center arena, and workmen were putting finishing touches on a judges' stand. Nearby, a covered boothlike structure had been built.

"Look, there's the royal box. The uncle of the king of England is to be the honored guest here." Goldie talked excitedly. "His proper title is His

Royal Highness, the Duke of Connaught. He's the new Governor General of Canada, and he's bringing his wife, the duchess, and their daughter, Princess Patricia."

Fannie and Rachel again exchanged glances.

Just then a commotion arose from the horse barn. A woman screamed, and a cowboy ran from the building shouting, "Call a doctor! Joe LaMar's been kicked!"

Del and Bernie dashed into the building. Fannie and the others followed, but Del, grim faced, reappeared and stopped them at the door. In the arena beyond, Fannie could see men hazing a frenzied sorrel horse and others crouched over the crumpled body of a cowboy. "Too late for the doctor," Del said. "Red Wing throwed him, then stomped him. He's dead."

Word of the accident spread fast, and an hour later a saddened troupe of riders assembled in the rain in front of the grandstand for the grand-entry rehearsal. Fannie felt disheartened and uncertain.

Guy Weadick, wearing his high-crowned white hat and astride a sleek black stallion, rode through the gate. He sat with proud bearing on a saddle that had finely tooled leather tapaderos over the stirrups. Turning his mount to face the riders, he surveyed their discouraged faces for a moment before he spoke. "We've had some sorry news here this morning. I know you feel as bad about it as I do. But we have a show to put on. And we're going to give the folks who buy the tickets their money's worth."

"Sure thing, Guy," one of the dispirited cowboys mumbled.

"We're going to dedicate today's opening to Joe LaMar," Weadick continued. "What would you think of contributing all of today's winnings to his family?"

"That's a decent thing to do," someone said. "I'm all for it, Guy."

"That's the least we can do," another said. Others nodded agreement. Some applauded.

"Just remember, we're doing this one for Joe," Weadick emphasized. "And we're not going to let the rain slow us up, either. We're going to ride like we've never ridden before." A cheer went up, and the riders fell in line behind Addison Day for a warm-up surge around the arena.

A spectacular parade through the streets of Calgary began the Stampede events. Weadick's depiction of the early West started with Indians from six tribes, Blackfeet, Blood, Sarcee, Cree, Stonie, and Piegan. Then came missionaries, the Hudson's Bay company, whiskey traders, and cowmen with their roundup crews, chuckwagons, and cavvy. Stagecoaches and prairie schooners with seasoned drivers carried old-time hunters, trappers, guides, scouts, and frontiersmen. A contingent of veterans of the Northwest Mounted Police wore their red coats. The mounted cowboy band preceded hundreds of marchers from Calgary labor organizations that, Fannie learned, Weadick had reimbursed $10,000 to cover any lost profits due to cancellation of their annual Labor Day sports program.

Fannie, wearing a white-satin shirt with a red-silk scarf over the hatband of her new white Stetson, rode a spirited palomino beside Clay McGonagill, whose black shirt and hat went handsomely with his black quarter horse. Following the mounted riders, a band of vaqueros from Old Mexico completed the 6-mile-long procession.

Thousands of cheering onlookers jammed the sidewalks as the parade passed under a Grecian archway constructed over the main street. The huge structure, outlined with electric lightbulbs, glowed through the mist, and Fannie read GOD SAVE THE KING across the top of the arch, and CALGARY WELCOMES THEIR ROYAL HIGHNESSES. A gigantic billboard advertising Sweet Corporal Cigarettes adorned the roof of a small cafe nearby. But most impressive of all, she thought, was City Hall, ablaze with thousands of electric lights outlining its tower, its four-story dormers, and its gigantic sign, WELCOME TO CALGARY.

Eager spectators were still scrambling for seats in the Victoria Park grandstand when a snappy thirty-piece citizens' band, decked out in green and gold uniforms, marched through the gate and spread out in formation, the big bass drum and two glittering gold tubas setting a bright tempo.

Following the band, Guy Weadick, mounted on his prancing black, and Addison Day, on a handsome Appaloosa, galloped into the arena carrying flags of the United States and Canada. They led the procession of colorfully dressed riders circling the field, two by two, then separating to form two lines going in opposite directions. Crossing diagonally, they laced into an intricate pattern before ending in a single line before the grandstand. Fannie, gazing at the thousands applauding from the stands, held the palomino in line between Clay and a cowboy named Doc Pardee.

Weadick and Day dismounted and placed the flags on either side of the judges' platform. Weadick greeted the crowd, his voice booming through a large megaphone. "Welcome to the Calgary Frontier Days and Stampede." He turned to each side of the stand and toward the bleachers so all could hear. "You're about to witness the greatest exhibition of roping and riding—the greatest aggregation of frontier cowboys and cowgirls—ever assembled in any one place till now."

Weadick waited for the roar of enthusiastic cheers and applause to fade. Then his voice softened. "But in spite of this happy occasion and the fine turnout, our hearts are heavy. Joe LaMar, one of our bronco riders, was killed today when he was thrown and kicked." A low murmur spread through the crowd.

"So all prize money from today's performance will be donated to Joe's widow and children." Applause. "And to make doubly sure Joe's family is taken care of, we're passing the hat so that every one of you can help. Let's show that we appreciate these cowboys and cowgirls, and that we don't forget one who has given his life doing what he loved to do."

Addison Day walked down the line of performers, holding his hat out for their contributions. Other hats, filled with coins and folding money, were brought from the stands.

"Thank you, folks," Weadick said. "I know Joe's family will truly appreciate this. And now . . . on with the Stampede!"

The band struck up as Lucille Mulhall, Florence LaDue, and Bertha Blancett galloped into the arena, twirling lariats in wide loops above their heads. Fannie stood with Goldie and Annie to watch. One by one the women showed the fancy roping feats that had made them champions. Bertha and Lucy performed flawlessly, and Florence LaDue was even more impressive. Her act climaxed with her keeping 65 feet of rope whirling around herself and her horse, a blaze-faced chestnut with one white-stockinged hind leg.

Strains of "The Dream of Old Mexico" filled the air when Senor Esteban Clemento and his Mexican vaqueros performed their intricate roping stunts. Tex McLeod gave an exhibition of trick riding that left the audience breathless. Twice his mount crashed against the fence, but McLeod was not thrown. Little Irene Palmer demonstrated her Cossack ride, winning a standing ovation from the crowd.

Adding comedy to the show, Ed Carr of St. Pierre, North Dakota, rode a bucking buffalo, and Bob Yokum drove a pair of wild buffalos in a chariot race, followed by a riotous wild-mule fiasco that tickled Fannie and her friends. Fannie applauded until her hands ached.

Then the bucking-horse riders drew for their broncs.

Goldie St. Clair shrieked as she looked at her number. "Oh, my God!"

"What's the matter?" Bernie ran to his wife's side.

"I got Red Wing." The glow faded from Goldie's cheeks.

"Why was that killer left in the draw? I won't let you ride him!" Bernie said.

Goldie composed herself and a change came over her face. "But I want to ride him. If I can ride Red Wing, I'll win. I know I will."

"You'll get yourself killed."

"No, this is my chance. Any one of you would ride him if you'd drawn him." She looked from one to another. "Well, wouldn't you?" No one could deny it.

"Don't worry," she said. "I'll ride that booger to a standstill."

Fannie drew a big black named Turkey Trot, and Annie and Bertha would ride Maple Leaf and Rooster in the first day's event. Hazel Walker, a dark-eyed young woman from Los Angeles who drew Hellcat, wore harem-type trousers that intrigued Fannie.

"We Montana Girls wore long black bloomers," she whispered to Bertha when the California entry was out of earshot, "but they were nowhere near so *formfitting*."

"I wouldn't mind revealing a little something," Bertha said, holding the folds of her long leather riding skirt at either side of her ample hips, "if I could sit those broncs without all this." The women laughed and turned to watch the men's bronc-riding event.

Bucking horses were to be saddled in the chutes. A ride would last from the time the horse cut loose until the whistle, which sounded when the bronc stopped bucking or when the rider bucked off, pulled leather, or lost a stirrup.

"Don't wrap the loose end of the lead around your hand," Bertha cautioned. "In this contest, that's as bad as pulling leather."

The event began with special exhibitions. Charles Tipkins, of Denver, rode a bronc with one stirrup only, and Bernie St. Clair rode a vicious bucker without any stirrups. In the competition, cowboys Art Acord, Jim Massey, Ralph Ackorn, and Ed McConnell tried Addison Day's broncs in turn. But the horses, not lively enough to challenge the riders, failed to give the crowd a good show.

Then Fred Walsh of Oklahoma came out on Caviota, an outlaw with a reputation. The animal belonged to Art Acord, who claimed it had been ridden only once. His claim remained undisputed. Walsh promptly took a header into the dust, rising to proclaim Caviota "a sunfishin' son-of-a-gun."

The women's bucking event began with Annie up first on Maple Leaf, a nervous mouse-colored mare who skittered across the field but failed to buck seriously. Fannie was next on Turkey Trot, who snorted in fury as she mounted, then bolted away from the chute in a halfhearted crowhopping stampede toward the far side of the arena, a disappointed Fannie aboard.

"What's the matter with these horses?" she complained as she rejoined the others.

The crowd applauded Bertha's passable ride on a rank gray called Rooster, but Del grumbled as he returned from hazing the horse back to the corral. "Weadick's mad as a wet hen about the poor bucking stock," he said. "He's having fresh broncs brought in for tomorrow."

Blanche McGaughey, a versatile rider from Oklahoma, rode the mustang, Toad. But it was Hazel Walker's harem trousers that brought the strongest response from spectators that afternoon. Her bronc, Hellcat, a sulky brown, at first refused to buck, then broke into a run, stumbled, and fell to his knees. Hazel's foot caught beneath his leg, and she was pulled to the ground, still holding one rein. The crowd rose to attention, but Hazel got to her feet while the misnamed Hellcat mustered a few more uninspired jumps. Fannie could see Hazel was in pain.

"What rotten luck," Bertha murmured.

"Not much of a performance, is it?" Fannie was now anxiously aware that only one more rider remained. Goldie on Red Wing.

Addison Day took the judges' stand. "Hazel Walker's going to be all right. Just a sprained ankle." He led the applause that followed the injured rider from the arena. "Now, folks, as you know, this has been a benefit for the family of Joe LaMar, the rider who was killed attempting to ride the outlaw bronco, Red Wing. I'm pleased to announce that you've all been generous. The collection amounted to nineteen hundred dollars, which will be presented to Mrs. LaMar tonight." An appreciative murmur rose from the crowd.

Goldie St. Clair stood near the chutes, visibly trembling despite her husband's arm around her, while the handlers struggled to saddle Red Wing in the end chute.

"And now for today's final event! Canada's Goldie St. Clair will attempt to ride that same killer horse . . . Red Wing!" Gasps of alarm rose over the rattle of the chute gate as Red Wing lunged against it.

"Are they crazy? She'll be hurt!"

"They're putting a woman on that devil?"

Amid the din of protest, Goldie climbed onto the chute. She paused for a moment, gathering courage, then lowered herself onto the defiant sorrel. The noise of the crowd ceased. Only the low rumble in Red Wing's throat could be heard as the gate opened. He plunged sideways into the arena, heaving into a high twisting jackknife, reversing ends as he hit the ground. Then another jackknife, his hind feet nearly under his chin. Goldie's body snapped with each roll, her feet and legs gripping the hobbled stirrups. Red Wing squealed, bucking in fury, then pounded to earth, plunging again and again in blind desperation.

Fannie winced more than once, but the determined rider sat through the ferocious ride, her free arm thrashing the air, until the whistle sounded. Kicking loose from the pitching bronc, she grasped the hazer's saddle horn and was carried to safety. Waves of applause and cheering rewarded her daring. She waved and bowed to acknowledge the ovation.

Lucy Mulhall stood beside Fannie. "She's some rider."

"What chance do the rest of us have?" Fannie said. "Except for Red Wing and Caviota, these broncs just aren't bucking."

"The men are demanding better stock, and Weadick knows these men deserve better. Del Blancett, Doc Pardee, Johnnie Mullens, Ed Echols, Henry Cramer, Ray Knight—I'd say this is about the biggest gathering ever of top riders interested in making roundup riding a sport."

"A sport?"

"That's right. Folks are tired of Wild West shows that exploit the so-called *romance* of the West. Weadick wants to build recognition for the skill and endurance, the dedication it takes to compete in these events. He's trying to preserve the real West, not a watered-down imitation. That's why some of us are trying to make what we do into a recognized sport."

Fannie looked intently at Lucy. "I'd sure like to help you do that."

Lady Bucking-Horse
Champion of the World

12

"No one can top Goldie's ride on Red Wing." Fannie confided her doubt to her mother the next morning as they prepared to leave for Victoria Park.

"Goldie's riding hobbled. Bertha's the one you got to beat."

"Lucy says they're bringing in better broncs."

"That Lucy Mulhall is smart," Rachel said. "Educated in a convent. And her pa, Colonel Zack Mulhall, who pioneered in Oklahoma, is one of the first ever to stage a Wild West show."

Fannie looked sharply at her mother. "How do you know she was educated in a convent?"

"Mr. Russell told me. I'll be sittin' with him today, so be sure you put on a good ride."

"Who's Mr. Russell?"

"Charles M. Russell. He paints pictures. He may sketch my portrait."

"You sat with Charlie Russell, the artist?"

"I met him in the exhibition building. They're showin' his paintings there along with some by a fella named Edward Borein. He told me he saw you ride at Pendleton." Rachel adjusted her new straw bonnet so the black feather curled over her left ear. "Oh, I do wish I had a smarter-looking dress."

"Ma, you look just fine." Fannie tied the bonnet strings under her mother's chin. "Charlie Russell will want to draw your picture for sure."

Despite the wet track, the opening relay race proved exciting. In a close finish, Fannie, who had not had a chance to work her mounts before the race, came in third. Bertha took first, and Mary McKenzie of Crossfield, second. The Indian pony races were won by Hoopenough, Cowtop, and Sittingdown. Clay McGonagill tied with Doc Pardee in the steer roping.

Then Addison Day announced that the bucking-horse events would be postponed. The judges agreed, he said, that the broncos did not have enough spirit to test the ability of the riders. Fresh broncs were on the way.

All contests took place in the open arena, but because of the dismal weather, additional performances were given that night under electric lights in the enclosed horse-show building, and spectators had to wade the sea of black mud, shoe-top deep, that clogged the area between the two facilities.

When fresh bucking stock arrived on the third day, Tex McCarty was first up to test one of the new broncs, Tornado. The horse began by plowing his nose into the ground, nearly turning a somersault. Flying mud prompted standing spectators to edge back as the bronc spun for almost fifty jumps, McCarty fighting him all the way.

Fannie and the others cheered, both for Tex and for the promising new crop of bucking horses. "Now we'll see some action," she said, grinning at Del and Bertha from under the rivulets of rain dripping from her hat. By the time the women's event was announced, she was soaked to the skin. But her bronc, Nett, turned in a wildcat performance that showed off her horsemanship in fine style. Fanning him with her hat throughout, she rode until the horse had had enough and quit cold.

Blanche McGaughey's little buckskin took only a small space to show what he could do. Whirling on a dime, bucking and bellowing, his stiff-legged jumps failed to unseat his rider. Annie Shaffer's bronc, Baby Reed, fought savagely in the chute, crashed the gate, and broke away into a stampede down the track before Annie could get on him. Annie waited, poised nonchalantly on the top rail, while two hazers drove him back into the chute. Then she mounted and rode a brief and unimpressive exhibition. "Too bad he showed his stuff before Annie got aboard," Bertha joked.

Goldie St. Clair drew a "ladies' horse" that pitched only a few weak jumps. Bertha sat a ducker and dodger named Bar Circle, who plowed indignantly across the field in an unsuccessful effort to shed saddle and rider.

Though stove up from her accident, Hazel Walker climbed aboard Rooster, the savage gray retained from the first day. He fought the saddle and appeared to be in a murderous mood when the California girl mounted, then he shot from the chute with a series of hard bucks and headed straight for the wire fence. The audience gasped, and some women turned their faces away, not wanting to witness another accident. As the bronc plunged against the wire, Hazel swung from the saddle and managed to avoid falling beneath him, but the animal struck back with its hind foot and struck her arm.

"Poor Hazel," Fannie murmured. "She's having terrible luck."

"That field is muddy as all get out." Lucy flicked at the globs of mud spattered over the front of her buckskin skirt. "Look at me. They won't be able to tell me from the steers." Then she slogged onto the field for the steer roping and gamely carried through an exhibition of tying down the wild longhorns.

Clay McGonagill, on his quarter horse Kelly, surprised his friends by failing to perform to his usual standard. "You can't even stand up out there," he said, "let alone get a toehold to throw a rope on one of them critters."

But the bulldogging continued wild and rough. Steers from the Blood Reserve weighing up to 1,200 pounds were given a 10-foot start, and each rider, after jumping from his horse, tried to twist the animal to the ground. Seven seconds was the fastest time, made by Esteban Clemento. Bertha Blancett competed in the men's steer bulldogging, then again won the women's relay by a wide margin.

"She's a splendid jockey," Fannie told her mother, "and her ability to mount, dismount, and change saddles is the best I've ever seen."

Fannie's disappointment with her own performance in the relay vanished into laughter as the Wild Horse Race got under way. Fifteen bucking horses were saddled and mounted, and an attempt to ride them across the field produced a muddy free-for-all of bucking and stampeding.

"Ladies and gentlemen." From the judges' stand, Addison Day shouted through the megaphone. "We've seen some fine performances here today. But we have one more event for you. Bill Rook will try to ride the notorious bronc Caviota on a bet of two hundred and fifty dollars." Spectators, holding wet newspapers and umbrellas over their heads, reseated themselves, and Fannie and the other riders edged closer for a better view. Caviota staged a desperate blowup and upheld his reputation by piling Rook, and Rook lost his bet.

Crowds increased as the daily rains subsided. By the fifth day, admission was limited to standing room only and performers had difficulty pushing through to the field. Newspapers advised that all of Calgary's 60,000 citizens, plus visitors from all over western Canada and the United States, were in attendance. And more continued to arrive each day by train. Weadick had arranged with the railroads to offer a special discount to Calgary-bound passengers and, to accommodate the growing numbers taking advantage of the discount price, he decided to extend the Stampede two extra days to make up for time lost to inclement weather and reluctant bucking horses.

Each day Fannie and Rachel clipped accounts of events from the *Calgary Herald*. Duly reported was the flurry of excitement that swept through the crowd when renown humorist Will Rogers appeared among the spectators, as were the comments of The Right Honorable Walter Long, a visiting Englishman.

Most extraordinary. In a nutshell, the Stampede can be summed up by one word—wonderful. Riders of those bucking horses must have the courage of a hundred people. Transplanted to England, such a show would attract millions if it were possible to stage it there in all its present entirety.

On the final day the September sky shone a crystal blue as Fannie, mounted on the palomino, awaited the grand entry and the arrival of the royal party. The gate opened, and two white horses pulling a low open coach moved into the arena, a top-hatted coachman seated high in front. The three members of the royal family smiled and waved as the coach carried them across to the royal box. The Duke of Connaught, in a medal-bedecked uniform and white naval-officer's hat, ascended the steps, followed by the pleasant-looking duchess, who wore a wide-brimmed hat trimmed with flowers and an elegant bustled dress, as did their pretty daughter.

When they were seated, the Ride to the Colors began. Mounted cowboys and cowgirls galloped, two abreast, around the arena, doffing their hats as they rode before the royal party. One cowpuncher rose in his saddle, waved his hat, and yelled, "Hey there, Duke." The duke laughed heartily and won a chorus of cheers when he gave his hat an extra flourish when returning the salute.

Johnnie Mullens opened the show riding Roman Candle, a rough bucker. Doc Pardee's bronc Black Reed bucked all over the arena, with a few furious twists down directly in front of the royal box. All occupants of the box applauded heartily.

Red Parker, of Alberta, was next up on Blue Roan. Parker refused to hold a lead rope and fanned the bronc with his hat while roweling him with his spurs. Blue Roan, disinclined to quit after circling the arena twice, displayed prodigious bucking that brought him, too, directly in front of the royal party. Parker had demonstrated flawless horsemanship until then, but when he eased his concentration for a split second to wave at the duke, the roan took advantage of it. Only by gripping the saddle horn did Parker miss being piled. The royal guests rose from their seats to show their delight in the performance.

An exhibition of stagecoach driving by a veteran of the early days also provoked enthusiastic applause. Bertha Blancett gave a demonstration of rough riding as practiced on the plains, including her "drunken cowboy" trick ride. Daring stunts by petite Dolly Mullins of New Mexico challenged the fancy riding of Montana's Otto Kline.

Florence LaDue performed the difficult feat of tying a double hitch in her slackened rope with only two movements of her wrist, and she showed agility and endurance by jumping through the loop and keeping it whirling while lying flat on the ground. She tied a man, hand and foot, with three motions of her swinging loop to win the judges' decision. Lucy Mulhall ran a close second, roping a rider by flipping the rope with her foot.

Then came the draw for the bucking horses. Fannie felt her pulse racing as she stepped up to the hat proffered by Addison Day and took the slip of paper that would decide her chances for the championship. Red Wing! A gasp of delight escaped her lips. She'd drawn Red Wing! Luck was with her after all. Here was her chance to beat Goldie's spectacular hobbled ride. Heart pounding, she joined the noisy crowd in the stands and tried to focus her attention on the arena as Annie, first up, burst from the chute on a white-footed bay named Tip.

Bertha's slick ride on a big red horse called Two Bars brought wild cheers from royalty and commoners alike. The big horse spun crazily, churning the dust with his thrashing hoofs, then he tried to reach the sky with high buckjumps. The cantle caught Bertha's lower back and snapped her head mercilessly. But her strength and skill prevailed. She stuck with the powerful high roller, alighted of her own accord, and waved to acknowledge the cheers. Bernie St. Clair congratulated her as she rejoined the group. "That's one of the best slick rides I ever saw made by a woman. *Or* a man."

Goldie, in a silver-spangled shirt, sat unsmiling. Fannie could see she was not pleased with Bertha's fine performance. She sat sullenly while Blanche McGaughey stuck through the gyrations of a red roan. Then Goldie's turn came.

"Remember to smile at the crowd," Bernie called to her. Goldie moved across the arena, both arms held high. Her skirt and spurs caught the light and glittered silver as she turned with a dazzling smile to face the royal box, waved to each section of the stands, then climbed to the top of the chute.

Would Goldie make another championship ride? Fannie tugged at her red-silk neckerchief and adjusted her sleeve holders. Nothing felt comfortable all of a sudden.

Goldie eased onto a wiry bronc called Dish Rag, whose name proved appropriate only in his flexibility. He reared from the chute, towering over the handlers, who scattered for the fence. The lethal front hoofs churned the air, and he twisted right and left with lightning speed. Goldie's hobbled stirrups held her legs firm. Then Dish Rag spun another sidewinder and Goldie, silver spangles flashing, seemed to lose her balance. Only the hobbled stirrups held her on. Her body whipped off center.

"She'll get her neck broke. Get her off."

But Goldie took the pounding. At the far end of the field, she grabbed the hazer's saddle horn and pulled herself free. Dish Rag stampeded, and the crowd went wild. Fannie saw that Goldie seemed shaken as she limped from the field, her hand to her forehead.

Del tapped Fannie's arm. "You're up next, Fannie."

Addison Day shouted from the judges' stand. "Folks, we've saved the best for last. You've been treated this week to the finest exhibition of lady bucking-horse riders ever presented. You've seen these women ride. You know they're second to none. And now you're going to see another attempt by one of these outstanding women . . . to ride the killer bronc, Red Wing!"

A hushed murmur, then a surge of shouts and applause from the stands. Day held up his hand for quiet before continuing. "And the brave little lady who'll make this attempt is . . . Montana State Champion Fannie Sperry!"

The spectators, primed for the excitement of this final ride, let go. A roar filled the arena, propelling Fannie toward the chutes on waves of sound. She held her white hat above her head to acknowledge the ovation, then climbed onto the chute above the glistening sorrel, who stood taut as a hair trigger.

Fannie lowered herself slowly onto the saddle. A shudder rippled across Red Wing's flanks. Positioning the toes of her boots in the stirrups, Fannie adjusted her grip on the buck rein. The familiar feel of her own saddle provided small comfort as she poised her body against the cantle and tightened her legs around the horse's girth. Take your time now. Be ready for the power in his first move. Get set. The only sounds she heard were the squeaks of leather as Red Wing tensed under the saddle, a low groan of protest coming from his throat. She signaled and the gate opened.

Red Wing squealed as he surged out of the chute. Whirling to the right, he rose in a high leap, swapping ends as he hit the ground, then sailed even higher with another twisting jump. Plunging his head low, he heaved into a homicidal bucking frenzy. Fannie succeeded in bringing up his head, but he reared, poised in a vertical stand, neck arched high, lips curled back around another squeal.

"Hold 'em, girl!"

"Stomp that bronc!"

A jackknife. Another high buck. With each, Fannie hit the cantle hard, then the pommel as she threw herself forward to keep her balance. But she felt nothing except the tension of her legs gripping the horse. Her task was to stay on this whirling devil horse. Sit light and go with him. Watch his head. Keep the stirrups down. Anticipate. The arena spun around her.

"She's dancin' that outlaw!"

"What a ride!"

The crowd alternately gasped, then cheered as she stayed with the killer bronc, never losing control, never sacrificing balance or style.

When the hazer pulled her free in front of the royal box and she dropped to her feet, a thunder of applause measured her triumph. Trembling, she saluted the audience with a bow and a wide sweep of her hat toward the

*Fannie shows the riding skill that won her the title of Lady Bucking Horse
Champion of the World at the first Calgary Stampede in 1912.*

visiting royalty. Then she glimpsed something that made her catch her breath. She saw her mother seated in the royal box beside the duchess.

"Ma?" Her lips formed the word, but the continuing cheers drowned the sound. The feather on her mother's hat bobbed merrily as the tiny woman led the royal applause.

The official announcement came almost immediately. "Your Highnesses. Ladies and gentlemen. May I have your attention please?" Finally, the noise quieted to complete stillness. "The judges' decision is unanimous. The Lady Bucking-Horse Champion of the World is . . . Fannie Sperry, of Mitchell, Montana!" Amid a tumult of sound that surged from the stands, Guy Weadick rode up beside her on his black stallion and dismounted. "Here, Fannie, get on and take a bow," he shouted, handing her the reins. When she stepped up into the saddle, her trembling was gone.

She felt she was riding a phantom horse, an ethereal charger carrying her into a kingdom beyond her wildest dreams. The handsome stallion pranced before the royal box, and at Fannie's command, a special slight tug on the reins, he stood on his hind legs, gallantly saluting the crowd. She acknowledged the applause with another sweep of her hat and a radiant smile.

When finally she rode from the arena to return Weadick's horse, her mother pushed through the throng. "I knew you could do it," she said. They embraced, both blinking back happy tears. "I'm so proud of you, Fannie."

Bertha joined them. "You sure deserve the title, Fannie."

"Congratulations, Fannie." Annie clapped her hands like a delighted little girl, while Blanche McGaughey offered a hearty handshake.

Bernie St. Clair took Fannie's hands in both of his. "Good going, Fannie. You're a real champ."

"Goldie did a fine job, too," Fannie said, looking around for the blond, spangle-clad rider. But Goldie was nowhere to be seen.

Rachel turned to the group, an expression of pure joy beneath her perky hat. "Well, did you see *me*?"

Fannie remembered her glimpse of Rachel sitting with the duchess. "Ma, how on earth . . . ?"

"The duke asked Mr. Russell and me to join the royal party. I had a nice chat with his Highness and the duchess." Fannie stared openmouthed at her mother. "The duke sends you his congratulations, and Mr. Russell wants to meet you." Rachel beamed with pride as Guy Weadick took Fannie's arm and led her toward the judges' platform, where the prizes were being presented. Another wave of applause rang through the park as she bounded up the steps.

"In the women's bucking-horse competition, first prize goes to this fine champion, Fannie Sperry." Ceremoniously, Addison Day handed her a check made out to her in the amount of $1,000. "Congratulations." Fannie stared at the check and accepted another handshake.

"But that's not all," Day continued. "We also have for Fannie this silver-mounted saddle." A handsome saddle, hand-tooled with roses over the cantle and tapaderos, was lifted onto the platform.

"And so you won't forget this grand occasion," he added, "here's a solid-gold engraved buckle for you." Day placed the elaborate buckle in her hand, and she read, LADY BUCKING-HORSE CHAMPION OF THE WORLD, CALGARY, 1912.

"Thank you." Her voice choked with emotion as applause washed across the field and wrapped itself around her.

"Now, Fannie, what are you going to do with your prize money?"

Back home on the Beartooth after winning the championship, Fannie shows off her prize saddle.

What would she do with . . . ? Suddenly, she realized the grand prize was actually hers. She had won a fortune. Without hesitation she knew what she would do with it. "I'm going to buy land for my pa."

Day looked surprised. "That's a mighty fine thing to do, Fannie. Speak louder so the folks can hear you."

He handed her the megaphone, and she spoke loud and clear. "I'm going to buy that piece of railroad land my pa's been wanting ever since he homesteaded."

A murmur of affection for this champion swept through the stands. Day's cheeks crinkled into a smile.

"Folks, she shouldn't have to give up her prize money. What do you say we help her get that land for her pa? Shall we pass the hat?" Applause and whistles confirmed audience approval of the idea.

Fannie was dumbstruck. What? They're going to give me still more? "No, no. I couldn't accept . . ."

But already a flurry of activity rippled through the stands as hats were passed down the rows. Fannie clutched the gold buckle and the check, while Day moved about the platform encouraging those who wished to show their appreciation of Fannie's unmatched performance to dig into their pockets. Guy Weadick himself brought the final collection to the platform.

"You earned this, Fannie," he said. "I'm mighty proud to have you in my Stampede." Someone produced a cigar box, and Day placed the coins and bills into it, then tucked it under Fannie's arm. "We'll see you next year."

And so the 1912 Calgary Stampede came to a close. The royal party departed, and reporters interviewed the winners. Fannie enjoyed the attention but, as the Blancetts drove her and her mother to the railroad station late that afternoon, she knew that the publicity, and even the championship, were not the most important aspects of her experience here. She had won the respect of the finest riders in the West. She had proved her skill among her peers. Nothing could ever take that satisfaction away from her. She knew now, too, that she would never give up riding. She would go back to the Beartooth and buy that land for her folks. And she would help on the ranch, of course. But she would never give up riding.

At the station the Stampede performers hurried about checking departure times and seeing each other off. Many new friends and well-wishers called to her as she and Rachel prepared to board the train for home. One face was still missing. She had not seen Goldie since the winning ride.

The hiss and screech of the locomotive drowned out the final goodbyes as she followed her mother up the steps of one of the passenger cars. Then, above the commotion, she heard someone calling.

"Fannie, wait." Goldie St. Clair pushed through the crowd, holding two ice cream cones in front of her. "I have something for you."

"Find seats, Ma. I'll be right there." Fannie stepped from the train and ran to meet the blond cowgirl.

"I saw you heading for the train," she said. "They're selling this ice cream in the depot." Goldie handed her a dripping cone, her eyes searching Fannie's face. "Can you forgive me for being such a poor loser?" she said. "It's just that, well, for a minute I was so disappointed."

"Think nothing of it," Fannie shouted above the shrill whistle. She licked the cone, grinning as some of the ice cream ran down her chin.

"I didn't mean it, Fannie. I don't know anyone I like as much as you."

"Thanks, Goldie. It was good of you to come." As the two hugged, the train began to move. "Holy Moses! They're leaving without me."

"Oh, hurry." Gesturing to help her through the thinning crowd, Goldie bumped Fannie's cone. The scoop of ice cream toppled down the front of Fannie's skirt and into her boot.

"Oh, Fannie, I'm sorry."

Fannie looked up in time to see her mother's anxious face at the window as the train chugged out of the station.

PART TWO

Romance on Horseback  13

Catching the next train, Fannie overtook her mother at Lethbridge where Rachel, miffed and worried, had gotten off the earlier train to wait for her. But the incident soon produced smiles when Fannie told her mother all about Goldie's apology, the pleasant supper she had shared with the St. Clairs while waiting for the next train, and the warm camaraderie of all the performers gathered in the afterglow of the Stampede. When Fannie and Rachel arrived in Helena, local reporters were waiting to interview the new world champion. Rachel, too, had gained celebrity status as a result of her afternoon with the duke and duchess.

Along with the congratulatory letters in her mail, Fannie found an invitation from the Powell County Fair Committee offering to pay her $100 for an exhibition ride in Deer Lodge the first week in October. She accepted, grateful that now she could afford to take both her parents and Walter, too, since Carrie offered to do the chores while they were gone.

From atop a chute at the Deer Lodge fairgrounds, Fannie acknowledged the greetings of other riders waiting in the warm October sun. Even those she hadn't met seemed to know her.

"How come a big-timer like you is bothering with the Deer Lodge Fair?" one lanky waddy teased.

A young boy called up to her. "Can I help you with your broncs, Fannie?"

"Hey, I saw her first," his pal countered.

Fannie grinned, her spirits soaring. As she prepared to ease down onto the rangy dappled bronc struggling under the saddle, a wrangler in clown makeup climbed up on the opposite side of the chute. A tattered hat hung like hound's ears on either side of his false red nose and blackened whiskers.

"Well, if it ain't Miss Knickers."

Fannie glanced sharply at the grinning clown.

"I hear those knickers got glued to a winner up at Calgary."

Fannie glared at him as she dropped onto the saddle, startling the nervous bronc. It lurched against the narrow confines of the chute, pinning Fannie's leg against the rough boards. But the clown at once gripped the hackamore to shift the animal, then bounded into the chute, bracing his body between horse and chute so that Fannie could free her leg. "You okay?" he asked. She nodded, and he climbed up out of the chute.

"Then let 'em buck!" At the clown's command, the wranglers swung the gate. The bronc spilled into the arena, and Fannie rode with all the grace and gumption of the champion she was. Spectators roared their admiration and affection for this golden girl of the West. When the ride ended, they continued to cheer as Fannie waved and ran from the field.

"Not a bad ride." The clown followed her, dabbing at his burnt-cork whiskers with a red bandana handkerchief. "I wanted to congratulate you on your win at Calgary, too." He held out his hand as he pulled off the rubber nose. His clear blue eyes held hers.

"Well, thanks." She shook his hand awkwardly.

"We met . . . sort of . . . at Pendleton," he said. "I'm Bill Steele."

Now she remembered. This was the same rude cowpoke who'd made fun of the knickers incident then, too. She started to turn away, still resenting the laugh he'd gotten at her expense.

"Please." He caught her arm. "I want to apologize if I've said anything out of line. I . . . I guess I'm a little envious of anyone who can sit a bronc like you can."

"It's all right." She pulled her arm free and started to walk away.

"No, wait." The smudged face remained at her side. "I said I'm sorry. Let's pass the peace pipe over a cup of coffee." An appealing grin spread across his grimy face. Fannie stopped and glared at him, hands on her hips. But seeing his amiable look, she chuckled.

"Sure, why not?"

Bill guided her through the crowd toward the refreshment wagon behind the bleachers. While Fannie found seats at one of the long tables set up for eaters, Bill fetched two tin mugs of steaming coffee. They sat silently for a few moments, Bill fingering his cup.

Fannie saw that he was older than she; his slender face also carried the etched lines that come from a life outdoors. "How come I haven't seen you around before?"

"I came up from New Mexico," he said. "Had a restaurant in Dawson."

"Never heard of Dawson."

"Just a no-count mining town. I'm working for Dad Elliott's outfit now outside of Deer Lodge. Got a string of bucking horses. Furnished stock for the fair here. I was glad to see you drew that dappled cuss. Gave you a chance to make a good showing."

Fannie nodded. "Do any bronc stomping yourself?"

"Some. But I ate a little dust this spring breaking colts. Stove me up. I'm getting too old for bronc stompin', but I sure do appreciate a good horse under me."

As she listened to the soft voice, Fannie studied his face, sensitive and handsome, despite the smudges of dirt and clown makeup.

"I'm supplying horses for C. B. Irwin's Wild West show in Cheyenne next summer," he continued.

Fannie knew about the three Irwin brothers and their families, all horse people. "The Irwins are pretty good riders, I guess."

"The best. When they put on a performance, it's the real thing. They won't work with anyone who doesn't know his stuff."

Was there something different about this cowboy? She liked his eyes. He seemed intelligent. And he was easy to talk to, a rare quality in most of the men she knew. She toyed with her still-full cup.

"What's the matter, your coffee cold?"

"No, but I take sugar in mine. I like a lot of sugar."

Bill grinned. "Come to think of it, so do I."

That evening as Fannie sliced the home-cured ham to fry with potatoes over the Sperry campfire, she thought about Bill Steele's steady blue eyes and the sound of his voice, soft yet straightforward and confident. "He's going to work with the Irwin brothers," she said aloud.

"Who is?"

"Bill Steele. I met him this afternoon. He's the hazer who plays the clown."

"He's pretty doggone good at it." Datus looked up from under the wagon, where he was attempting a nap. "Did you see how he moved in when that Missoula cowboy almost got stomped by that black bull?" His praise pleased Fannie.

Walter seemed amused as he fanned the campfire coals. "He must be powerful brave to stand up to Fannie when she ruffles her feathers the way she did this afternoon."

"Well, he deserved it." She hoped she wasn't blushing, yet she had never felt such strange delight in just talking about a person. "He was so forward. I thought he must be a masher."

"Why? What happened?" Datus came from under the wagon and took a seat on a log before the fire.

"Nothing. He's a real gentleman. In fact, we're riding out to Dad Elliott's in the morning to see some of his horses." Three of the Sperrys exchanged glances, and Fannie knew she hadn't been successful in concealing her interest in Bill Steele.

Sleep was not a high priority with Fannie that night. Cocooned in quilts, she lay beside her mother in the open wagon box, watching the dark dome of sky swallow the stars one by one. She scarcely noticed her father's wheezing from beneath the wagon where he and Walter had spread their bedrolls.

Bill Steele. Even his name had a good sound to it. He was the finest-looking man she had ever met, even with whisker-black smudged on his chin. Yes, even in the red clown nose, his eyes had looked right through her. She pulled the covers closer. Life was full of surprises.

Startling awake with the sounds of the camp stirring, Fannie peered from under her quilts. In the early light, frost sparkled across the grassy field and fringed the golden aspen at the far side, where she saw her father and brother waiting in line at the pump. Had October ever been more beautiful? She sat up, clasping her arms around her knees.

"Better get out of there, sleepyhead." Rachel, rummaging in the grub box, took out bread and leftover ham and placed them on the tailgate.

Fannie reached for a fresh shirt in her pack. Today, she would wear her best, the white satin. Huddling beneath the quilt, she changed quickly, then climbed from the wagon to wash her face in the washpan on the tailgate. As she brushed her hair, peering into the fragment of mirror hanging on the brake lever, she heard hoofbeats. She turned and saw Bill Steele riding toward them on a splendid blaze-faced sorrel gelding and leading a sleek bay.

"Mornin', ladies." Fairly gleaming from meticulous grooming, he tipped his Stetson. Even his boots had been polished to a fare-thee-well. He dismounted and stood looking at Fannie for a moment, tapping the sorrel's reins against his hand. "Brought us a couple of ponies for our ride. This is Blaze and that's Ginger."

"Ma, this is Bill Steele." Fannie, embarrassed that he should see her with her hair half combed, quickly pinned it into a bun at the back of her neck.

"Wallace S. Steele. Pleased to meet you, ma'am." He looped both sets of reins over a wagon wheel, then removed his hat and held it politely in both hands.

"Howdy do." Rachel held out her hand to him. In the morning light, Bill looked to Fannie even older than he had the day before, but the boyish grin and steady blue eyes were just as she remembered. And Fannie knew her mother had already taken in everything there was to see about this stranger.

"Would you like to join us for breakfast, Mr. Steele?" Rachel glanced at Fannie. "Then you two can go along on your ride."

"I'd be much obliged," Bill said, "if I'm not putting you out. Here, let me give you a hand." And he scurried to help build the fire. Rachel placed a frying pan over it and stirred in the ham and potatoes.

"Are you a horseman, Mr. Steele?"

"Yes, ma'am. Rode all my life. But I've took about as many headers from ornery broncs as I care to. Aim to let others do that from now on."

"Fannie tells me you brought bucking stock for the fair here."

"That's right. Keep my string out at the Elliotts."

Datus and Walter, returning with the bucket and coffeepot filled with fresh water, looked surprised to find their family circle had grown.

"Pa, Walter, this is Bill Steele." Fannie ignored Walter's slyly raised eyebrow.

"I sure am pleased to meet you, Mr. Sperry." Bill gripped the older man's hand. "I've heard about those draft horses of yours. I may come up to trade with you one of these days. Dad Elliott has asked me to keep an eye out for another team."

"That so?" Datus scrutinized the man who seemed to be so eager to please.

"Better eat while the vittles are hot." Rachel, having spooned the food onto the four tin plates for the others, sat down to eat her portion from the skillet.

"Now, just a minute, ma'am." Bill sprang to her side and exchanged his plate for the frying pan. "I'm not letting any lady as pretty as you eat from no frying pan. I'm used to such accommodations." He seated himself across from Fannie and began to devour his breakfast, talking all the while about horses and stampedes.

When they finished eating, he started to collect the plates, but Rachel rose quickly and took them from him. "Here, I'll tend to that. You and Fannie better get a move on if you're going to be back in time for the bronc riding this afternoon."

"Thanks, ma'am," Bill said. "And much obliged for the breakfast. It's been a real pleasure." He took the horses' reins from the wagon wheel, then held the bay's stirrup so Fannie could step into it. "We'll be back in plenty of time," he called as he mounted the sorrel. The three Sperrys stood motionless beside the wagon and watched Fannie ride away with the cowboy.

"First time I ever saw anyone hold a stirrup for Fannie," Walter said.

"First time she's ever allowed it," Rachel summed up.

When the sun cleared the mountains, warming the valley, frost winked out on the sage and grasses, and the songs of meadowlarks accompanied the two riders along the road toward the Elliott ranch. Clusters of yellow aspen nestled among spruce and fir on the ridges while, in the valley, golden cottonwoods edged the winding Clark's Fork River. "Someday I hope to own a spread here," Bill said, sweeping his hand toward the mountain peaks of the Continental Divide to the east that curved around to border the valley far to the south.

"It's a beautiful valley." Fannie breathed deeply, savoring the autumn fragrance as the well-trained bay she rode stepped smartly beside the sorrel. Chatting easily, they soon passed under the high crossbar that marked the gate to the Elliott ranch. As they neared the big, log ranch house, a man and woman came out across the porch toward a horse and buggy hitched in front.

"Howdy, Dad. Mrs. Elliott," Bill said, "Rode out to see the horses. Got to get right back though." He dismounted and looped his reins over the hitching post. "This is Fannie Sperry."

"It's nice to meet you, Fannie. We saw you ride yesterday." Mrs. Elliott's warmth put Fannie at ease.

"We're just now leaving for the fair." Dad Elliott strung the lines over the horse's rump to the buggy. "You folks make yourselves at home. Bill, why don't you show her my new colts?"

"Sure thing." Bill helped Mrs. Elliott into the buggy and stood watching as the older couple drove across the range toward the main road. Then he and Fannie walked out past a barn, bunkhouse, and other outbuildings to a corral that held several saddle horses.

Fannie reached through the rails to pat the nose of a tan-and-white paint. "I like pintos," she said.

"Smart saddle horses if you break them in right." The paint nuzzled Bill's shirt pocket while he stroked its neck. "Want to ride him?"

"I'd like to, but we don't have much time."

Neither moved. They stood looking at each other across the paint's forelock. Then Bill spoke. "Guess you're right. They can't start the bull riding without the clown."

Bill went with Fannie to draw for the bucking horses. A cowboy named Tink Van Horn drew Pioneer Outlaw, a spinner that had thrown him the day before. Slamming his hat into the dirt, Van Horn gritted his teeth in a curse. "I'm not gettin' back on that bastard!"

The surprised wranglers concealed any reaction, but a bronc rider never refused his draw, and Van Horn was setting himself up for ridicule. Bill seized the moment to say to Fannie in a voice that could be heard by all, "Why don't you show him how it's done, Fannie?" And before she could respond, he shouted, "Fannie Sperry will ride that spinner." She not only rode Pioneer Outlaw to a standstill that day, but two other broncs as well, and the fair committee paid her $100 for her exhibition performances.

Supper time found Bill Steele once more around the Sperry campfire, this time sitting next to Fannie. She knew her folks were pleased. This is what they've been waiting for, she thought. For me to find someone and settle down. But she also knew that if she hitched up with Bill, settling down would be different from what they might expect. He wanted his own stampede. She would help him.

That evening Fannie and Bill strolled through the fair exhibits. They visited the livestock barns and the fruit and vegetable displays. Finally, Bill had had enough. "Do we have to see every damn turnip and rutabaga in Powell County?" He took her arm and led her out across the darkened field beyond the corrals. The moon cast silvery light over the expanse of rangeland clear up to the high rocks of the distant Divide. For once, Bill seemed at a loss for words. "Fannie . . ."

For her, it was lovely just to hear him say her name.

As they walked, he kicked at the stubble beneath their feet. "I sure hate to see you go tomorrow. I . . . I've come to like you . . . a lot. I think you're the finest girl I ever met. Not silly-headed like so many women." He stopped and took both her hands in his. "Fannie . . ." For a moment Fannie thought her heart had stopped, too. He pulled her to him and gently kissed her lips.

"I like you a lot, too," she murmured. They kissed again.

"Fannie, I'm older than you. I'm thirty-six. Do you think we'd have a chance if we threw in together?" Though his lips tasted salty, this moment was the sweetest Fannie had ever known—next to winning the championship.

The following day at the close of the fair, she prepared to leave with her folks. She hadn't told them that, after knowing Bill Steele only two days, she had decided to marry him. And when Bill came to say good-bye but didn't kiss her in front of the family, she understood why. They needed more time to get used to the idea.

"Why don't you come up for Thanksgiving, Bill?" her mother said, and he accepted the invitation. Thanksgiving. A month away. An eternity.

"See you then, Fannie." He waved, his blue eyes looking right into her heart. And as the wagon pulled away, already she ached with loneliness.

During the November that elected Woodrow Wilson to the Presidency of the United States, Fannie filed a claim and purchased for her father the half-section of railroad land, 320 acres, adjoining the ranch. Thanksgiving week found her helping with the holiday cleaning and baking as well as with outside chores.

Dusk had fallen on Thanksgiving eve when she heard Blaze's hoofbeats on the frozen road. She looked from the window to see Bill riding up the road, bundled against the cold wind in a heavy sheep-lined overcoat, a woolen muffler tied over his hat. She grabbed her mackinaw and ran outside, but as he dismounted, his beet-red face making his eyes even bluer, she felt suddenly shy. Had she been presumptuous to think this handsome cowboy, this commanding horseman, cared deeply about her?

Walter came from the barn with two full milk pails. "Bill, good to see you again," he called.

"Good to be here." Bill untied the muffler, but his eyes remained on Fannie. She had piled her hair in a stylish high puff, and now she felt foolish. She pulled her mackinaw up around her neck.

"Fannie. I've missed you."

"I've missed you." She fell into his arms and raised her face to his. His kiss dissolved any doubt. After a long moment, she eased from his embrace, smiling. "Come on, I'll show you where to grain this broomtail of yours."

In the darkness of the barn, their lips touched again before Fannie lit the lantern and hung it on a peg near the door. Bill led Blaze into a stall and pitched down some hay. When his horse was taken care of, he again held Fannie in his arms. "It's been hell being away from you, Fannie. I want to marry you." He looped his muffler around her neck, binding her to him in the stall. "I don't have much to offer you right now, but . . ." Reaching inside his coat, he took a folded paper from his shirt pocket. ". . . here, I wrote you a poem."

"You write poems, too?"

"I wanted to explain the kind of guy I am."

"I know what kind you are."

"No, you don't. Your folks think I'm just another saddle bum."

"They do not!" She kissed him again to quiet any such talk.

"Well, tell me if you like this." He moved closer to the lantern and peered at the paper. Fannie leaned against his shoulder to peer at the handwriting on the page, and Bill began to read aloud.

Only a Bronc Twister

He's only a bronco twister, the people say,
As they pass him by and give him the way,
For his spurs with a rattle and bang
Strike many ears with their unpleasant clang.
His dress is not tidy, his face is all tanned,
But note his walk, like a man not ashamed
Of his friends, nor afraid of his foes,
When every morning to the corral he goes,
Not knowing the chances he's taking
From each bronco he rides.
Confidence in his skill and the unseen danger
Give strength to his arm and light to his eye.
He fears not to ride the outlaws wild.

"That's good," Fannie whispered. Bill continued.

I've seen in a corral a few days ago,
By only a bronc a twister was laid low,
His pals stood by with tears falling fast
And not a word was spoken till he breathed his last.
They said of their comrade lying dead at their feet,
'He's only a bronco twister, ever tidy and neat,
But his heart was as big as the world,' they said.
'We'll defend his good name now that he's dead.'
And in brotherly love was the reunion of twisters that day,
By the side of their comrade in clay,
Who loved his friends, feared not his foes,
And had a big heart for humanity's woes.

Bill looked at Fannie. "Well, what do you think?"

She saw pride and tenderness in his eyes. "I love it."

"And I love you, Fannie Sperry."

Later that evening when the family gathered around the fireplace, Bill popped popcorn in the long-handled skillet. Rachel paused in her mending. "Where'd you say you were from, Bill?"

"Missouri." Bill shook the skillet back and forth.

"Missouri?" Fannie looked at him in surprise. "I thought you said you were from New Mexico."

"I am. Missouri was earlier. Winfield, Missouri. But Montana's my home now." He dumped the fluffy, hot kernels into a dishpan, and Fannie filled small bowls and passed them to her parents and Walter.

"Bill, why don't you read your poem for the folks?"

"You mean we have a man of letters here," Datus said.

"It's not much," Bill protested. But at Fannie's urging, he took the folded paper from his pocket, settled himself before the fire, and read "Only a Bronc Twister." When he finished he looked up and shrugged.

"That's real good, Bill," Datus said.

"*Real* good," Walter echoed.

"It should be printed in the paper," Rachel suggested.

"I wrote it for Fannie."

Fannie returned his smile in the dancing firelight. There's depth to this man, she thought, and no end to what he can do.

Bill made two more trips from Deer Lodge to the Beartooth that winter, riding the 60 miles over the Divide and arriving nearly frozen. Fannie soon had him thawed out and holding forth before the fire with amusing horse stories and accounts of his adventures as a wrangler and ranch ramrod. During his New Year's visit, Fannie agreed to marry him in April. They would honeymoon on the Elliott place during the roundup and branding.

"Fannie, are you sure this is what you want to do?" her mother said as they worked in the kitchen after Bill had gone.

Fannie sat at the wooden butter churn, plunging the dasher up and down in a dreamy rhythm, while her mother poured a fresh supply of cream into appropriate containers for souring and for storing fresh. "It's what I've wanted all my life. Bill is everything I could ever want. He's thoughtful and kind. He's smart. And he loves horses as much as I do. How could anything be more perfect?"

"He doesn't say much about his background or family."

"What is there to say? He's been on his own since his early teens. Wrangling. Breaking and riding broncs. Hazing. That's one of the hardest jobs there is when you do it on foot as a clown. Lives depend on his judgment and knowledge of bulls and broncs."

"I know that." Her mother smiled. "I will say this for him. He sure can tell a good story. Writes good poems, too."

"Seems like he's done just about everything." Datus stood at the kitchen door. "But he sure don't have much to show for it. He must be close to forty, and he's still bumming around."

"Bumming around?" Fannie glared at her father. "He's foreman at the Elliotts. He has a string of horses. He supplies stock for stampedes. The Irwins want him next summer. I don't call that bumming around."

Datus smiled. Fannie never defended anything except horses with such intensity.

"And he's only thirty-six," she continued. "You and Ma were in your thirties when you got married. What's so different about Bill and me?"

"Now, Fannie." Her mother wiped her hands on her apron to take a turn at the churn. "We like Bill. But your pa thinks you should think about a place where you can settle down, have something to show for your years. There's no future in wrangling at stampedes."

"We'll have our own place. I can earn enough riding exhibition to get us a stake in no time."

Fannie longed with all her heart to reassure her parents, but something in their faces left her feeling uneasy.

The Newlyweds  14

The faded pattern on the carpet in Arthur's parlor stared back at Fannie throughout the ceremony. Cabbage roses entwined with gray vines. Something like the pink floribunda that bloomed beneath her window each summer. A heady fragrance came from the corsage Bill had pinned over her heart. Red roses. Perfect, she thought, against the lace that filled the neckline of her ankle-length navy-gabardine dress.

The worn, high-topped shoes on the pastor's feet shifted back and forth as he intoned the vows. The Reverend James McNamee. Fannie's eyes swept upward to his balding head, held in place, it seemed, by an overly tight collar, and her hand shifted nervously to the dark mass of her own hair piled high and held with bone hairpins.

She didn't trust herself to look at Bill, so near tears as she was. But when she promised to love, honor, and obey, and he slipped a gold wedding ring on her finger, she did look at him and saw that his eyes, too, brimmed with tears. He blinked them away and tucked his chin, unaccustomed, into the high white collar and tie that set off his new black suit.

"I now pronounce you, man . . . and wife."

Wife. The title had worn well for her courageous and strong mother, who had crossed a wilderness to join the man she loved and had tamed an arid homestead into the ranch that nurtured them all. Fannie wondered if she would be able to do as much. Would her marriage be as right? For Carrie

Fannie Sperry marries Bill Steele, April 16, 1913.

and Bertha the babies were coming nearly every year. Carrie was in the family way again with her sixth; she hardly ever left the ranch. And the kids scattered like wild rabbits when anyone came onto the place. Bertha's oldest, the sweet five-year-old William, had died of scarlet fever just before her fourth baby, Bryan, was born. Fannie loved the children. And she loved her sisters. Now she would be like them. Married.

Wife. She knew that Arthur and Edith, maybe even Walter, had doubted she'd ever settle down. And she had felt the glances of neighbors at local gatherings. Glances intended to emphasize the fact that their own daughters her age were long since safely wed, and their sons, too. But just being married is not enough, Fannie thought. Marriage has to mean something. Marriage has to guarantee your right to a life of your own choosing.

Wife. She raised her face to Bill's kiss. From that moment, her life and Bill's would be one. She would give him happiness just as he had already given her more than she had dreamed possible. His eyes met hers. And the moment held in its promise a magnificent soaring of spirit, strong enough to chin the moon.

Carrie stepped forward to embrace her, murmuring, "Be happy, Fannie."

Bertha hugged them both. "Now we each have a wedding dress for special occasions." She laughed, but her eyes glistened, too.

"Be good to her, son." Datus cleared his throat as he shook Bill's hand, then kissed Fannie's flushed cheek.

Rachel beamed at the newlyweds as she clasped their hands in hers. "You do make a handsome-looking couple."

"I knew the minute I saw *you*," Bill told his new mother-in-law, "that your daughter was the one for me."

"Oh, go on." Rachel hadn't looked so happy since her day with the duchess.

"Don't I get any of the credit," Datus joked.

"Pa, if Bill turns out to be half as fine as you, he'll be one in a million." Fannie gave her father a hug.

"Good luck, Fannie." Her brother Arthur pecked her on the cheek.

"Thanks, Arthur, to you and Edith, for letting us be married at your apartment. It's a good beginning."

Walter waited, almost shy, and when Fannie turned to her younger brother, her words stuck in her throat. Dear Walter. Always he seemed to be on the sidelines wishing her well.

Dad Elliott stole a kiss from the bride, while Mrs. Elliott said she had never seen a lovelier wedding. Edith came from the kitchen carrying a small cake and placed it on the side table where Bertha cut it and served generous portions on Edith's pretty wedding china.

Fannie looked at the happy faces around her. "If only Christine could have come." Christine, in her third month of pregnancy, had not been feeling well and could not make the trip to Helena to attend. Still, as Bill steadied Fannie's hand on the cake knife, she murmured, "Oh, Bill, isn't this the most perfect day?"

"Even better'n the day you won the championship?" he teased.

"Well . . ." She pretended to hesitate. "Darn near."

As they prepared to leave for the Elliott ranch, a knock sounded. Bill answered the door and admitted a reporter from the *Herald*. "Finish your good-byes," he told Fannie. "I'll talk to him." He guided the reporter outside, and they sat talking in the buggy he'd borrowed from the Elliotts for the wedding, now hitched to a team of Morgans, a gift from Fannie's parents.

The days that followed seemed pure joy to Fannie—sharing Bill's small bunkhouse, brightened with the quilt Clara had given her for a wedding present; rising before dawn in the early spring chill to round up cattle; riding over the broad expanse of valley between the tree lines, and up to where snow still lay on the crests. The mountain air, she thought, was every bit as crisp and refreshing as it was on the Beartooth, and at night, after supper with the other wranglers in the ranch-house kitchen, she and Bill retired to their own private world.

The *Helena Herald's* report of their wedding arrived a week later. The headline, *Miss Fannie Sperry Wedded to Horseman. World's Champion Woman Bronco Buster Married to W. S. Steele*, was followed by a brief item. *Miss Fannie E. Sperry, of Beartooth, was married here yesterday afternoon to Wallace S. Steele, a horseman of Deer Lodge. The wedding took place in the apartments of relatives in the Diamond Block. Mr. and Mrs. Steele will reside on Mr. Steele's large ranch near Deer Lodge.*

"How did they get the idea you own a large ranch?" Fannie wondered aloud.

Working with the other wranglers and waddies, they completed the Elliott roundup in record time. Too soon, Fannie thought. She wanted the blissful, carefree time, riding the range by day and lying in Bill's arms at night, to last forever. Bill, protective and solicitous of her comfort, never seemed to mind the good-natured attentions the other hands paid her. And when they raced Blaze and Ginger across the slopes, he seemed proud of her, even when she outrode him, which was usual. With Bill she never had to hold back. She felt she could truly be herself. Their sharing and caring deepened day by day.

She liked the Elliotts, too. They complimented her on her work in the roundup and expressed appreciation when she helped with the branding, holding the calves while Dad Elliott wielded the red-hot irons from the campfire to seer his brand into the hide of each, and Bill applied the knife to castrate the bull calves before each bounded back to its mother.

That night in their tiny bunkhouse, after the Rocky Mountain oyster feed, Fannie rubbed Bill's back and shoulders with liniment. "It's good to see all the calves back on the range," she mused. Bill moaned softly as she kneaded his sore muscles. "If I were getting wages like the other hands . . ." Fannie's thoughts focused into a question. "Do you think the Elliotts might pay me to help with the haying? We could put by a little money if they would."

A negative grunt came from deep in his pillow.

"Why don't we ask if I could get on as a regular hand?"

"No need to," he mumbled. "We're leaving."

"Leaving?" Fannie stopped massaging. "What do you mean?"

Bill raised his head. "Dad Elliott needs someone here for the whole season. He'd be in a fix when we go to Cheyenne in July."

"But we'll only be with the Irwin show for a few days." Fannie couldn't imagine giving up the place where they'd been so happy. Where would they go? What would they do until July? And after? "Can't Dad Elliott spare us just for those few days, then we could come back."

Bill rolled over to face her. He took the liniment bottle and set it on the floor beside the bed. "Look, we'll be away in August, too, when you defend your title at Winnipeg." He grinned and pulled her down onto his chest. "I figure this is as good a time as any to make the break. We'll hit the trail this summer and you can ride exhibitions. If you win in Winnipeg, we'll come back with enough of a stake to do whatever we want next year."

Fannie smiled. "Sounds good." She kissed him lightly on the lips and nestled against his neck.

"I think the best thing would be to rig up a wagon to live in," Bill said. "Then we'll have a place to sleep and eat, no matter where we are, rain or shine. I won't have you sleeping out in the open."

"Sounds real good."

"You just stick with old Bill." He turned to blow out the lamp, then took her in his arms. "You ain't seen nothing yet."

Wildflowers, awakened by late May rains, bloomed along the roadside, and the fragrance of spring grasses wafted before them as they rode out of the Elliott gate and headed toward the Beartooth. Mounted on Ginger and Blaze, they trailed Bill's string of twenty-five bucking horses and the Morgan team. They would stay with Fannie's folks, helping with the ranch work till they left for Cheyenne.

At the Sperry ranch, Bill spent long hours outfitting the new wagon with tools and equipment. He rigged a tentlike cover over the box and purchased a small kerosene stove, a tin oven, a tub and washboard, and a lantern. Then he wrote to sponsors of stampedes in towns where the C. B. Irwin's Wild West show was scheduled to appear, entering Fannie in the bucking-horse events.

While Bill planned their tour down to the smallest detail, Fannie helped her mother and Walter around the ranch, fixing fence, mending tack, planting the garden, and preparing for the busy summer when they would have to manage without her.

Immediately after the first haying in late June, the Steeles loaded the wagon and prepared to leave. Rachel stocked their grub box with her fresh bread, butter, jellies, and a lemon cake, along with a slab of bacon and enough ham and boiled potatoes for several days. In a small crock, Fannie packed two dozen eggs in straw. After rounding up the bucking stock, she cinched her prize saddle on Napoleon and stepped aboard, slipping her boots into the handsome tapaderos. Datus and Rachel watched the testy bucking horses uneasily, and Fannie smiled to reassure them as she fanned her hat at the lead mare to haze her along. "If I keep Whirlwind in line, the rest will follow."

"Don't you worry now," Bill said. Seated in the wagon, he flicked the lines to the Morgans. "We'll be back after the Winnipeg Stampede."

The procession moved down the narrow road and, as they reached the first bend, Fannie turned to wave one last time at Walter and her parents standing beside the floribunda bush.

The day passed uneventfully with the cheerful tinkling of Whirlwind's bell setting the pace for the horses under Fannie's watchful eye, and Bill in the wagon bringing up the rear. That night they camped under cottonwoods next to a creek. Fannie watered the stock and turned them loose to graze, hobbling Whirlwind, while Bill took the kerosene stove from the wagon and placed the tin oven on top. By the time Fannie had washed up, he had baked steaming-hot baking-powder biscuits to go with the fried ham and gravy.

"I never could make biscuits like these." She savored the light texture mingled with that of her mother's sweet butter.

"Learned to make 'em when I had my cafe." Bill spooned a second helping onto his plate. "Wait till you taste my peach cobbler."

"Ma and Bertha used to do most of the cooking," Fannie confessed as she mopped up the gravy on her tin plate.

"What?" Bill threw up his hands in mock alarm. "You mean my little bride can't cook?"

"I can cook," she said. "We're talking about biscuits."

Bill cut the lemon cake and handed a piece to Fannie. They sat, leaning against the wagon wheel, balancing cake and coffee, and watched the last light fade behind the western mountains.

"This isn't such a bad life, is it?" Bill nodded toward the wagon, where their bedrolls lay on the floor surrounded by crates and boxes of supplies and tack.

"Not too bad." Fannie raised her eyebrow. "If the stock don't run off and the wolves don't get us." They giggled like schoolchildren.

Then Bill said, "Did I tell you there'll be several Indian tribes with the Irwin show? Red Cloud, son of the great Oglala Sioux chief, will bring a delegation from the Pine Ridge Reservation."

"How do you know that?"

"It's my business to know. Ain't I the manager of this outfit?" He smooched her cheek. "Irwin wants to stage what he calls Scenes of 'Forty Nine, with the Indians attacking and burning a prairie schooner while cowboys rescue the settlers."

As they talked, the deepening darkness inspired a chorus of crickets with a few frog soloists near the creek. They sat on the tailgate and gazed at the low-hanging stars.

"What'll we do if a bear comes?" Fannie teased.

"Well, we could always invite him to join the show. You could teach him to ride a bucking horse."

"You teach him," Fannie quipped. "I'll keep this handy just in case he don't want to learn." She patted her Winchester tucked under the quilts at her shoulder.

"You're right about one thing." Bill stretched his arms above his head. "That wagon seat is no feather bed."

"You asked for it, cowboy." She pulled off her boots. "I offered to drive the team."

"Trailing broncs is even worse." He yawned. "And I can see that it's better if I make the biscuits."

Just as Bill had planned, they arrived at the Cheyenne fairgrounds on July third, the day before the Frontier Days Celebration was to begin. Charles B. Irwin, a portly man of nearly 300 pounds, stepping lightly through the soggy corral, called to them as they trailed the horses toward the stock pens. "Well, Bill Steele." His round, rosy face sported a wide yellow-toothed grin. "And this must be Fannie. Welcome to Cheyenne."

Fannie leaned over Napoleon's neck to grip Irwin's hand. It felt good to be part of the excitement again. She looked around for someone she would recognize from Pendleton or Calgary.

"You'll be riding relay, Fannie," Irwin said. "And we've set up a bucking-horse exhibition for you with Prairie Rose Henderson." Fannie knew Prairie Rose had won a ladies' bucking-horse championship in Los Angeles the previous year.

"She travels with our show now," Irwin continued. "Great little rider. With the broncs you brought and a couple of Wyoming strings, you should pull some good buckers. Even the notorious Old Steamboat is here."

"Come on over to the cook tent after you put up your stock," Irwin said. "Want you to meet the family." He moved off to oversee the setting up of the Indian camp.

They drove the wagon toward a shady spot beyond the line of tepees, where a group of Sioux clustered around a tall buckskin-clad Indian. A bone-pipe breastplate and a small fur medicine bag dangled from his neck, and his hair was twisted into a long lock and knotted at the end with a piece of red trade cloth. "That looks like Chief Red Cloud there," Bill said, nodding politely as they passed. The chief returned the nod, the short feather in his topknot bobbing over his forehead. "He's a ghost dancer, like his famous father," Bill said when they were out of hearing.

C. B. Irwin greeted them in the cook tent and introduced his brothers, Frank, a bronc buster, and Floyd, a trick rider and roper. Their daughters, Pauline, Joella, and Gladys, sat with a young woman wearing a big sombrero.

"And this is Prairie Rose Henderson." The dishwater-blonde turned toward them, her eyes narrowed as she peered from under the brim of her big hat. Fannie could see that behind her comely face was a will of iron.

"I'm looking forward to seeing you ride," Fannie said.

"Likewise." Prairie Rose also seemed to specialize in an economy of words.

The Irwins put on a dazzling show. And, as advertised, the skills exhibited were authentic. To open the performance, Napoleon and Blaze, with Fannie and Bill astride, pranced through a quadrille featuring mounted cowboys and cowgirls.

When crack-shot Frank Miller, billed as the world's greatest sharp-shooter, galloped around the arena shooting from horseback, Fannie stood transfixed. "He hasn't missed a single target," she whispered to Bill.

"Why don't *you* start practicing on horseback?" he whispered back.

A mock holdup of the Deadwood stagecoach, complete with its original driver, Spittin' Bill Davis, on the box, brought spectators to a standing ovation.

Fannie's bucking-horse exhibition against Prairie Rose competed for audience attention but not for prize money. And in the three days of women's relay races, Fannie, riding against Vera McGinnis, Rose Wenger, and the Irwin cousins, came in first only once. She placed second twice, behind Joella Irwin, and was awarded the second-place prize money of $50.

Early each morning, she practiced shooting at small glass balls tossed by Bill while she galloped Napoleon around the track. Frank Miller had given her the targets and a few tips on technique.

From Cheyenne, the Irwin show moved on to a frontier celebration in Grand Forks, North Dakota, for ten days in mid-July. Advance publicity by the Irwins played up Fannie's appearance with the show. Bill, recruited to clown, was put in charge of the horses.

Opening night in Sioux City, Iowa, July 20, the show took place in the ballpark under newly installed electric lights. As Fannie prepared to ride, the bright ring of illumination frightened her bucking horse, Red Sandy, and Bill had trouble earing him down. "Get on," he shouted. "I can't hold him." Fannie jammed her boot into the stirrup and swung aboard. With his first explosive pitch, the panicked bronc lost his footing and rolled a complete somersault. Fannie fell beneath him, taking his weight momentarily as he twisted to his feet. The crowd strained to see what was happening, and a buzz of speculation passed through the stands.

Fannie got to her feet and stood unsteadily, her eyes searching the circle of light for Bill's familiar clown garb. She felt her senses dimming, then she crumpled to the ground.

Bill ran to her. "Somebody get a doctor."

"She's sustained severe back sprain," the doctor announced after checking Fannie. "She must have complete bed rest for a while."

"Honey, you've got to be well for Winnipeg," Bill told her. "I'm putting you on the train for home."

Too miserable with acute pain in her back and hip to protest, Fannie took her first ride in a Pullman car. Bill and their horses continued the tour with the Irwin show, fulfilling their contract. Barely a month remained before the Winnipeg Stampede, where Fannie would defend her world championship.

Defending Her Championship  15

W hat the hell's going on here?" Bill's angry voice startled Fannie. "They've got you riding with Weadick's group, and I'm in with a bunch of waddies." He crumpled the leaflet listing the Winnipeg Stampede parade lineup, picked up his saddle, and stomped off toward the field. Fannie followed him, carrying her own saddle. Her injured back had healed, but she tried to guard against straining it.

"Now, don't get sore, Bill. It doesn't mean anything."

"Sore? How am I supposed to feel when I'm shoved aside while you ride in like a queen?"

"As lady champion, I have to ride in the special honor formation that closes the parade." She hurried along beside her fuming husband. "You know that."

"If that's the way they're gonna treat me, I won't be in their damn parade."

"But you have to. It's in the contract. All performers must ride in full costume."

"Damn the contract." He stormed off.

Prairie Rose Henderson heard the exchange. "Ain't that just like a man." She chuckled as she stooped to adjust her spurs. Her big sombrero now sported a flamboyant, multicolored scarf looped through the hatband and trailing down her back. "I never seen a man yet who could take a backseat to his wife."

"Take a backseat?" Fannie bristled. "Bill doesn't take a backseat to me."

"Then how come he ain't ridin'?"

"He is. He's entered in the cowboy's bucking event." Fannie turned away, her cheeks burning. Bill had insisted on entering even though he had done little bronc riding in recent months.

At the parade lineup, Addison Day, arena director again this year, moved along the line of assembled riders and directed them into position. Fannie was relieved to see that Bill, riding Blaze, had taken his assigned place among the cowboys, directly preceding the Blackfeet Indians. Other tribes, Stoneys, Piegan, Blood, Sarcee, and Cree, were interspersed between the groups of performers that included top cowgirls Lucille Mulhall and Tillie Baldwin, steer ropers from Oklahoma and New Mexico, old-time cowpunchers from Wyoming, vaqueros from Old Mexico, and, riding alone, the mysterious Russian Cossack rider Zarofezromatzy Rofelbustoltrozy.

Then came the headliners. Champion fancy-rider Otto Kline riding beside Fannie, champion fancy-roper Tex McLeod beside roper Florence LaDue, champion bareback bronc-rider Jim Macey beside cowpuncher-turned-movie-actor Fred Stone. Addison Day and Guy Weadick held the final places of honor at the rear.

Following the parade, Lucy Mulhall and Fannie sat on the ground in front of the bleachers and watched Indian ceremonial dancers on the infield while trick and fancy riders performed on the track. Fannie kept her eyes on the clown, only halfheartedly watching the bareback riding and the Indian half-mile race, wondering if Bill was still angry. But she gave full attention when Tillie Baldwin came out standing full up on two horses in a Roman race against Johnnie Mullens and A. J. Bryson.

"Tillie's got the strength of an ox," Lucy said, getting to her feet. "She's not riding broncs here, but she'll be your main competition at Pendleton." Then she ran to the chutes for the longhorn-steer roping, the only woman in the event against eight men.

The women's bucking-horse event came after the bulldogging. Fannie drew a horse called Blackboy. She would compete against Prairie Rose on Railroad, Hazel Walker on Grey Goose, and Blanche McGaughey on Snake. Each of the women turned in a good ride. Fannie came in third in the cowgirls' relay race, behind Joella and Pauline Irwin, while Rose Wenger, Vera McGinnis, and Tillie Baldwin trailed her across the finish line.

The women had scarcely cleared the track when the cowboys' bucking event was called, and Bill was announced as the first rider on a buckskin bronc, Hyena. Fannie hurried toward the south infield, where she saw Bill atop the end chute. She hoped he had cooled off. It wasn't good to ride when feeling out of sorts.

Settled onto the horse, Bill gave the ready signal, and Hyena sidled out of the chute. For a moment, he seemed inclined not to buck. Then he broke loose with a high twist and a pile driver, followed by another snorting gut buster that left his rider sitting in midair. Bill landed on his hands and knees, barely escaping the flashing hoofs as the buckskin careened away. Immediately, he was up and waving to the crowd, but he hadn't qualified for the finals. Fannie breathed a sigh of relief.

"That bronc really is a hyena," she said, joining him amid the group of busters around the chute. She hooked her arm through his.

Bill hardly looked at Fannie. "I'm going into town with the boys for a little snort. You go on over to the wagon and get some rest. We'll be back in an hour or so." Fannie could see that he was still angry, if not about the parade, about his mediocre showing on the bronc. Maybe a few laughs with the boys would improve his spirits.

"All right," she said. "I could do with a nap." Turning away, she walked past the line of Indian tepees back to the wagon, where she washed up, brushed the dust from her hair, and, suddenly weary to the bone, lay down to rest.

Sometime later, she woke with a start to discover that dark had fallen. She glanced around for Bill. Wasn't he back yet? She could hear laughter from a group around a campfire. Smoothing her hair, she left the wagon and walked toward the circle of dark silhouettes outlined against the orange of the fire.

"Hey, Fannie." Prairie Rose and Lucy were there, along with Tex McLeod, Otto Kline, and a Miles City cowboy named Rufus Rollen.

"Anyone seen Bill?" she asked. "I guess I fell asleep."

Tex, hunkered down against a saddle, moved over to make room for Fannie in the circle. "We saw him earlier at the saloon. His yarns kept the whole place in stitches."

"That husband of yours is some storyteller," Otto said.

"And you're some rider." Rose, a bottle of beer in her hand, tipped it toward Fannie. "Want some beer?"

"No, thanks. I . . . I don't drink." Fannie studied Rose's face in the flickering light that emphasized the circles under her eyes.

Prairie Rose shrugged. "If you stay in this business, you'll soon learn that a nip just before climbing onto a bronc is the best insurance in the world that you'll loosen up and climb off in one piece." She saluted again with the bottle. "I aim to beat you tomorrow."

Fannie grinned. "You're sure welcome to try." The others chuckled.

After a while, one by one, the tired riders began drifting away, and Fannie stood to leave. "Think I'll hit the hay, too." She didn't want them to see that she was disturbed by Bill's leaving her alone so long. "Those broncs won't be any easier tomorrow."

"That's for damn sure. Good night, Fannie."

In the dim moonlight, she didn't bother to light the lantern. She found the loaf of bread, broke off a piece and nibbled it, but it stuck in her throat. She tossed it aside and sat down against the wagon wheel to wait. Before long, the laughter of several men could be heard across the field. Jolly farewells floated through the sleeping camp, then Bill came toward the wagon, singing to himself.

"Sounds like somebody had a good time." Her voice coming from the shadow of the wagon wheel surprised him.

"Fannie. Honey. You still awake?"

"I had a nap earlier. I was waiting for you."

"The boys and I got to talking and time just slipped away." He sat down beside her. She could smell whiskey on his breath but he didn't seem drunk. "I didn't mean to keep you waiting here by yourself. Why didn't you join the others? Did you have supper?"

"I wasn't hungry. I sat around the fire with Lucy and Prairie Rose for a while."

Bill put his arm around her. "Honey, I'm real sorry. But after that spill I took, I was feeling pretty low. I needed to relax. You should have come, too."

"Into a saloon?"

Seeing that she was shocked by such a suggestion, he said, "I got an idea. After the finals, we'll go into town, and I'll buy you a swell supper. How's that?" He seemed genuinely sorry.

"I'd like that," she said.

Next day, Fannie drew Eagle Butte and turned in a fine ride. Hazel Walker rode Sage Hen, and Blanche McGaughey stayed with a wild paint named John. Prairie Rose drew Terrasses Buck, a terror of a horse, and after her outstanding ride Fannie knew that Rose was the top contender. The third day's draw gave Fannie an advantage when she won the crowd's approval with her ride on Snake, while Rose's performance on Blackboy was not up to snuff.

On the final day, riding slick on the tricky Terrasses Buck, Fannie brought the spectators to their feet, cheering. The outlaw horse broke his buck rein, but she stayed in the saddle, her free arm outstretched in perfect balance. He bellowed and heaved through a series of swift and clever contortions that left the old-timers white-knuckled. Still Fannie stuck, outriding Prairie Rose. And slick saddle to boot. Audience reaction left little doubt as to their choice. The judges agreed. Fannie had retained her world championship.

When the official announcement came, Bill clasped her in his arms and swung her around, her feet skimming the ground. "You've done it! You're still Lady Champion of the World!" he said. "Tonight we're going to take some of that prize money and celebrate."

After the tension of the Winnipeg Stampede—defending her championship while worrying about reinjuring her back—Fannie relaxed and enjoyed trailing the stock with Bill from the Helena station back to the Sperry ranch. She was still champion. And the Winnipeg prize of $1,000 represented a healthy nest egg for their future.

As they pulled the wagon into the yard, Walter came from the house to open the corral gate for the horses. He looked distraught.

"Walter, what's wrong?"

His expression grim, Walter took her reins as she dismounted.

"What is it?" Fannie searched his face.

"It's Christine. She . . . she died."

"What?" Fannie, uncomprehending, stared at her brother.

"After her baby . . . well . . . she hadn't been well," he stammered.

"Christine? But it can't be."

"It happened right after you left."

Fannie defends her championship title at Winnipeg, 1913.

She reached out for Bill, her eyes searching his. "Not Chris. Why, she was so good. So healthy. Oh, her poor baby."

"We'll go tomorrow to see Will," Bill said.

Rachel came from the house, and Fannie cried in her mother's arms. "It's a terrible thing," Rachel said, leading her into the kitchen. Through the door to the front room, Fannie saw her father, propped in his chair and struggling for each breath. Weak with grief, she turned to her mother. "Isn't there something we can do to help Pa?"

"If there is," her mother murmured, "I don't know what it is."

Sharpshooting and Bronc Stomping

16

To relieve Bill's increasing boredom while wintering at the Sperry ranch, Fannie arranged a visit with Carrie and Bertha and their families. Carrie's seventh child had been born sickly, but Bill enjoyed entertaining the other children—Florence, Beatrice, Nick, George, Mathew, and little Betty, now two years old—with Wild West tales. He could make an amusing story out of the most trifling incident, and the children loved him. But Fannie's sisters and their husbands had never fully accepted Bill's way of life, which they considered irresponsible, and the visit, though polite, was brief.

Datus's asthma grew worse day by day. Fannie spent more and more of her time caring for him, and Bill, too, sat long hours talking with him, mostly about horses. But the illness had taken its toll. On a still night in March, seventy-four-year-old Datus Sperry drew his last labored breath, and the grieving family laid the stalwart pioneer homesteader to his final rest in a small cemetery on the prairie north of Helena.

Her father's death so soon after Christine's was hard for Fannie. She now felt even more responsibility to help her mother and brother on the ranch, but pitching into the hard work did little to ease her sorrow.

She stepped up her practice of shooting clay pigeons from horseback, a skill she planned to use in their Wild West performance. Deciding that was not exciting enough for audiences, Bill, unflinching, held a china egg between his thumb and index finger while she shattered it with a bullet from her .22 pistol. Her unfailing marksmanship prompted him to suggest she shoot the ashes off a cigar held between his teeth. "Just be a trifle more careful with your aim," he cautioned.

"Why? The cigar is farther from your face than the egg is from your fingers. It's easier than shooting the egg."

"True. But I can do without a finger easier than I can do without a nose."

During the warm spring, Bill completed the itinerary for their first season on their own. They added two wild horses to the string of bucking stock, a dun stallion Fannie named Skyrocket and a rugged little black mare Bill called Bangtail. The wagon supplies and other essentials now included cigars and china eggs ordered from Minneapolis.

On May 4, 1914, the fledgling Wild West show bumped down the narrow road from the Sperry ranch onto the flats, Bill at the wagon lines and Fannie trailing the eighteen head of stock. They rode west to the small settlement of Elliston, where Bill had made arrangements with a rancher to put on their first performance in a grassy field outside of town. He picked a spot to camp and unhitched the wagon. Then, while Fannie watered the stock at the nearby creek and set up camp, he saddled Blaze and rode the mile into town to talk up the next afternoon's show. He returned before sundown.

"I don't know how much business we'll do here. The ranchers are busy with spring work," he reported. "But I got word around at the stores. I'll go back after supper and get to know a few of the boys at the saloon." He placed bread and fresh milk, purchased in Elliston, on the tailgate, then washed up for supper. "Come along if you want to." But he knew Fannie was not comfortable entering a saloon. Or waiting outside.

After he again rode off toward Elliston, she cleaned up the supper leavings and tidied the wagon. When the twilight faded to darkness, she wrapped up in Clara's quilt and sat on the tailgate. Sounds of the horses grazing and the shifting of their feet were all she had to keep her company.

The black night sky deepened toward the east—toward the Beartooth. She thought of her mother and Walter alone at the ranch. Though she knew

Fannie continues to perfect her marksmanship by shooting from horseback at glass balls tossed by Bill.

they would manage somehow, she planned to get back to help them as much as she could. Hugging her shoulders in the evening chill, she watched the road for signs of Bill returning. The range seemed vast and lonely with only a few scattered pinpoints of light in the distance that marked the small settlement. Even with Napoleon and the Morgan team nearby, even with eighteen head of bucking horses, she felt far from home.

After a while, she heard the sound of Blaze's hoofbeats. Bill brimmed with enthusiasm as he pulled the saddle and bridle from his horse. "I passed the word that we'd pay five dollars to the best bronc rider and twenty-five dollars to anyone who could ride Bangtail. That ought to bring out the local cowboys. We'll pass the hat, and I figure we should clear the prize money and then some."

"It's a little scary," Fannie said as they lay awake in the tented wagon, "to know the show depends on just us. There's no Lucy Mulhall or Guy Weadick to draw a crowd."

"Listen, Fannie Steele's the biggest attraction in Montana right now. Folks will stampede to see you. And when they get a load of your shooting—a woman handling a rifle and pistol the way you do—they'll turn out in droves."

"I hope so."

"We'll get some newspaper publicity when we get to Deer Lodge. I'll have some notices printed up. Word will get around."

"But what about tomorrow afternoon. What if no one shows up? What if they don't put anything in the hat? How will we come up with the prize money?"

Bill nuzzled her cheek. "You just stick to the riding and shooting and let me do the worrying."

Morning dawned clear and cool. While Fannie groomed the saddle horses, Bill staked out an arena with strips of cloth tied to sticks, allowing plenty of room for the bucking arena and the sharpshooting by confining spectators to an area next to the road. Shortly after noon, wagons began to arrive. By two o'clock, the road was lined with teams and saddle horses, with people milling about among the assortment of wagons and buggies. Some had spread blankets on the ground down in front.

Bill walked out onto the field and raised his hand to get the crowd's attention. "Howdy, everybody," he began. "I'm Wallace S. Steele. But my friends call me Bill." His friendly grin drew return smiles from the spectators. "And here's Fannie Steele, the champion you all came to see." Fannie stepped forward. "We're going to start with the bucking-horse riding," Bill continued. "I got five dollars here for the cowboy that does the best job of staying on one of them ornery broncs. And after Fannie's sharpshooting, we'll give the grand prize of twenty-five dollars to anyone who can ride Bangtail, that little black mare."

A hush of anticipation settled over the crowd as Bill brought out a feisty strawberry roan for the first cowboy. When a young waddy offered to give Bill a hand, Fannie greeted him with surprise. "Well, Brian O'Connell." Now in his late teens, he still had the same freckles and mop of red hair. "I haven't see you for years. How's that gray mare I traded you?"

"Best horse I ever rode." His eyes still showed admiration for Fannie. "And how about the pinto you traded her for?"

"That's Napoleon over there." Fannie pointed toward the sleek piebald who stood saddled with her prize saddle.

Brian stared at the big horse. "Gosh, he's a dandy."

Several young cowboys lined up to try the bucking stock and, after all had ridden, spectator applause determined the winner of the $5.00 prize. Fannie studied the broncs' performances and planned to suggest to Bill that two of the weaker buckers be traded off.

"And now," Bill announced, "Fannie will show you her sharpshooting." He stepped off about 50 feet down the field. "All you kids stay back." Fannie loaded her pistol ceremoniously, and the onlookers stirred with anticipation.

Bill held up a china egg for all to see, placed it between his left thumb and forefinger, and extended it at arm's length. Fannie raised the pistol to shoulder height and sighted along the barrel. The crowd hushed as she steadied her aim and squeezed the trigger. The egg shattered. Bill held up his hand to show he was unhurt, and the crowd applauded enthusiastically. He then took another egg from his pocket and held it as before. Again Fannie took careful aim and fired. Another egg shattered. They repeated the stunt a third time. Three out of three.

"Don't she ever miss?" someone hollered out.

"If she did, would I be up here holding these things?" Bill responded. The spectators laughed.

Then Bill took a 5-inch cigar from his shirt pocket, placed it in his mouth, and lighted it. He jutted his chin in profile, and the crowd realized they were about to witness an even more daring feat. Fannie picked up her .22 Winchester. The only other sound as she chambered a cartridge was the whuffle and stomp of a workhorse harnessed to one of the wagons.

She took aim. The shot rang out. Ashes flew. And Bill waved the clean-cut cigar. "I'll use this stub again next time," he announced. Cheers rose from those gathered.

Next, with the help of Brian O'Connell, Bill blindfolded Bangtail and brought her forward. The little black mare reared, wild with fear at the noise of the crowd. Bill eared her down and Brian jerked the blindfold as the first cowboy settled into the saddle. At the mare's first lunge, the cowboy bit the dust. The second rider, too, departed Bangtail pronto. The third buster stuck through a challenging ride, then left the bronc of his own volition. Bill paid the rider $25 on the spot.

"Now you're going to see the Lady Bucking-Horse Champion of the World do her stuff!" Bill announced as Brian brought the blindfolded

Fannie shoots the end off a cigar that Bill holds in his mouth, 1915.

Skyrocket onto the field. Hackamore in place, the saddle was cinched up, and Fannie stepped up onto the dun stallion.

"Turn him loose," she shouted, and Brian pulled the blindfold. The dun let go, arching into an unpredictable series of high rolling jumps, twisting right and left, but Fannie stayed through all of his devilish moves until he paused long enough for her to jump off. It was a good exhibition ride. The crowd showed its appreciation.

Bill caught Fannie's hand and held it high. "Let's show some enthusiasm for the champ! Fannie Steele!" Folks continued cheering and applauding until Bill waved to quiet them.

"Ladies and gentlemen. Thank you all for coming this afternoon. I know you got a kick out of the fine horsemanship and marksmanship you've seen here today. Now, just so my wife and me can continue to feed these broncs and bring you these fine shows, we're going to pass a hat among you." Brian moved down the line with the hat, and the men dug into their pockets.

"We'll be here again next week on our way back from Deer Lodge," Bill continued. "So tell your friends, and we'll see you here on Sunday, same time."

After the crowd cleared and Brian had agreed to come with them to Deer Lodge to help with their Wednesday performance, Fannie counted $39 from the hat collection. "After our thirty-dollar expense for prize money, we cleared nine dollars." She patted the cigar box that would serve as their cash box.

"Well, now, you're a pretty good little accountant," Bill teased, flipping open the lid and taking a handful of coins.

"Somebody has to keep track," she said. "How else will we know where we stand." She showed him the notes she'd made on her tablet. Under "Income," she'd listed $39. Under "Expenses," Bangtail rider, $25. Bronc winner, $5.00.

"How much did you spend for groceries?" she asked.

"Let's see. The bread was a nickel. Milk, a dime."

"And at the saloon?" She poised her pencil above the tablet.

"Now, wait a minute We don't have to write down every damn penny."

"But we do, Bill. What did you spend?"

"I don't remember," he snapped. "Now, let's peel up some spuds for supper. Brian here looks powerful hungry."

The next Sunday the crowd doubled for their return performance in Elliston, and so did the take. In the following weeks, they performed to increasing numbers of spectators at nearly every town or large ranch along their route. Wolf Creek, Cascade, Ulm, and the Valentine Ranch, then on to Great Falls. There Bill had postcards printed up with a photograph taken by Marcell of Miles City, which showed Fannie riding at Calgary. They sold the postcards for 5 cents each, clearing an extra $2.00 to $5.00 at each performance in Fort Benton, Square Butte, Denton, Deerfield, Carter Road, Lewistown, the Kline Ranch, and Grass Range. Fannie's account books showed a profit of $436.99 between Elliston and the coming challenge, the prestigious Miles City Roundup.

Disappointments at the Miles City Roundup

17

The jingle of harness. The thump of wagon wheels falling over rocks. The squeak of saddle leather. Day after day the familiar sounds accompanied Fannie and Bill across the pitch and swell of Montana's austere rangeland. As the gentle sweep of the Yellowstone River Valley beckoned them eastward, scrub junipers clung to the rocky bluffs that flanked their journey, and sparse willows and cottonwoods struggled in the dry country to retain a toehold on the river and creek banks.

Miles City lay at the confluence of the Yellowstone and the Tongue Rivers, flowing full now at the end of June. Camping outside of town among the sagebrush along the Tongue, the Steeles left the wagon and trailed the bucking horses to the fairgrounds. After the quiet of the trail, they welcomed the noisy bustle of the town, where carriages and drays, cowboys, and livestock jammed the dusty main street. In the midst of it all, a number of automobiles added to the excitement, honking horns, frightening stock, and scattering folks to safety.

"We should get us one of them autos," Bill mused.

"I can't stand the noisy, smelly things," Fannie said. "Besides, they cost money."

"We could *afford* a *Ford*. Only seven hundred and fifty dollars." As usual, Bill tried to be funny when he wanted something. "Has eighteen horse-power."

Fannie chuckled. "Give me the eighteen horses any day."

She liked Miles City. For many years it was the northernmost point of the long cattle drives up from the Southwest, and nearly all cattle entering Montana had been dispersed from that point. The town still boasted the state's most widely attended stock sales, offering as many as 4,000 horses each month. The first Miles City Roundup, held the previous year, 1913, commemorated the thirty-fifth anniversary of the town's founding.

At the fairgrounds they drove their bucking horses into one of the corrals. Bawling longhorns filled another. Crow and Cheyenne Indians in feathered war bonnets and other native finery moved about in front of their encampments, clearly visible from the stands since all fences were of wire so as not to interfere with the view of events from all sides. One side was reserved for automobiles, where the occupants could sit in their machines to watch the events.

Bill had been hired to oversee the bucking stock. His string of broncs and those supplied by local ranchers totaled more than a hundred. While he grained the horses, Fannie rode back to the riverside camp. Wanting everything to be fresh for the Roundup, she got out the washtub and set up the stove, then hauled water from the river and heated it for washing clothes. After scrubbing the heaviest soil on the washboard, she rinsed everything in a bucket of cool water, twisting each garment to wring out the excess, and draped her washing over surrounding sagebrush to dry.

As she finished spreading and smoothing wrinkles from the last garment, she looked up to see two horsemen racing toward her in a cloud of dust, whooping it up in high spirits. One was Bill. She didn't recognize the other. She started toward them, her arms upraised. Too late. They thundered into camp, scattering dust all over her washing, knocking some garments into the dirt.

"Hellooo, Fannie," Bill called, waving his hat in greeting as Blaze trampled one of his best shirts. The other man pulled up short. Fannie stood fuming, hands on hips, too angry to speak. "Honey, this is my old pal, Harry Combs." Bill dismounted unsteadily and came forward to plant a peck on her cheek. He gestured toward the friend, who climbed down from his horse and walked toward her, holding out his hand. "Howdy, ma'am."

"Bill Steele, I could kill you," she raged. "Didn't you see my washing drying?"

Bill looked around sheepishly. "Gee, honey, I didn't."

"That's for darn sure."

"Here, I'll help you pick them up." He began scurrying around, shaking grit from the garments and smoothing them carefully over the sagebrush.

"I'm awful sorry, ma'am." Combs, clean shaven and neatly dressed, pitched in to help Bill. They seemed so remorseful, Fannie felt her anger lifting.

"Well, you two sure take the cake," she said. Then, managing a smile, she offered her hand to Combs, much to Bill's relief. "Welcome to Montana."

"Gol darn, Bill." Combs showed a row of gold-filled teeth when he grinned. "Your wife's a dandy. Pretty, too. Only I remembered her more blonde. When I used to see you two in Sedalia . . ."

Bill shot a startled glance at Combs. "That wasn't her."

"But I thought . . ." Combs looked from Bill to Fannie.

Bill picked up a trampled shirt. "Here, honey. I'll help you wash up these dirty ones. Then we'll all ride into town for supper." Fannie saw an evasiveness in Bill's face she hadn't seen before. Who was this woman Combs mentioned? When Bill took a bucket to the river for more wash water, she questioned the man from Missouri.

"You and Bill were good friends down in Missouri?"

"Oh, yes, ma'am. Met him in a saloon in Sedalia. Thought he was the funniest guy I ever saw—and one of the nicest, too. We got to be friends right away."

She decided to out with it. "Who was the woman you saw him with?"

"Oh, you know Bill. Always a charmer with the ladies."

"But you thought he was married to her?"

"Well, uh, I couldn't say about that."

Bill, returning with the water, had overheard. "Fannie, you might as well know. I was married once before."

His words hit like a lightning bolt. Why hadn't he told her?

"Hell, Bill," Combs stammered. "I didn't know."

"That's okay, Harry. It's just as well out." Bill's tone softened, and he moved toward Fannie. "Honey, I should have told you, but it happened so long ago. And it was for such a brief time. It didn't work out, and I left when we realized it was a mistake."

Fannie dropped the shirts into the tub and, fighting tears, ran toward the river. Bill overtook her.

"Fannie, it was nothing. . . ." He tried to put his arms around her but she pushed him away.

"Nothing? Being married is nothing?" Her voice broke.

"I didn't mean the marriage was nothing. But that was so long ago. It means nothing to me now." He drew her to him. "You know you're all that matters to me."

She stiffened to resist his embrace. "Why didn't you tell me? That's what hurts."

"I should have. But to tell the truth I'd almost forgotten it myself." His eyes were the same earnest blue they had always been. "Come on, now. Let's not make Harry feel he's done something terrible."

Her heart felt leaden, but she tried to compose herself as they walked back toward the wagon, where Combs sat cleaning his fingernails with his pocketknife. "Sorry, folks. Didn't mean to stir up trouble."

"Forget it. That's all in the past. Now, let's get these things up out of the dirt." Bill poured more water into the washtub, and he and Combs talked about good times they had shared in Missouri while they rinsed the clothes for Fannie to once again spread on the sagebrush.

Early the next morning, after a breakfast of Bill's biscuits and gravy, they rode into town to feed the stock. Harry wanted to see the eleven o'clock ball game between Miles City and neighboring Glendive, so Fannie and Bill rode out to the Fort Keogh Remount Station, a 100-square-mile horse ranch run by the U.S. Army, where Smoky Moore, the corral boss, showed them the army horses. Fannie commented on a sleek roan with white tail and mane.

"That's Silvertail," Moore said, squinting at the handsome mare. "Mighty good lines."

Bill turned his attention to the other stock. "Let's see what else you have. I may want to do a little trading after the roundup."

That afternoon, while Bill went about his chores at the fairgrounds, Fannie mingled with people moving toward the stands. Two marching bands rendering sprightly marches at either side of the field emphasized the holiday mood, while the bright shirts and bandanas of riders blended with the colorful costumes of Indians preparing for the grand entry. Amid the hubbub, she saw two men with cameras—one was Marcell of Miles City, who had taken her picture at Calgary.

A young woman beside her had noticed the cameramen, too. "That other one's with a moving-picture company, here to film the roundup," she said. Then, offering her hand to Fannie, "I'm Brida Randall." She brushed at strands of her auburn hair blowing in the brisk breeze. "And these two horse-happy characters are Marie and Cage Johnson." Dark-haired Marie offered a friendly smile, and her lanky husband showed a bucktoothed grin.

"I'm Fannie Steele."

"I know. And hanging on the fence there is Jesse Coates and the Coleman brothers, Lloyd and Ray." Lloyd Coleman held out his hand. "I hear you Steeles brought in bucking stock. Got some ornery ones for us?"

"You bet," Fannie said.

The movie man, grinding a large camera, cut in front of them. His black suit and string tie, dusty and rumpled in the heat, looked as outlandish as his wild, windblown hair. "Would you people move out of the way, please," he said without taking his eyes from the camera viewfinder. "I'm trying to get a long shot of the Indians." Fannie and the others moved to the side. But the cameraman had already hurried off across the arena toward the bull pen, his eye still pressed to the camera.

Mounted and waiting with Brida for the grand entry, Fannie patted Napoleon's neck and adjusted the red, white, and blue banner draped across his chest, identical to the banners provided by the roundup committee for each horse in the parade. The riders had paused on the sidelines while the Miles City mayor took the small platform at center front and signaled for the band to stop playing.

"Welcome to the second-annual Miles City Roundup." The mayor shouted over the quieting crowd. "Ladies and gentlemen, we're pleased to have some mighty distinguished guests with us today. Governor Stewart is here for the roundup." The governor stood for a round of applause, and the mayor continued his introductions.

"Two Moons, war chief of the Northern Cheyenne and last survivor of the chiefs who fought General Custer. Curly, the only scout in Custer's command who survived to tell the story. And Captain Grant March, the steamboat man who waited Custer's return at the mouth to the Big Horn." More applause for each veteran of history. "I wish we had time to bring all the old-timers to the stand, but I know you're anxious to get on with the roundup." He added with a wide sweep of his hat to the cameraman, "And I know these moving-picture folks are rarin' to capture the action on film."

That afternoon in the men's relay, Ben Ford, Cage Johnson, Toots Ayres, and Crow Indian Samson Bird-in-ground competed. The heats proved exciting, with Bird-in-ground well in the lead at the end of the third round. But he stopped just short of the finish line, unsaddled his mount, saddled a waiting horse, and took off around the track for a fourth lap.

"What's he doing?" Fannie said. "Doesn't he know there are only three rounds?"

The other riders came under the wire, and Toots Ayres was declared the winner just as Bird-in-ground pounded in to end his fourth round, shouting angrily at the judges.

"I think Bird should have won," Brida said. "He was ahead all three rounds. He must have thought it was a four-round race like last year."

"Too bad he didn't cross the finish line before he unsaddled his third mount."

Fannie and Brida moved toward the field as the cowgirls' bucking event began. Katie Wilkes, a short, sturdy girl with blond braids hanging down her back, was up first on a shifty-looking horse called Two Timer. Fannie could see Katie was in trouble with the bronc's first off-balance plunge, but the girl managed to free her feet from the hobbled stirrups as the horse went down. She landed hard on one knee, and she clasped it in pain as she was carried from the arena. Marie Johnson, her dark eyes wide with apprehension, made a good ride, as did Brida.

Then Fannie was introduced as the Lady Bucking-Horse Champion of the World. She had drawn White Diamond, a sorrel with a white star and four white feet, whose ears flattened as she mounted. At the ready signal, the horse reared out of the chute, neck arched, mouth distorted with fury. Fannie gripped the heaving sides, concentrating her leg strength. Another high and hard-bucking twist. When that failed to throw the rider, White Diamond shifted his energy to a series of sidewinders. Fannie sat the bronc with ease, and the movie man ground his camera throughout, capturing on film this graceful rider on the star-faced sorrel, then moving in to get a close-up as she alighted. As she rejoined the women behind the chutes, the cameraman followed.

"Miss!" he called to her. "I got some fine shots of you on that horse. You look good up there." He wiped his dusty sleeve across his face, leaving a sweaty smudge on his forehead. "I think you should talk to my boss when he gets here tomorrow." Then he dashed back onto the field to continue filming as the catch-and-saddle race began.

One of the judges, Henry Grierson of Forsyth, took the platform to announce the day's winners. "In the men's relay, Toots Ayres takes first place." A murmur of protest rippled through the stand.

"Bird-in-ground had Ayres beat by a mile."

The judge raised his hand to quiet the dissension. "Samson Bird-in-ground will receive the second-place money. Because he was out in front all the way, the judges thought he deserved second place." Then he emphasized, "Even though he didn't cross the finish line with his third mount."

Brida clearly didn't approve. "I don't think that's fair."

"There have to be rules," Fannie said. "Still, it's a shame he didn't get first. Sam Bird's the best horse racer in the West."

It was after six o'clock when the Steeles, Brida Randall, and the Johnsons headed into town for supper. Streets teemed with the lively holiday crowd, and the bands, having set up at the corner of Eighth and Main, provided continuous music to spark the yells and howls, serpentine marches, confetti tossing, firecrackers, and other devices for making a racket. The group found a table in a small cafe, and Bill issued an invitation.

"Any of you interested in joining up with Fannie and me? We need good performers for our new show. We're calling it the Powder River Wild West Show."

"We are?" Fannie laughed. "First I heard of it."

"I just thought up the name today," Bill said.

Cage grinned. "Me and Marie are thinking of taking off for

Hollywood. Don't you think Marie would make a beautiful move star?" He beamed at his wife. "They're looking for riders and pretty girls out there."

"That's pie in the sky," Bill said. "What do you say, Cage? Want a job? I'm recruiting as many as I can here at the roundup. We'll get the show organized and hit the trail about the first of August."

"Can't this year. Got to get home," Cage said. "I was just kidding about Hollywood."

"That man with the camera ain't kidding," Brida said. "He told Fannie this afternoon he liked the way she looks. Maybe he wants to put you in the movies, Fannie."

Bill shot a glance at Fannie. "What did he say?"

Fannie shrugged. "Just that he liked my riding. And that he wants me to talk to his boss tomorrow."

"That's great, honey. When we get our show rolling, we'll offer it to the movies, lock, stock, and barrel. Don't kid yourself, these moving pictures are going to be big someday."

The second day of the roundup dawned especially warm. By showtime the temperature had climbed to ninety-two in the shade, and the grandstand, packed to overflowing, had acquired extra rows of plank benches down front to accommodate the 4,000 paid admissions.

In the bucking contests one rider was slightly injured when he was thrown and kicked. Then the steers broke through the stock gate onto the track and had to be pursued by a posse of cowboys. Photographer Marcell got caught in front of a runaway steer and was scraped up a bit. It took every available hazer to get one of the renegades back to the pen, each looping a lariat around the steer's anatomy in one place or another—all of which Marcell recorded with his camera.

The bulldogging fizzled as only one horse, Smith White's, could be gotten near enough to a wild steer to allow a rider to grab its horns. And White was not an entry, but a hazer. The best bucking of the day was by a mule named Steam Chinaman in the catch-and-saddle race. Events moved rapidly. At times the arena was as busy as a three-ring circus, and necks grew stiff just trying to keep up with all that was going on.

Fannie again won the judges' decision in the cowbelles' bucking-horse event, riding against Brida. Katie Wilkes, after her spill, was not up to participating. In the relay, Marie edged out Fannie by a nose.

Though his camera continued to record each event, the movie man said nothing more to Fannie that day. Maybe his boss didn't get here, she reasoned.

That night when the friends gathered at the cafe, the Johnsons brought newspapers carrying details of the two days' events and touting the grand finale the next day, July Fourth. "It says here that the stands are all sold out already," Cage reported. "They're estimating at least five thousand will show up, including a group from the local reform school."

"That's quite a piece of change," Bill said. "You know, Fannie, I think that's the way we should handle our show. An admission charge. Charge everybody fifty cents to see it. We ain't getting rich passing the hat."

Fannie nodded. "Maybe so."

"Of course, you should charge," Brida said. "As good a show as you two put on."

"It would take more advance publicity," Bill continued. "I'd have to go on ahead to make arrangements for printing tickets, run advertisements in the papers, that sort of thing."

Above the noise of revelers in the street came the beat of the Crow drums, signaling the beginning of the tribe's war dance. Bill hurriedly paid the check and the group moved out into the street. Throngs of spectators had already claimed most of the viewing spots from which they could see the Indian pageantry, and Fannie stood on a nail keg to get a better view.

"Indian drums always give me goose bumps," she whispered as the dancers in war bonnets, leggings, and feathered bustles moved in a steady twisting rhythm around drummers seated in the center of the intersection beating tom-toms.

"Me, too," Brida replied. "But aren't the costumes splendid?" Fannie nodded, absorbed in the tribal display. Finally, after standing for more than an hour, Bill said he was in danger of falling asleep on his feet, and the friends agreed to get together again after the next day's finals.

The July Fourth crowd proved even larger than predicted, with people standing three deep along the sidelines and milling about over the grounds.

Bands, playing their loudest, strutted for the cameras. Marcell, limping from his encounter with the steer, was back on the job and trying to keep up with the movie crew.

Accidents increased with the fever pitch of the contests. Harry Neitzer of Fort Keogh was shot in the left side by a ricocheting bullet fired into the ground by a hazer trying to head off a rambunctious steer. Earl Onweiler, also of Fort Keogh, dislocated an elbow getting off a steer, and a cowboy named Olson broke his ankle trying to land a longhorn.

Marie Johnson was up first for the cowbelles' bucking-horse event. Riding hobbled, she stayed aboard a gaunt-looking Appaloosa, but her ride was not up to her usual, Fannie thought. Myrle Wilcox did well on a wiry black horse.

When Brida Randall came up on White Diamond, the outlaw sorrel lurched from the handlers and plunged to one side, ducking his head between his legs. The rider's boots pulled free, and she was hurled through the air, landing with a dull thud, her head striking the ground. Cage rushed to where she lay, out cold.

"She's hurt!" He patted her cheek to bring her around. Two men came running from the sidelines carrying a canvas stretcher, and Cage followed as they carried her from the field.

"Do you want me to go with you?" Fannie asked.

"No," Cage said, "you're up next."

Fannie had drawn a wild bucker, Oatmeal. Despite her concern over Brida's accident, Fannie intended to give the crowd what they had come to expect of her, a championship ride. Concentrating on the task at hand, she swung aboard, barely settling herself before the gate opened and the dappled bronc plunged into a bucking tantrum that brought the crowd to its feet. But Fannie remained aboard. Daring yet commanding, she leaned expertly into each move of the sinewy horse. Strength. Anticipation. Balance. Quick reflex. She had never ridden better. She was at her peak and she knew it.

As she bounded to the ground and waved to acknowledge the wild applause, Fannie looked around for the movie man. He hadn't photographed her ride this time, her best of the roundup. She saw him posing Sam Bird near the pens.

Bill followed her gaze. "I told that camera guy you weren't interested."

"You what? But why? I *am* interested."

"I talked to him this afternoon. He only wanted to do some test shots of you. He wasn't interested in our whole show, and I knew you wouldn't want to give that up just now. I've hired several riders to finish out the season with us, and you know I can't do it without you." Bill smiled and put his arm around her. "Wait till we get the show on solid ground. There's plenty of time to impress the movie people." He squeezed her affectionately. "By the way. Up there on Oatmeal. You were sensational."

They stopped at the roundup headquarters downtown to pick up her prize money and then crossed the street to the cafe. As they entered, a cheer went up from the row of cowboys at the bar.

"Here's our champion cowgirl," one said, touching the brim of his hat in salute. "You had that snuffy Oatmeal purrin' like a pussycat."

"Good going, Fannie."

"Quite a woman you got there, Bill."

Bill led the way to a back table where Marie and Cage Johnson were waiting for them. Brida Randall entered the cafe alone looking pale and shaken. She saw the group and came to join them. "I'm okay," she said, seeing their concern. "Just knocked out for a few minutes. But the doctor says I'll be fine." She sank into the chair Bill pulled up for her. "And Harry Neitzer is going to be okay, too. That bullet just missed his lung. Said he wished he could join us tonight to celebrate."

"And a celebration it is." Cage pulled a roll of bills from his pocket. "Let's see. Marie got a first and two seconds, and I won two seconds and two thirds. Looks like we cleared over seven hundred smackers. That ought to keep us in groceries this winter, huh, kid?" He nuzzled Marie's dark curls.

Bill took Fannie's prize money from his pocket. "Fannie has pulled down two firsts and a second. Her take is four hundred twenty-five, and we got a hundred thirty-five for bringing the bucking string and for my services tending stock. We're about five hundred sixty to the good."

Brida looked glum. "About all I got is a darn nasty goose egg on the back of my head. I took the five-dollar second-place money in the first day's bucking is all. Came out with a near goose egg there, too." The group laughed.

"Then I think it's up to your friends to buy you a drink," Bill said. He ordered whiskey all around.

"Not for me." Fannie fluttered her hand in a negative gesture. "I'd probably keel over if I drank anything."

"I'll have whiskey," Brida said. "After today, I need it."

"I don't know what you women are so worked up about," Bill said. "The only decent bucker in Miles City is that crazy mule Steam Chinaman." More laughter.

"I didn't see *you* on White Diamond." Brida's usually bright eyes had dulled in her ashen face.

"Or Oatmeal," Fannie countered. "That bronc knows what he's here for."

"Now, girls." Cage held his arms in front of his face, feigning evasion of an attack. "Just because you're the world's greatest women riders doesn't mean any one of us men couldn't outride you any day. Ain't that right, Bill?"

"Look, cowboy," Marie spoke sharply to her husband. "We draw for our mounts from the same hat as you men. What makes it less of an honor when we ride one to a standstill than when you do?"

"Hobbled stirrups give you the advantage." Cage raised his glass in mock salute.

"Fannie don't hobble." Brida downed her whiskey in two hefty draughts.

"So she don't." Cage squinted one eye at Fannie. "Well, maybe she's just a little bit foolish."

Wild West Headliner

18

"Why, that cameraman hung back like a borrowed dog when Steam Chinaman blew his plug." Laughter flowed easily among the riders after the roundup, and Bill reveled in telling his stories.

A stocky figure in a Montana-peak hat entered the cafe. He wore a red sash tied around his waist.

"Charlie!" someone called out. "Hey, it's Charlie Russell."

The artist greeted all with jovial remarks. With him were Lee Caldwell and Rufus Rollen, first- and second-place winners in the men's bucking contest. Russell saw Fannie and came toward her table.

"Well, Fannie Sperry. You did it again. Every time I see you ride, I'm more convinced you're one of the best damn bronc twisters ever lived." Russell's friendliness to Fannie surprised Bill and the others.

Fannie shook his hand. "My name is Steele now. This is my husband, Bill."

"Say, you're some lucky son-of-a-gun." Russell's ruddy cheeks crinkled with good humor as he acknowledged the other introductions, then he took a chair and straddled it backwards. "How's that spunky ma of yours, Fannie?"

"Fit as a fiddle." She nodded to Caldwell and Rollen. "You boys pulled off some good rides today."

"And *you* rode even better'n you did at Calgary, Fannie." Rollen winked at her. Young Caldwell, her male counterpart for the world title, nodded.

"What is this, a mutual admiration society? Let's celebrate!" Bill signaled the barmaid. "How about another round?"

"It darn right should be a mutual admiration society," Russell drawled, "because this here Miles City Roundup is the best of any of them. I've been around to Pendleton, Calgary, Winnipeg—hell, I've seen them all—and this shindig has 'em all cheated. Except in the matter of purses, of course."

"Charlie's right," Caldwell said. "Best riders in the country here, but the money ain't hardly worth comin' for."

"If I didn't live here, I wouldn't show up for what little they give out," Rollen said.

Cage patted the roll of bills in his pocket, grinning at his wife. "*We* did all right. Two of us riding makes a difference."

"I heard about one guy who found a way to make it pay." Bill leaned back on his chair, thumbs in his vest pockets. "Seems the sheriff nabbed a cowpoke at the depot last night making off with a load of loot that'd choke a buffalo. He'd stole everything he could get his hands on—jewelry, pocketbooks, even some shoes and silk stockings. Said it all belonged to his grandma."

Russell laughed heartily, his cigar fluttering between his teeth. "I heard some liquored-up waddy *borrowed* the sheriff's Appaloosa this forenoon. Rode the pony right down Main Street. When the sheriff spotted him single-footin' through town just as pretty as you please, his passion for law and order boiled up. He pulled that hog leg he wears strapped to his hip and hustled the horse thief off to the clink. That puncher's homesteadin' there now till he sobers up." The group found considerable humor in Russell's account.

"I'm hungry," Marie said. "I need something to eat."

"I feel great." Brida's voice carried above the others as she raised her glass for a refill. "Can't no cross-brained bronc get me down."

"Why don't you all come out to the camp?" Bill said, picking up the bar check. "And we'll light up a campfire."

"Fine idea," Cage said.

"How about it, Charlie?" Bill clasped his arm around the artist's shoulders.

"Why not? Might as well make a night of it. This *is* our country's birthday." He walked with Fannie and the others out into the night. By the time the group had mounted their saddle horses, Bill had invited several more to join the campfire party. Fannie simply wanted to crawl into her bedroll but, seeing that Bill was having a good time, she said nothing.

The night was warm, and while Bill's blazing campfire kept mosquitoes at bay the stories grew lengthy and the laughter loud. But long before the voices quieted and the revelers drifted off, Fannie slept soundly in the wagon.

The Steeles remained in Miles City through the month of July, resting the stock and reorganizing costumes and supplies. They interviewed cowboys for their new Powder River Wild West Show and recruited several more hands. Bill McKnight, a top bronc buster, trick rider, and roper, agreed to finish out the season with them. Others would join them at various towns along the way, supplying steers for bulldogging.

Bill wrote letters to arrange for advertising and to reserve show arenas in upcoming towns, picking up his mail from general delivery at the Miles City post office. He also made a few livestock trades. Oatmeal and White Diamond were now among their bucking stock, and Silvertail, from the Fort Keogh Remount Station, had been added to their string of saddle horses.

Fannie faithfully recorded their expenses for the month. Pair of chaps for Bill, $10. One bale of hay, 75 cents. Pasture for twenty head of horses, $22.50. With her prize money, Fannie ordered a fine riding skirt of brown-and-white unborn calfskin from Al Furstnow, a well-known Miles City saddle maker. Wearing the calfskin skirt and mounted on Silvertail in her prize saddle, Fannie was ready to headline their own Powder River Wild West Show.

They left Miles City on August 4, 1914, retracing their route along the Yellowstone River, with Fannie helping Bill McKnight and the other hands trail the stock. Silvertail, a well-trained quarter horse, soon became her favorite mount.

The new 50-cent admission charge did not keep people from attending in Rosebud on August 5. Nor in Hysham on August 9. Fannie took her bows as the featured crowd pleaser before large audiences drawn from the surrounding countryside. As usual, she clipped reports from local newspapers for her mother.

Fannie, wearing her new calfskin riding skirt, poses with Bill for a portrait advertising their Wild West show.

Fannie Sperry Steele, the world's champion lady bucking-horse rider, and her company of reckless riders will give an exhibition in Hysham at 2:30 Sunday afternoon. Mrs. Steele also holds the championship of Montana and is herself a product of this state. She was the one big attraction at the Miles City Roundup, and people who have seen her ride say it is well worth the price of 50 cents, which will be charged for her exhibition here.

Fannie smiled at the words *the one big attraction.* Bill's handiwork again. But perhaps it was true. She *was* the champion, and reviews of their show were beginning to sound like those of the Irwin Brothers or the Miller Brother's 101. With bronc riding, steer riding, and bulldogging, plus Bill McKnight's trick riding and roping, and her sharpshooting act, they had become a real Wild West show.

From Hysham, they traveled north to Melstone on the Musselshell River for an August 12 performance, trailed west along the river to the town of Musselshell for a show on August 16, then on to Roundup, where Bill organized an August 21 women's relay in which Fannie won the $10 first prize.

From Roundup, the Powder River procession headed north again to Flat Willow, skirting the Lewis and Clark National Forest to Straw, and following westward along the Musselshell to Harlowton, Two Dot, and White Sulphur Springs, less than 100 miles from home.

At White Sulphur Springs, a heavy downpour dampened the afternoon show and the troupe bedded down early. Bill lay listening to the rain on the wagon tent, while Fannie recorded the day's proceeds and expenses before turning in.

"The show went well today," Bill said, "even with the rain."

"Better than I expected."

"The men make a good group. But it's going to be tough to keep all twenty of the hands between here and Pendleton. That's almost a month away, and I haven't got anything else lined up."

Fannie turned to look at her husband, frowning. "But if they drift off to other jobs, they won't be available for Pendleton."

"That's about it. They have to eat." Bill paused as if formulating an idea. "Do you think your ma would mind if we camped them at the ranch? We'd pay for what they eat, and they could sleep in the barn."

Fannie visualized her mother's surprise when they trooped in with twenty extra mouths to feed. "She'll probably enjoy it."

Rachel did enjoy it—at first. The men sat around drinking and telling stories, and Rachel, Walter, Fannie, and Bill joined in. But by the end of the first week, the novelty of having twenty cowboys underfoot was growing thin. Rachel began to complain to Fannie about the quantities of food they were eating. Walter was peeved at the amount of drinking.

"They don't mean no harm," Bill said. "They're just lettin' off steam after a hard summer."

"Some of them got no more manners than a hop toad," Rachel snapped. "Except that Bill McKnight. He's nice. He showed me how he does some of his trick riding. I may try it myself."

"You'll do no such thing," Fannie interrupted. "Trick riding is not a sport for a sixty-nine-year-old lady."

"Fannie's right," Bill teased. "You better stick to catching wild broncs."

"Oh, go on, all of you." Rachel bustled about the kitchen, helping Fannie prepare kettles of food for the cowboys' next meal.

"Ma, I want you to see the show," Fannie said. "We'll ride in Townsend on September fifteenth on the way to Pendleton. Why don't you come down there with us? With Arthur and Edith living there now, you can stay with them."

"Maybe *we* can stay with them, too, Fannie," Bill mused. "Just us, I mean. Not the whole troupe."

A Place to Call Home  19

The steady click of the locomotive wheels on rails ticked off the miles, and Fannie sat restlessly while the train carrying the Powder River Wild West Show climbed over the Great Divide toward Oregon on September 22, 1914. Fannie felt nervous about the Pendleton Roundup after the hurriedly arranged performance in Townsend, where her mother and Walter finally saw the show in action after their harried month of boarding the troupe.

"We shouldn't have piled in there for so long," Fannie said.

"What could we do?" Bill snapped. "We had to hold on to the men till after Pendleton."

She knew he was doing his best to reduce expenses while keeping their riders together. Now he worried about losing them to the army because of the outbreak of hostilities in Europe. Germany had declared war on Russia and France, and when German troops marched into Belgium in August, England retaliated by declaring war on Germany.

Fannie tried to work at crocheting a lacy edge on a pillowcase. "President Wilson says the United States will stay neutral."

"Maybe so, but some of the boys are talking about joining up." Bill sighed and stretched his long legs into the aisle. "I'm getting stove up just sitting here. Come on, let's see what the others are up to." The parlor car reverberated with noisy bronc busters, bulldoggers, ropers, and wranglers telling stories, singing songs, playing cards, and drinking. Bill moved easily among them, joking and teasing. Ordering two beers at the bar, he motioned Fannie toward a group at one of the tables, and the revelry continued throughout the evening. Toward midnight, Fannie left the parlor car and tried to get comfortable in her seat for a few hours of sleep. They would arrive in Pendleton about noon and immediately drive the stock to the fairgrounds for the 2:30 P.M. opening.

When the train pulled into the station, the troupe emerged washed and groomed, wearing fresh shirts and colorful bandanas, seemingly alert and ready to get on with the show. While the wranglers took care of the stock at the fairgrounds, Fannie and Bill signed their group on for all events. Bill again insisted on entering the bronc riding, and Fannie pinned number 117 onto the back of his blue-satin shirt. She wore a pink-satin shirt and a new maroon riding skirt and vest Rachel had made for her, along with her championship belt and a new white Stetson. As Bill fastened number 118 to her back, she saw two old friends approaching.

"Bertha and Del Blancett!" she called, suddenly feeling lighthearted. Bertha was the one woman whose bronc riding she most respected.

"Fannie, if you ain't a sight for sore eyes. I hoped you'd be here."

"You two haven't met my husband, Bill Steele."

The Blancetts shook hands with Bill, Bertha showing her chipped-tooth grin. "We heard you was married, Fannie. Dang if it don't look like you got the pick of the litter."

"*I'm* the one who got the pick," Bill said.

"You can say that for sure." Bertha's good humor was contagious. "Lucy Mulhall is here again, too," she said. "And so many others. Hey, Peggy. Hank." She called to two riders moving toward the check-in. Sandy-haired Hank Warren stood nearly 6-feet tall, towering over his wife, whose short, round figure and common features were softened by a halo of curly brown hair.

"The Warrens are both bronc riders, too. Peggy and Hank, meet Fannie Sperry and her hubby, Bill."

"Fannie *Steele*," Fannie corrected. "I'm a married lady now."

"This is quite a reunion," Bertha said.

"Yeah, even William S. Hart is here." Del draped an arm around his wife's shoulders. "He's riding broncs with Yakima Canutt and that tall, blond ladies' man, Art Accord. Someone said they've all signed up for the movies."

"So has Vera McGinnis." A look of disapproval clouded Peggy's blue eyes. "She's pretty, but some say she's the kind who gets into hair-pulling brawls."

Bertha patted her own stringy hair, tied back with a leather thong. "I better primp up, there may be a scout here today." She broke up at the idea and they all laughed with her.

Fannie lost first-place honors to Bertha in the ladies' bucking-horse event, in which Peggy Warren took a spill that broke her wrist. In the cowgirls' relay race, Fannie again took second money, coming in behind Ruth Glasgow. Bill failed to place in the men's bucking contest.

Perhaps as a consolation prize for their having missed the top money, Bill bought Fannie a black gelding, as pretty a high-stepper as she had ever seen. Delighted, she stroked the animal's nose while scrutinizing the well-shaped head and withers. "What's his name?"

Bill chuckled. "They call him Bonehead."

Fannie grinned at the misnomer. "He looks like a Thoroughbred. Hello there, Bonehead." She climbed into the saddle and patted the gleaming mane.

"You can change his name if you want," Bill said.

The Powder River troupe moved on to The Dalles, Oregon, for an end-of-season three-day roundup. Peggy and Hank went with them, although the cast on Peggy's broken wrist prevented her from riding bucking horses.

"It's good having you along," Fannie said as she and Peggy shared a quiet moment in camp. Comfortable in each other's company, they had become the best of friends.

"Nothing like having another woman to talk to, is there?" Peggy's clear eyes and rosy cheeks attested to her energy and good health. "I would have died of boredom nursing this wrist if we hadn't hooked up with you."

"I guess you know Hank and Bill have worked it out so you'll be traveling with us next summer."

"I'll sure be looking forward to it."

"Me, too," Fannie said sincerely.

While the train chugged back over the Divide toward Helena, Fannie once again pored over her account books. She figured all their earnings and expenses for the months of May through October. "We've cleared more than nine hundred dollars," she announced to Bill, "not counting horse trades." Having recorded the names of horses sold or traded and for how much, she knew that though they often merely broke even on the trades, their stock was being continually upgraded.

Bill dabbed at the pencil smudge on her cheek with his thumb. "We'll do even better next year. There's going to be a big stampede in Banff that will last all summer. The man who helped Guy Weadick produce the Calgary Stampede, H. C. McMullen, is getting up this one. Calls it the Rocky Mountain Park Stampede."

"You mean we could stay in one place all season?"

"That'd be the deal. I'm writing to McMullen and offering to supply horses and suggesting you for the featured bronc rider and shooting act."

McMullen responded enthusiastically, confirming in a letter dated April 11, 1915, that he wanted the Powder River Show, headlining Fannie, for the whole summer season. With the right publicity, he said, the opening May 24, birthday of Queen Victoria and a national Canadian holiday, should generate huge crowds. And members of the British royal family would be the guests of honor.

Frost still clung to the Beartooth as the Steeles left for Banff a week before the May 24 opening. At McMullen's suggestion, Bill had the horses inspected by the American Inspector in Helena so there was no delay in crossing the Canadian border.

Since Fannie was to head the Banff parade directly behind the drum major and marching band, she decided to show off Bonehead. She hadn't gotten around to changing his name, even though on the ranch the horse had proved to be intelligent and responsive. Sleek and shining ebony black, Bonehead looked his best that cold, misty morning as Fannie, wearing a warm mackinaw and rain slicker over her parade outfit, guided him into position behind the band.

With the paraders all in place, the drum major raised his baton and the band struck up. At the first blare of trumpets, Bonehead charged like a mad bull through the band formation, scattering instruments right and left. Fannie tried to hold him back, but the terrified horse stampeded along the main street, knocking over souvenir stands and becoming more panicked with each maneuver. Fannie stuck with him, but before she could get him stopped, the handsome horse had put nearly a mile between him and the parade. Bonehead did not take part in the festivities that day. Instead, hurriedly recruited Silvertail pranced admirably in the place of honor.

But the stands were barely half filled. Skies remained leaden, and the temperature dipped below freezing, changing a fine mist to snow flurries. Attendance the next day was even worse, but McMullen maintained an optimistic outlook. "This little cold snap will clear," he told the riders. "By the weekend, attendance should pick up." But the weather did not clear. Snow remained on the ground, and continuing sleet slowed gate receipts almost to nothing. At the end of the first week, McMullen could not pay the performers and stockmen.

"I don't see how we can hang on here very long," Bill told Fannie. "Most of the men are already talking about looking for something else."

"But we can't just walk out on McMullen," Fannie argued. "We have a three-month contract."

That night McMullen called a meeting and a vote was taken to close the show at the end of the second week if the inclement spring weather didn't moderate. No such break occurred. The show closed, leaving the Powder River Wild West Show without plans for the summer.

Bill sprang into action. He hired some of the dismissed performers on the spot, contracting them to be in Marysville, Montana, on the Fourth of July. The show, opening there to a large, encouraging crowd, then moved south to Silver, Boulder, Basin, and Whitehall. They performed at Dad Elliott's ranch near Deer Lodge on July 29, then traveled back north through Avon to the communities of Augusta and Gilman.

Day after day, Fannie trailed stock, grateful for Peggy Warren's good company and cheerful humor. In the small towns of Valier, Conrad, Chester, Bingham, Havre, Big Sandy, Fort Benton, and Geraldine, local bronc riders and steer ropers signed up to compete for the modest prize money.

By mid-September, Fannie had wearied of the endless moving, the hard work, and trying to make ends meet with the larger troupe. After expenses, it was barely a living. Working over her books by lantern light in the back of the wagon, she felt exhausted and discouraged.

"Bill . . ." she began. "Peggy and Hank are talking about pulling out. They want to get a ranch. Don't you think it's time we put something into a place of our own, too?" She closed her books. "I'm happy about the way things have gone, but it's time to put down roots."

"How can we prove up on a homestead when we're gone all summer?"

"We could get someone to look after it while we travel."

"I thought you wanted to help your ma over the winter. She likes having you around her place."

"I'm not so sure about that after we dumped the whole troupe on her last fall." She shook her head, remembering the miserable month at the ranch. "Anyway, Walter will have the folks' place someday. Then where will we be? We need our own home, Bill."

Bill considered Fannie's words. "It would be good to have somewhere to winter the stock. And the riders. When we get back to the Beartooth, let's look around."

Fannie grinned. "I already know of a nice quarter section." She put the account books in the trunk and sat down beside him, dangling her feet over the tailgate. "It's down on Towhead Creek just a mile from the homeplace. We could still use Ma's corrals for the stock till we get some built, and it's close enough to round up more wild horses from the mountains." Bill's interest banished her fatigue. She hugged his arm and leaned her head against his shoulder. "I can't wait for you to see it."

Shortly after arriving back at the Beartooth, she took him to inspect the property, 160 rocky acres sloping up from Towhead Creek across a browned-out stand of bunchgrass to a few small clusters of scrub pine.

"It's a good location, Fannie," Bill said after he had walked over the property. "But to prove up on a homestead, we'd have to live on the place. We couldn't afford to build a cabin till after next season."

"I know. But we can get a tent and live in that." She scanned the acreage for a good spot. "Right there next to the creek."

"All winter?"

"You bet. We've been camping out everywhere else. What's so different about camping on our own land?"

"Well, for one thing, it might get a little chilly this winter." Then, seeing that Fannie was determined, "But if you can take it, I reckon I can."

"Just think," Fannie mused. "Our own place. We can build it up into a fine horse ranch. We'll keep a few cows for milk. Maybe sell a little butter. You can trade horses. I'll ride exhibition in the summer . . . but only at special events. Oh, Bill, it's perfect."

She ran toward a little rise above the creek. "Here's where we can put the cabin. And over there, the barn and corrals."

"I like it," Bill said. "Let's go into Helena to file on it before somebody beats us to the draw."

The Steeles moved onto their homestead on October 26, 1915. For her new domesticity, Fannie purchased a small iron cookstove, which would serve to warm the 8-by-10-foot tent as well as to prepare their meals. The stove left barely room for their trunk, a bed, a packing-crate cupboard, a table, and two chairs. Supplies that wouldn't fit under the bed or in the trunk were stored outside in the wagon.

She also bought two good milk cows from Rachel, and Walter helped them build a lean-to for the stock and fence a small corral. Most of their horses would be wintered at the homeplace, where hay was readily available. They hauled just enough to the homestead to feed Napoleon and Silvertail, piling it around the tent and the lean-to for extra warmth for them and the horses.

The first snow caught them still cutting wood among the scrub pine. Working in the freezing cold, they gathered and sized deadfall, using Walter's wood sled to haul it. As they piled it near the tent, Rachel drove up with the mules and spring wagon on her first visit to the bleak little camp.

"I still say this is the silliest thing I ever heard of." She climbed down from the wagon, which held a small coop containing four fat hens for Fannie's egg supply. "I thought it was crazy in the beginning, and now I'm sure of it." She kicked snow from her boots before stepping into the tent. "Why don't you come home where you belong?"

"Now, Ma. We went through all that. Bill and I like it here. It's our own place. You can understand that."

"But look at you." Fannie wore several layers of nondescript clothing, including Bill's heavy rubber overshoes and an old cowhide coat that had belonged to her father. "How can you fix a decent meal in here?" Rachel edged through the tent between the makeshift packing-crate cupboard and the table, piled high with Bill's newspapers, pamphlets, and writing materials.

Fannie was quick to explain the clutter. "Bill's getting out letters for our tour next summer."

"If you live that long."

"Now, Ma, you sit down here, and I'll make us some coffee." While she added a stick of wood to the coals in the stove, measured coffee into the tin pot, and dipped water from a bucket of melting snow, her mother sat down at the table and picked up one of the pamphlets.

"The Passing of the West? What's this all about?"

Fannie was pleased by her mother's interest. "We're going to be in one of the best Wild West shows ever. A whole trainload of top performers—including Bill and me—will tour for two weeks in July. Mr. C. L. Harris, a Billings businessman, is organizing it. And he's paying us five hundred dollars, guaranteed, all expenses paid."

"That's good money. But how are you going to prove up on this place if you're traipsing all over the country?"

Bill came into the tent, his face beet-red from the cold. "That blasted creek. Freezes over as fast as I can chop a hole in the ice."

"The cows are still giving milk," Fannie said brightly. "We've already sold twenty pounds of butter in Wolf Creek." She pointed with pride to the new cream separator in the corner next to the stove.

"You see we're not entirely primitive around here," Bill said. While Fannie poured coffee for the three of them, he sat down on the bed, smoothing the rumpled quilts to conceal the bare ticking. "Fannie's making some pillowcases."

"I don't mean to criticize," Rachel said. "I just hate to see you living the way your pa and me had to when we first homesteaded—only we at least had a cabin."

They laughed. "See," Fannie said, "roughing it didn't hurt you."

"No, I guess it didn't." The older woman chuckled as she placed her coffee cup on the table. "Well, me and Walter will be looking for you for Thanksgiving. If you get froze out before then, come on home. Your room's waitin' for you." She wrapped herself, put on her mittens, and went out into the sharp wind to help Bill and Fannie unload the chicken coop and feed she'd brought. "Those hens are good layers," she called as she climbed on to the driver's seat and drove off toward the Beartooth.

That night a coyote howled along the creek, so close to the tent that Fannie startled awake. She heard Napoleon and Silvertail shuffling in the lean-to, where the chicken coop had been snugged next to the hay. "I suppose those critters are after the hens." She slipped from under the heavy quilts and pulled on her boots over the woolen socks she slept in. Donning the cowhide coat over her woolen union suit, she took the Winchester from under the bed and peered from the tent flap. A low howl sounded from the slope above the lean-to. Stepping outside, she raised the rifle to her shoulder and fired in the direction of the sound. A soft whuffle from Napoleon. Then all was still.

January temperatures dropped to thirty below zero. Fannie and Bill could do little more than sit beside the cookstove, with Fannie sewing while Bill continued his correspondence.

"I've written to every two-bit promoter in the West," he complained. "Half of them don't bother to answer."

"But the weather's been too bad for you to get to the post office," Fannie said. "You probably have letters waiting."

"Waiting. God Almighty, I'm tired of waiting in this miserable place." He kicked at a chair, tipping it against the stove and bumping the handle of a hot skillet in which potatoes were frying for their supper.

"Watch out! That's the last of the potatoes."

"And this is the last of my patience," he shouted.

"*Your* patience? You don't even try to make the best of things."

"It was your idea to hole up on this stinking homestead. It's not worth a hill of beans . . . with or without buildings."

A long high-pitched howl sounded near the lean-to. Anger rising, Fannie threw on the cowhide coat, grabbed the rifle, and ran out into the January dusk. As the coyote scooted off up the snowy slope, Fannie dashed to the lean-to, where Napoleon stood hunched against the wind. In one leap she gained his back, urging him, without bridle or saddle, into a full gallop after the coyote.

"Hie!" A cry escaped her throat as she saw the coyote crouching next to a scrub pine, and she drove Napoleon directly toward it. The snarling canine yelped in pain as the horse, seemingly aware of Fannie's intent, ran over him, striking him with one hoof. Fannie jumped down and took aim as the injured coyote prepared to spring at her. The gun failed to fire. She quickly shifted her grip to the barrel and, swinging the rifle as if it were a club, smashed a powerful blow against the snarling coyote's skull. It fell dead.

Fannie later listed the coyote pelt in her ledger, along with the sale of two horses, Ginger, who brought $40, and Bonehead, $60. Under expenditures, she itemized the cream separator, $32.50, and a new hat for Bill, $7.50.

When the weather moderated with an early February chinook, Bill returned from the post office waving a packet of letters. "We got the Passing of the West contract." His eyes showed the old excitement. "We start in Butte on July first." He handed the contract to Fannie, and she read the fine print.

It is understood and agreed that said W. S. and Fannie Sperry Steele are known as professional hands in the Wild West game, and they recognize and appreciate the danger and hazards of their occupation and the danger of the particular work, which they have agreed to do as herein outlined. It is understood and agreed that they hereby assume all risk of injury, and that C. L. Harris, Management, will not be responsible for any injury received by the said Steeles during the performance of their work and acts as herein outlined.

They were to furnish ten bucking horses, two workhorses, and six saddle horses. Fannie would ride bucking horses and perform her shooting act. Bill was to *ride bucking horses, steers and bulls, rope wild steers, and do such other work as said W. S. Steele may be accustomed to doing.*

The creek began to melt, relieving them of the daily chore of chopping a hole in the ice so the stock could drink. The slope greened, but with disappointingly little grass. One of the cows freshened, and Fannie once again delighted in the newness of a Montana spring. She rode up into the mountains with Bill and Walter, and after a long search, they rounded up three wild horses.

Before Fannie and Bill left for Butte and the Passing of the West Show on June 23, Walter came over to take the milk cows and the new calf to the Sperry ranch.

"Have you met the new teacher yet?" Fannie teased. A one-room schoolhouse had been moved down below the Beartooth and a teacher hired to accommodate the growing number of children in the area. Carrie's six older ones (she had borne her eighth, Dorothy, in December) were school age, as were two of Bertha's and the children of a few scattered neighbors.

Walter grinned as he rode off after the ambling stock. "No, but I'm aiming to."

"I don't know what we'd do without him," Fannie commented. "But I hate to impose on him the way we do."

"Look, how can we be in two places at once?"

"I don't want to quit riding, but I do hope we can get the cabin started before another winter sets in."

"You want too much." Bill turned to face her. "Either you're going to be a champion rider or you can be a two-bit rancher. Make up your mind."

The Passing of the West Show opened in Butte on July 1, 1916, a day providing just enough wind to keep the streamers and flags waving above the thousands of spectators streaming into Columbia Gardens. The afternoon lineup touted renowned Wild West performers Lucille Mulhall, Vera McGinnis and her cowboy-husband Earl Simpson, Tex McLeod, Sammy Garrett, Jesse Coates, Wild Bill Revelle, and others in daring, hair-raising stunts. Circus acts sparked the evening show, with Charles Gaylor and his giant frog act; Capt. George Webb's sensational 85-foot dive into a net; and Shaft and Shaft, a comedy-knockabout act. Also featured were the biplane flights that had boosted aviators Emil Laird and Frank Champion to national stardom.

Harris presented scenes of the early frontier by erecting a model Old-West town he called Cowitchie, with a replica of Calamity Jane's dance hall centering the action in the mock town. Fannie's sharpshooting act, performed on the make-believe streets, prompted one newspaper to compare her with Annie Oakley, who, the paper stated, was at present in Portsmouth, New Hampshire, giving lessons in the art of shooting to some eastern society folks.

After the opening in Butte, 140 performers, including a thirty-two-piece band, boarded the train chartered for the Passing of the West tour. The entourage included carload after carload of animals and equipment. For the next two weeks, Fannie and Bill lived onboard, alternating between it and the big white circus tents set up in each town where they performed.

In Billings, on July 16, the final day of the tour, an open competition was held in which Fannie won the ladies' slick-bucking contest, and Peggy Warren took the hobbled event. Bill confined his participation to clowning and hazing.

At the close of the show, Fannie sat mending tack with Peggy when Bill came running across the field, waving a letter. "I got news!" he called. "We're headed for New York City!"

"New York City?" Peggy's eyes opened wide at the prospect.

"Weadick wants us for a stampede there next month." Bill grabbed Fannie and swung her around. "Honey, we've made the big time. Hank and Peg and most of the troupe are coming, too."

Fannie felt some hesitation at going so far from home. And to the biggest city she could imagine. "Does he want the horses, too?"

"Yup. And that ain't all. From New York, we go to Chicago," he paused to emphasize his words, "to appear with Buffalo Bill Cody."

Buffalo Bill? She would be riding in the same arena with her old idol. An image of Walter, Arthur, Carrie, and Bertha playing Buffalo Bill flashed across her memory.

Peggy jumped up and down. She hugged Fannie and Bill, then Hank, who ran to join them. Hank's words came in excited spurts. "Weadick's booked the Sheepshead Bay Speedway on Long Island. And purses will total fifty thousand dollars paid in American gold." Hank smacked his lips on the letter in a mock kiss while Fannie and Peggy looked at each other in delighted amazement.

"And listen to this," Bill interjected. "First money in the men's bucking is fifteen hundred; with second, a thousand; and third, seven hundred fifty. Now that's worth getting back in the saddle for."

"How about the women?" Fannie asked.

"First for women is a thousand; second, seven hundred fifty; and third, five hundred."

"I guess those broncs don't buck as hard for us girls," Peggy pouted.

"No, they never have," Fannie said dryly.

"Helloooo, Broadway!" Hank tossed his hat into the air. "Yahoo!"

Bill's hat, too, went flying high. "New York City, here we come."

Big Cities and Buffalo Bill  20

We do as we advertise. Guy Weadick's slogan for the 1916 Stampede at New York's Sheepshead Bay Speedway promised a fair deal for participants. Bill reread the flyer as they clicked off the final rail miles across Pennsylvania.

The Original Stampede crowns its winners with the official title of World's Champion. He glanced at Fannie, who, weary from the long hours on the train, sat staring out the window at mountains and pine forests that made her think of the Beartooth. *And our Stampede enjoys the reputation of paying the largest cash purses ever offered at a celebration of this nature.*

Wild Bill Revelle, seated across the aisle, looked up from his newspaper. "New York City is having an outbreak of infantile paralysis. Says here theaters are either closed or scarce on customers. That don't sound too good for attendance at the stampede."

"We'll be out on Long Island performing in an open arena," Bill reassured.

"But it says the city may have a transit strike, too." Wild Bill perused another item. "There won't be any public transportation running."

"What?" Bill took the paper and scanned the stories. "Well, if that don't beat all. How'll folks get out to the Speedway? That stadium holds twenty thousand."

"New Yorkers have automobiles," Hank offered.

Fannie, looking over Bill's shoulder at the newspaper, expressed concern. "It says hundreds of kids are dying. They get a headache and a stiff neck, then paralysis sets in, and . . . if they live . . . they're left crippled." She turned to Peggy. "No wonder people are staying away from public places."

"This war scare ain't helpin' either," Wild Bill said. "I'd sure like to go over there and help beat those heinies. They got no business runnin' over everybody like they're doin'. If Wilson declares war, I'll sure be one of the first to sign up."

"Don't be too hasty," Bill cautioned. "People get hurt in war, you know."

"That's why I got to be in there helpin' put a stop to it." Wild Bill's grim expression told the others he meant what he said.

Guy Weadick himself welcomed them to the Speedway on August 4 during a continuing New York heat wave.

"We may have a tough time of it here," the tall, self-assured promoter told those assembled near the stables after having settled into quarters provided for the performers. "Harry Harkness, president of the Speedway Company, says business is slow due to the threatened transportation strike and the infantile paralysis scare. We're going to have to give an opening performance tomorrow that will have people crawling to get here if they have to."

"We will, Guy. Don't you worry."

"And be careful if you go out on the streets," Weadick cautioned. "Howard Lemands got brushed by a car this morning and won't be able to do much bulldogging. I can't afford to lose any more of you."

Opening day, August 5, dawned hot and muggy, and by two o'clock the heat and humidity were oppressive. In the huge, nearly full grandstand, reputed to be the largest in America if not the whole world, perspiring spectators fluttering paper fans awaited the grand entry. Even the bleacher seats began to fill, despite newspaper headlines predicting that the limited subway, elevated, and surface lines still operating would be stalled before evening.

New Yorkers sat astonished through the opening fancy roping by Lucy Mulhall, Tex and Millie McLeod, Florence LaDue, Sam Garrett, and Floyd and Frances Irwin. The daring riders delighted the novice audience, but the cowboys' bucking event was the first to bring them to their feet. Jesse Coates, Rufus Rollen, Art Accord, Jack Thompson, Lee Caldwell, and Clay McGonagill demonstrated spellbinding horsemanship. Even Fannie had never seen better riding. Tillie Baldwin and Dolly Mullins maintained the pace with their fancy trick riding.

The women's bucking-horse event stunned the spectators, then drew enthusiastic cheers for Fannie, Prairie Rose Henderson, Tillie Baldwin, Peggy Warren, Ollie Osborn, Dot Vernon, Louise Thompson, Dorothy Morrell, and Prairie Lillie Allen.

Fannie also raced relay against Joella and Pauline Irwin and Helen Maish to the satisfaction of the now hooting and hollering audience, many of whom had come on foot from some distance to attend the city's first stampede. Adding to the thrills was the spectacle of a one-armed cowhand who bulldogged right along with his better-equipped competition. Another cowboy, fresh from a western hospital, rode with hunks of plaster bracing a leg that was still knitting. Dorothy Morrell, also recovering after months of suffering from injuries received the previous season, rode gamely and well.

The evening newspaper headlines touted the event.

Guy Weadick's Stampede Goes Over Mightily in the Big City.
Bored and Jaded New York Stirred by New Thrills.
Vast Throng First Stares Tolerantly, Then Gasps, Then Abandons Itself to Tumultuous and Wild Acclaim.

The *New York Times* reported that 15,000 had viewed the opening show.

A new amusement has been born. If it hadn't been for the threatened car strike, 100,000 people would have attended. On the whole, if enthusiasm is any indication, signs point to the Stampede as an annual and profitable event. Guy Weadick has mounted another rung in the ladder of fame, and New York has found something new to rave about.

New Yorkers may have thought they knew something about cowboys, but after watching the skills and tricks presented by the cowboys and cowgirls in the arena, life in the West seems a little more dangerous than at first thought.

The *Herald* commented, *When a bunch of New Yorkers sit to see a show that lasts till after 7 o'clock, it's good. And say, these old western boys sure had 'em standing up and yelling like drunken Injuns.*

Fannie smiled at the paper's attempt at western talk, then read aloud.

Dot Vernon made one of the most spectacular rides of the afternoon, her mount resorting to all tricks peculiar to outlaw horses, then throwing her to the ground. Prairie Lillie Allen was thrown off her horse, right over his head, then the horse rolled on top of her. Luckily, neither woman was badly injured, but the shock of the accidents caused several women in the audience to faint.

"Ain't that just the way," Bill said. "They report an accident but don't say a thing about the outstanding riding by those who weren't thrown."

"Listen to what they say about Weadick," Fannie continued.

Weadick was cool, collected, efficient, capable, anticipative, resourceful, and confident. He mobilized, marshalled, and generaled his forces and literally forced and compelled the immense success freely conceded to New York City's first stampede. There were waits and hitches aplenty, but Weadick always got things going before impatience became marked. There were tame numbers that did not hit the New York fancy, but Weadick was quick to sense it and speeded them up and got them by before they became tedious. He did ten men's work—did it without turning a hair, did it easily, did it smoothly.

"Holy smokes!" Bill reviewed the glowing tribute. "It's clear we're in good hands. I may even get some ideas for our show."

"If fifteen thousand show up every day, he'll more than make the prize money," Fannie said. "Guess we worried for nothing."

But the next day, another scorcher with the temperature hovering in the nineties, the crowd dwindled as fewer New Yorkers managed to get to the Speedway. Afternoon events began with an accident in the men's bucking contest. Tom Eckerd of Miles City was kicked in the stomach, and an ambulance was brought onto the field to take him to a hospital.

The incident made Fannie edgy. Bill was up next. He never should have signed on, she thought. He's too out of shape to ride broncs, no matter how much prize money is offered.

Bill drew a sinewy buckskin, Moonshine. Wiping sweat from his face with his bandana, he eased, stiff and scowling, onto the horse. The buckskin hurtled from the gate, and with the first high bucking twist Bill sailed through the air, landing in a heap on the ground. A lightning-quick hoof hit Bill's shoulder.

Fannie caught her breath and started to run across the field toward him.

"What next?" Weadick said, running with her and Wild Bill Revelle toward the injured rider. "We can't lose any more."

"Don't worry," Wild Bill called out. "Fannie will ride these broncs if Bill Steele and every other bronc stomper is dead and buried."

"How can you joke when he's hurt?" Fannie flashed the question at her friend. But she knew he was right. She had climbed onto killer outlaws many times after a friend had been injured. But now it was Bill lying there in the dirt. If she were up next . . . ? Yes, she would ride no matter what.

But she wasn't put to the test. Bill stirred. And before she could reach his side, he had struggled to his feet.

"It's my shoulder." He grimaced in pain, sweat beading on his forehead. Revelle and Weadick helped him to a spot behind the chutes to await the doctor.

"A dislocated shoulder," the doctor announced. "He'll have to be taped up for a few days."

Bill's face was ashen. "Looks like you'll have to bring home the bacon, honey."

Feeling shaky after his shoulder was set and taped, Bill went to their quarters. He didn't see Fannie's extraordinary ride on Midnight, a cantankerous bronc with a national reputation, nor her first-place win in the relay.

The next day was Teddy Roosevelt Day at the stampede, honoring the former president. Roosevelt arrived with his sons, Theodore Jr. and Kermit, along with Police Commissioner Arthur Woods and Mrs. Woods. "This is the greatest exhibition I've ever seen in New York," the stocky Roosevelt announced as he was introduced to the crowd. "It's the real thing. And I've spent enough time on the great western frontier to know."

At the close of the performance, Roosevelt came to the arena to congratulate the riders and pose for photographs with them. "It's good to see there are still some real Americans left," he said. "You're the real stuff of the West. Man or woman, our country is built on the kind of courage and fortitude that all of you have shown here today." Then, lifting his straw skimmer, he added, "I salute you."

But even Teddy Roosevelt's visit to the Speedway did not perk up gate receipts. By midweek the stands were largely bare. Following the afternoon performance, a group of riders gathered outside their quarters hoping to catch a cooling breeze in the stifling heat. Weadick had brought in a tubful of iced beer.

"So much for *We do as we advertise*." Bill fished with his good arm for a beer in the tub of melting ice.

"Weadick can't even meet expenses," Rufus Rollen said. "Everyone's broke. Some of the boys are talkin' about hittin' the rods to get back home."

"Well, I ain't ridin' no freight train." Prairie Rose, decked out in a shirt of red sequin-trimmed silk with black brocade bloomers brushing the tops of her spangled boots, held a cool beer bottle to her forehead.

Millie McLeod joined in. "Me neither. I just can't believe this. First, we suffer through all this heat, now they can't pay us. I counted on having a good time this week."

"Ain't you havin' a good time, Millie?" Tex put his arm around his wife. Fannie knew that Tex had won a nice purse with the world's roping championship in Walla Walla two years before, and that Millie had gotten used to his bringing home sizable wins.

"I've had better times swilling hogs," Millie pouted.

The stampede closed without the customary finals, and Weadick announced he would be able to make good on only 25 percent of the daily prize money. The Steeles were sympathetic to his dilemma even though it took money out of their own pockets. Fannie's share of the winnings would barely pay their way to Chicago.

Bill tried to cheer her. "The Irwins want us to go on with them from Chicago. We'll perform in Milwaukee and Kansas City, so it won't be too bad a season after all . . . except for this." He indicated his injured shoulder.

The Chicago Shan-Kive and Roundup represented the combined effort of Buffalo Bill's Wild West and the Miller Brothers 101 Real Wild West extravaganzas. Held in the Cubs ballpark, the event attracted nearly every top rider in the country.

"Cody don't call it a show," Bill cautioned. "He feels that *show* means something theatrical and contrived and takes away from the genuine skills.

He claims he's presenting a picture of actual frontier life, not just producing a show."

"But calling it a Shan-Kive . . . ?" Fannie disliked the name. "No one knows what that means."

"Shan-Kive is an Indian word meaning 'a good time.' I think it's a fine title," Bill said. "All the roundups and stampedes in the country are coming together here. Pendleton, Cheyenne, Calgary, Winnipeg, even Los Angeles. There's keen competition. Should be a darn good time."

"Lucy says the Shan-Kive is the turning point . . . when exhibition riding truly becomes a sport. In California, they're calling it rodeo."

Buffalo Bill Cody, seated in a phaeton, drove a team of white horses to head the grand entry. Still a dashing figure in a fringed buckskin coat with brass buttons, buckskin riding pants buttoned from calf to knee, and tall military boots with spurs, he waved to the crowd. His familiar white goatee, mustache, and long hair flowing beneath a high-crowned Stetson were as Fannie had always pictured. But his cheeks were sunken, his gestures feeble.

"He looks old and sick," Fannie whispered to Lucy as the phaeton passed them. She hadn't imagined Col. William F. Cody as an aging invalid.

"He's nearly seventy." Lucy gazed after the Wild West show pioneer. "Had to stage these big spectaculars and hire extra circus acts to flesh out his show, to hide the fact that he's getting tired."

"I read that he lost his whole stable of three hundred horses to glanders disease," Fannie added.

"Yes," Lucy said. "Quite a jolt to a man who loves horses like he does. And he's lost money in mining and other ventures, so he's obliged to make all these 'farewell tours' to pay his debts."

Fannie felt sorry for her longtime hero. "He's still a handsome figure of a man, though," she said, as if to keep an old dream alive.

One of the acts in Cody's show, two highly trained pintos billed as "high-school horses," fascinated Fannie. The brown-and-white pair, Sultan and Daisy, coached by their owner, Homer Wilson, appeared to answer questions by tapping a front hoof. Returning from a session of watching Wilson work the equine stars, Fannie commented to Bill, "A smart horse like Sultan or Daisy would be a big attraction in our show. I'm going to

Fannie (left, rear) and other riders pause for a photo with Buffalo Bill Cody at the Chicago Shan-Kive Wild West Show, 1916.

learn how he does it." And with Bill's go-ahead, she spent hours working with the high-school horses and their trainer.

She also picked up prize money, winning the daily bucking-horse event every day for four days. One day she rode eight broncs because other girls were ailing.

A Chicago newspaper editorialized:

American cowboys and cowgirls are the greatest roughriders in the world. Riding "outlaw" ponies is a commonplace experience with them. No horse is too wild for them to attempt to ride. As ropers, also, they are unexcelled. Their work on the ranch often makes it essential for them to rope the wildest steers under circumstances that would mean injury or death in case of failure. Naturally, among them there develops a spirit of rivalry which leads to the most strenuous and exciting contests of skill. The roundup fosters the legitimate rivalry and brings out all that is best and most daring in the people of ranchland. Prizes here are so generous that the cleverest of the entire West have come to compete. Only one spirit prevails: Let the best man—or woman—win!

That evening Bill took Fannie to the Howard Hotel in downtown Chicago for supper. Fannie, dressed in her best western attire, became the center of attention as the headwaiter ushered them to a table near the back of the fashionable dining room.

"Folks are looking at you, Fannie," Bill whispered as they seated themselves. "They recognize you from the Shan-Kive. You're famous."

Fannie ignored the stares of some of the diners, but, as they ordered beer and beefsteak, a burly reporter approached their table. "Excuse me, ma'am. You must be with the Wild West show."

"That's right."

"You're . . . ?"

"Fannie Sperry Steele," Bill said, gesturing to the extra chair. The reporter seated himself and, while they continued to eat, directed questions to Fannie.

"Mrs. Steele, what do you think of today's styles?"

"Styles?" Fannie was taken off guard. She had never thought much about styles. "They're awful," she said. "I don't like them a bit."

The reporter tried a different tack. "When did you first begin to ride?"

"Oh, I don't remember. I know I was riding bucking horses at roundups when I was fourteen."

"And who is your toughest competition?"

"I don't have much real competition among the women because I ride slick."

"She's the best woman rider in the world," Bill interrupted. "Beats 'em all."

Fannie grinned modestly. "Well, I don't know. Bertha Blancett's hard to beat. And I'd hate to have to compete against my ma. She's one of the finest riders I ever saw. And that's strange, considering she isn't a product of the West. But in her day, I think she could have won any contest."

After a few more questions, the reporter excused himself, and Fannie finished her cooling steak. "Some of those people are obnoxious," she whispered.

"Don't be too hard on them. They're part of our bread and butter." Bill wiped his mouth with the linen napkin.

Next morning, Bill rose early, as usual, and went out to buy a paper.

"Fannie, that interview guy wrote about you," he announced as he returned and raised the shades to another bright, hot day. Fannie pulled the sheet over her head to blot out the realization that she must get up and ease her aching body into riding clothes for the day's bucking and relay events.

"Listen to this." Bill read rapidly:

"Present styles in women's clothes? They're awful," said Fannie Sperry Steele, world's champion woman rider and bronco buster, as she sat with her husband in the dining room of the Howard Hotel last night.

> *Mrs. Steele's own clothing spoke fully as emphatically of her disregard for convention and her opposition to the uncomfortable dress of the "East," as she considers this part of the country. She wore a riding skirt of deep maroon that showed hard wear in the saddle. The sleeves of her orange shirt—it was not a shirtwaist—were held up by black elastic. Around her waist was a wide leather belt with gold buckle, a trophy won, together with $1000 cash, at Calgary, Canada. On her breast was a medal presented to the "Champion Lady Rider of Montana," while the stick pin in the red necktie had been won in a twenty-four-mile relay race in Minnesota. A wide, high crowned sombrero covered her head, while two long braids of hair hung down her back.*

"He's making fun of me." Fannie sat up in bed. "Let me see that."

Mrs. Steele, who cannot remember far enough back to recall her first horseback ride, but who began to ride bucking horses at the age of fourteen, will meet all women riders during the frontier celebration. She admits no peer, with the possible exception of her sixty-seven-year-old mother.

"Good Lord! He makes me sound like an idiot. That's the last time I talk to one of these eastern reporters."

"Don't worry." Bill seemed amused. "The others will be green with envy that you got your name in the paper."

The Shan-Kive drew crowds filled with enthusiasm for the budding sport of rodeo and the lore of the Old West. But the *Chicago Tribune* was not as complimentary as the *New York Times* had been. On the editorial page, a protest was printed under the heading *Steers and Horses Subjected to Cruelty.*

Every person of intelligence having a spark of humanity should stay away from the "Roundup" now showing on the west side at the Old Cubs Park. The city does not permit prize fights, but they are mush and milk compared to the brutality shown at the Roundup. I refer particularly to the roping of steers. There is absolutely no call for this act but to put dollars in the company's pocket. If these animals were loose and it were necessary to catch them, I would not complain, but they are chased all over the lot and thrown with violence, sometimes going way up in the air, rolling over and over, breaking their horns, and I expect, sometimes their legs.

Bill scoffed. "That shows how little they know about anything." The editorial continued:

Even the audience called out "Cut it out!" I suppose they claim these animals are not injured, but it is cruelty just the same. The main part of the whole show is cruelty. Striking spurs in the sides of horses so they can show how they stick on the saddle. If these horses jumped and tore around of their own volition, it would be a different thing. Then there is bulldogging, consisting mainly of twisting a poor animal's neck until it has to fall down. Mr. Official, responsible for the granting of this permit, I call your attention to the above.

The criticism bothered Fannie. "A few of the boys do get a little rough sometimes," she said thoughtfully. "But it's rare. What city folks don't understand is that these animals are our lives. We love them like family."

"I don't know of any sport that gets full approval from the Ladies Aid Society," Bill scoffed.

"I wouldn't hurt an animal for anything in the world." Fannie had never thought of riding bucking horses as cruelty. "Do you think this editorial will make people think less of us?"

"There's always a rider who's willing to climb on a rough bronc, and there's always a crowd that wants to see it." He tossed the paper aside.

Bill's comment proved prophetic. The performances continued before packed audiences. From Chicago they made a side trip to Milwaukee to appear in a show produced by Homer Wilson. At Wilson's invitation, Fannie took his place in the arena to put Sultan and Daisy, the high-school horses, through their tricks. She made Sultan sit at attention, then asked, "Do you like these folks who come to see you?" Her hand signal, unnoticed by the audience, clued the horse to nod his head up and down.

"That's nice. Are you going to give them a good show?" Another signal and the pinto shook his head from side to side.

"No? Well, how many smart horses are there here today, Sultan?" Sultan stomped his foot once.

"Only one? What about you, Daisy?" She turned to the sleek mare standing nearby. "How many smart horses do you say are here today?" Daisy tapped her foot twice.

The audience loved it. Fannie concluded the act by giving signals for a series of foot stomps in answer to simple arithmetic questions.

"You're doing a good job with Sultan and Daisy," Wilson said as they led the pintos back to the barns.

"I've gotten attached to them." Fannie patted Daisy's jaw, while Sultan tried to nose in closer.

"I'll tell you what." Wilson had an easygoing way about him. "I ain't gettin' any younger, and I been wantin' to sell these two smart critters. But I couldn't let them go to just anyone. With you, I know they'd be in good hands. How'd you like to take them with you? I'll give you a good price on them."

Fannie could hardly believe her ears. Owning these two favorites would be the answer to her fondest dream—and Bill's, too, since they would be a special attraction for their own show. She gave the quiet, awkward man an affectionate hug. "Thanks. I'll talk to Bill."

A travel crisis developed when the railroad agent would not let Fannie ride in the stockcar with her new pintos, and Bill had to convince her that Sultan and Daisy would fare just fine enroute to Kansas City.

They stopped in Omaha, where Fannie was to be featured in the bucking event at the local roundup, but that day, too, proved disappointing. Omaha rules stated that all women must ride with stirrups hobbled. The management would not allow Fannie to ride slick saddle, and she refused to ride hobbled. Despite her advertised appearance, the Lady Bucking-Horse Champion of the World did not ride in Omaha.

But at the Royal Fat Stock Show in Kansas City, she walked off with the top prize in the bucking event for successfully riding the famous bronc Cannonball, who had thrown some of the best male riders in the country.

Fannie continued at the peak of her prowess. Her thirtieth birthday the following March would be a milestone in a life that completely suited her in every detail, she thought. She had been a professional horsewoman for nearly half of that life, riding some of the wildest broncs that ever bucked beneath a saddle. She had earned money, medals, saddles, and other trophies, plus the deep inner satisfaction of having won the respect of her peers.

She could hardly wait to get Daisy and Sultan back home to continue their education.

A Troubling Revelation

21

But Fannie's joy faded when they arrived at the bleak homestead on Towhead Creek. The land lay parched from late-summer drought, and dust sifted in the wind around the sagging tent, which had been blackened with soot from the fallen stovepipe. Not even a magpie turned out to welcome them.

"Not much of a homecoming, is it?" Bill gazed blankly at the dismal scene. Fannie dismounted and set about picking up the pieces of rusted stovepipe.

"Come on, Fannie, let's stay at your ma's. We can't spend another winter here."

"But it's our home." She lifted the tattered tent flap. A wave of intense heat and the musty smell of mildew came from within. A mouse skittered across the dusty cookstove.

Bill stayed on his horse. "This is no home, honey. Just look at it. It's not fit for man nor beast. Sultan and Daisy deserve better than this. Let's take them to your ma's with the rest of the stock. We'll bring the wagon back to pick up this stuff."

Fannie stood for a moment over the fragments of her shattered hopes. Then she walked away from the drooping canvas, swung into her saddle, and turned toward the Beartooth.

In January, during the comfortable winter they spent on the Sperry ranch, they read about the death of Buffalo Bill. He had made only one last public appearance after the Chicago Shan-Kive.

"I'm glad we got to meet the old gentleman," Fannie said, feeling bereaved somehow at the passing of an era.

Walter joked to cheer her up. "Aw, he's probably running a string of horses right now at that great roundup in the sky."

Fannie chuckled. "He better be. If heaven don't have horses, *I'm* not going."

On April 5, President Wilson declared war on Germany. Shortly afterward, the Steeles received a package from Wild Bill Revelle. Inside was a pair of spurs with a note that read, "Keep these for me till I get back."

Fannie was glad her Bill was over the age limit for military service, and that Walter had a deferment—in addition to having inherited his father's asthma, he remained the only one to operate the ranch. Many of their riders, too, were classified 4F due to poorly healed broken bones and other injuries.

So the roundup season proceeded as usual, bigger and better than ever for the Powder River Wild West aggregation, with Fannie and her high-school horses headlining the show. Americans needed relief from the stress of war, and publicity for the Great Northern Montana Stampede, which opened in Havre on July 4, 1917, left no doubt as to the intent of the celebration:

> *The man or woman who indulges in serious thought in Havre within the next four days is disloyal and unpatriotic.*

Nearly 9,000 Montanans watched from within the grounds, and almost as many viewed the contests from the tops of nearby freight cars and other vantage points in the surrounding hills. Again, a moving-picture camera recorded the thrilling events.

Rufus Rollen showed the stuff that kept him in a class by himself. No man could beat him in bronc busting, Fannie thought. She also admired the horsemanship of Jackson Sundown, considered the world's top Indian rider.

At fifty-six years old, Sundown had won the championship at Pendleton the previous year.

Fannie watched the proceedings with confidence and a deep feeling of belonging. The audience seemed to know personally each individual performer, and many exchanges of greetings and good wishes passed from the stands to the arena. But she and Bill also heard some critical comments.

"I can't see why these strong, young cowboys ain't in the army." The shrill voice of a lady of advanced years carried through the bleachers. "What're they doin' here when they could be helpin' Uncle Sam?"

Someone responded, "These busters are so stove up they can't hardly move on land. Most of 'em walk like their 'spenders was caught around their necks."

"Just the same, looks like they could be doin' somethin' for their country."

Fannie saw that Bill, too, was troubled by the remarks. "I'd be happy to serve," he said as they moved out of earshot. "But they won't take a guy my age. You know, Fannie, maybe I should dress up like Uncle Sam when I clown. That would show we're just as patriotic as anybody. Maybe we could sponsor some Liberty Bond sales at the shows."

"That's a wonderful idea." She enjoyed his enthusiasm. "We'll have a long-tailed coat and a tall hat made up in red, white, and blue."

The Powder River Wild West Show moved south across Montana and Wyoming to participate in Cheyenne's Golden Anniversary July 23 through 28, then traveled north again into Canada for the Calgary Stampede August 2 through 5. But their appearances were not limited to the larger events. On the way back they performed in small Montana towns, such as Winnett, Gilman, Shelby, and others. Bill's Uncle Sam costume, including a tuft of cotton glued to his chin, went over well, and at his urging, war-bond sales increased in towns where they performed.

Returning to the Beartooth late in September, they made another visit to the forlorn homestead on Towhead Creek. Now only the lonely lean-to remained on the browned-out land.

"Some horse ranch," Fannie said glumly.

Bill grinned as if harboring a secret he now intended to share. "I heard about a little place down by Helena that we could get cheap."

*Bill wears an Uncle Sam costume for their performances to show his
patriotism during World War I.*

Fannie caught her breath. "Oh, Bill, you have? Where?"

"Over on Jackson Creek. Good grass. It's close to town, and it has a well,
a shed, and a two-room house. What say we go down and take a look at it."

Fannie fell in love with the Jackson Creek property. Situated on a hillside, the small log house and shed nestled in a stand of pine surrounded by
hay and pastureland. A pump outside the kitchen door brought up a ready
supply of spring water.

"The place needs repair," Bill acknowledged, "but it's closer to Helena
and Unionville, where we'll be able to find more customers for our butter

and cream. And there should be good hunting this winter up in those hills." He turned to her. "Well, what do you think?"

Fannie had never felt happier. "I think you're a peach for finding it."

They settled in on Jackson Creek in the late fall of 1917. Purchasing hay for winter feed, they soon had the shed and fences in shape for the stock. Then Fannie went to work on the house, cleaning and polishing. The cookstove and separator shone against the fresh paint on the table, chairs, and a secondhand Hoosier cupboard. In the tiny bedroom, she set up her new sewing machine beside the window and made flannel sheets and pillowcases for the bed. During the lengthening winter evenings, she braided rag rugs and hemmed flour-sack dish towels.

"Now don't you go and get too domestic on me," Bill teased. "This place alone won't support us, you know. You've still got broncs to ride next season."

"Don't you fret. We'll go up to the Beartooth and run down some wild ones as soon as the weather breaks." Fannie felt a comfortable balance now between her professional life and the security of their own place. "And I've got some ideas for new tricks for Daisy and Sultan."

With war news continuing to occupy the nation, Bill spent more and more time in town during that long, cold winter of 1917–1918, while Fannie set up a trapline and skinned out enough pelts to buy him a new overcoat.

When spring warmed into summer, they began their Powder River Wild West junket once more, with Bill in his Uncle Sam costume again promoting the sale of Liberty Bonds at each performance.

The sad news came that Del Blancett had been killed on the western front at Château-Thierry, where the Allies stopped the German advance that had seemed to be unstoppable from March until June. Throughout the summer and fall, they received no word of Wild Bill Revelle. Then, following Allied victories in battles at Argonne and Ypres, an armistice was signed on November 11, 1918. Bill rode into Helena to celebrate, and Fannie picked up her pen to write her weekly letter to widowed Bertha Blancett.

On Fannie's thirty-second birthday, March 27, 1919, she rode up to the Beartooth, leaving Bill to tend the stock at Jackson Creek. She and Walter searched the hills above the ranch for wild horses but came back empty-handed. The wild ones were scarcer than ever, many having been picked off and sold to the army during the war.

Rachel, delighted with the visit, heaped the table with Fannie's favorite foods. "You're so skinny, Fannie." She touched the clear, taut skin of her daughter's cheeks.

"I'm not skinny, Ma. I'm in great shape. You can't be fat and sluggish if you're going to stay aboard those broncs."

"She's just right, Ma." Walter stretched his long legs under the table and leaned back with a toothpick between his lips. "Prettier than ever. But she won't be skinny long if she sticks around here eatin' your cooking."

Rachel gave her son a playful cuff. "It hasn't put any meat on *your* bones." Then, looking directly into her daughter's eyes, she asked, "Fannie, when are you and Bill going to settle down and have a family?"

"Now, Ma, I don't have time for kids. I have to think of my riding. A woman in the family way has no place on a bucking horse."

Rachel sighed. "If you don't watch out, your brother will get ahead of you. He's keeping company with the new schoolteacher, you know."

Walter grinned. "Her name is Fleta Isham."

"She's college educated," Rachel said proudly.

Walter winked. "Rides good, too. Came up the Missouri with her folks when she was fifteen. They homesteaded near Fort Benton, but she had a strong yen for learning and went to teacher's college at Pierre."

"She and Walter have a lot in common," Rachel summed up.

"She sounds wonderful. I can't wait to meet her." Fannie picked up her embroidery, and a feeling of contentment rose in her. Dear, sensitive Walter would have a home of his own and a loving wife after all.

Shortly after Fannie returned home, a Montana blizzard settled over Jackson Creek, and snow piled up around the little log house. Fannie, keeping busy with household tasks, sat near the stove mending their costumes for the coming season. Bill glowered over his correspondence, and she sensed his growing restlessness.

"Are you worried that this place isn't going to work for us either?" she said quietly.

"It's a roof over our heads."

"But we're not making plans. What happened to the fine horse ranch we were going to have?"

"Takes money."

Fannie put down her mending. "Nothing ever seems to work out the way you plan it."

"Look, you're a world's champion. Don't that mean anything to you?"

"But I'm thirty-two years old. I can't go on riding at stampedes forever. Most everyone my age is having babies."

"I suppose you're blaming me for that, too?"

"I didn't say that."

"How can you expect to carry a baby when you're bouncing around on top of a bucking horse?"

"I don't think riding has anything to do with the fact that we haven't had kids."

Bill stood up and faced her, his eyes blazing. "Are you saying it's my fault?"

"No, I didn't mean it that way. I'm not blaming you. But it can be the man's fault."

"Well, you just get that out of your head right now. Maybe it's you. There's nothing wrong with me."

"My sisters haven't had any trouble having kids."

"Look, I *know* I can become a father," Bill shouted.

She was startled by his vehemence. "How can you know that?"

"Because . . . I have a son." His words hung in the air.

"You . . . you have a son?"

"I've never seen him. But . . . well . . . my first wife . . . she was in the family way when I left her."

Fannie caught her breath. "You left her in . . . in . . . ?"

"I didn't plan it that way. We didn't get along, and after I'd gone to New Mexico, I heard from a cowhand that she'd had a baby."

Tears came to Fannie's eyes. "Why didn't you tell me?"

"I didn't want to hurt you, Fannie."

She turned her back and buried her face in her hands. Bill made a movement forward but didn't touch her. "Now, don't take on so. Things are no different between us than they've ever been. I told you I'd put that part of my life behind me."

Tears spilled down Fannie's cheeks.

"I thought you and I would have a bunch of kids, and it wouldn't make any difference," Bill continued. "But since we haven't . . . well . . . you might as well know. I've been thinking of trying to find the boy."

Fannie whirled, glaring at the stranger before her. This was the man she thought she knew. Anger erupted in her. She sprang at him, lashing out with both fists, but he caught her in his arms and held her close against his chest.

"Fannie, you know you're all I care about." He pressed his cheek against her hair, and they stood for a long time in the rays of cold sunlight streaking through the frosty window.

Bill gently rocked her back and forth, cradling her in his arms until her hurt and anger drained to weariness. It was nearly sunset. Chores had to be done. Cows milked. Horses and chickens fed. Her lips felt swollen as she licked away tears that had dried there. Finally, she spoke.

"Do you know his name?"

"Ivan."

PART THREE

The Fading Dream

22

Ivan. The name of Bill's son haunted Fannie. Ivan. Sometimes it came to her as a furtive, pleading murmur that left her with vague, uncomfortable feelings. Sometimes as a soft, lyrical ripple that brought images of a small laughing face. If only she and Bill had been blessed with children.

With the heavy December snow, the temperature dropped to thirty below zero and stayed there for nearly two months. Livestock bunched up in secluded corners of the ranch, and each morning Fannie loaded the wagon with hay and drove the team through the drifts, her mittened fingers stinging with the cold as she gripped the lines.

But she preferred the bleak desolation of the snow-swept range to the cold silence that hung over the cabin when Bill was in one of his moods. Her daily forays across the frozen land looking for cattle relieved the tension, and when she found the stock standing with frost-covered backs, icicles forming in their nostrils, she pitched the hay down to them with determined vigor.

With the depth of the early 1919 winter came another difficulty for Bill. Prohibition. The new law hampered his social life. He continued to join the boys in town at the local saloons, but as liquor stocks depleted, riding 9 miles in frigid weather to slog down endless cups of coffee dampened his enthusiasm for "promoting."

He moped about the cabin for days at a time, halfheartedly scanning stampede brochures or writing inquiries to fair committees. He paced the tiny kitchen, back and forth between the frosty windows, where he scraped off small patches of icy white crystals and stared out toward the mountains. He looked tired, Fannie thought, though he had little reason to be. Yet, despite his disagreeable moods, she was glad they were isolated from the influenza epidemic that was claiming countless lives across the country.

At such times, Fannie took her rifle and hiked up through the timber looking for coyotes. Sometimes she brought back a grouse for the table, and occasionally she saw deer tracks. Deer and elk, hunted off by settlers, had been scarce in Montana since the turn of the century. But in recent years, naturalists had made efforts to repopulate the wild stock, and Fannie could see the results. The sight of her first whitetail grazing near the creek thrilled her so she couldn't bring herself to shoot it even though they needed meat. Occasionally, she stopped by to see their neighbors, Arley and Jack Burt. Arley was a helpful, motherly sort, and Fannie enjoyed having a woman friend nearby.

In March, with the first chinook winds, she saddled Silvertail and rode out across the hills, exhilarated by the surge of renewed spirit and freedom she always felt with her horses. She scared up a cottontail and brought it down with her .22. Back at the cabin while she fed and watered the horses, Bill cleaned and fried the rabbit for their supper, making red-eye gravy to go over his hot biscuits.

As the days lengthened into a warm May, a young cowboy-marksman named Elmer Keith often came by for a day or two of fun riding bucking horses with them, and after Bill ordered another supply of china eggs, Elmer and Fannie staged their own keenly competitive shooting matches. Fannie also worked Daisy and Sultan for Elmer's amusement, and the high-school horses performed well when the Powder River Wild West Show began its annual tour of Montana in June. Peacetime audiences increased, and Fannie noticed that her husband was never happier than when crowds lined the fields where they performed.

Fannie rode a mousy bronc called Dismal Dick for an exhibition ride in Windham on August 20, 1920, during their summer tour. The *Gilman Optimist* on Friday, August 27, 1920, reported, *"W. S. and Fannie Steele are here with a string of bucking horses that Mr. Steele doubts can be ridden at this stampede."* The

Fannie rides Dismal Dick for an outstanding exhibition of her skills at the Windham Roundup, August 20, 1920.

September 14, 1920, issue of the *Augusta News* mentioned, *"Mrs. Fannie Sperry Steele gave a wonderful exhibition of riding and her stunts received the approval of the crowd."*

But the approval of the crowd wasn't enough for Fannie anymore. Dreams of further championships had lost their appeal. She knew she had to think of the future even if Bill wouldn't.

"What can I do except manage livestock," he said, showing his annoyance as he clipped the news items to be reprinted in the Helena papers. "That's what I'm good at."

"We've taken in barely enough to get us through till spring, Bill. We've got to find something else."

"Maybe we should enlarge the show."

"We've tried that." She found it hard to be patient with his same old answers. "It hasn't worked."

"If we bought some Percheron, we could breed them and . . ."

"We don't have enough money to invest in a donkey."

In June 1921, after arranging for Arley Burt to milk their cows and tend the chickens, Fannie and Bill started their summer tour with a performance at the Winnett Stampede. Bill had scheduled a full calendar with long treks between performances, and the tedious season dragged to a close before they could keep an ongoing promise to Fannie's mother to visit Bertha and N. D. on the Hilger homeplace. Bertha came from the house to welcome them, her hair carefully arranged in a neat pompadour. She wore a new gingham dress. N. D., scowling, sauntered from the corral and greeted Bill curtly. "Stampede season over?"

"Howdy, N. D." Bill shook hands with his brother-in-law. "We're on our way home."

"Fannie, it's good to see you," Bertha murmured as the sisters embraced. "The kids ask about you every single day." The four children came running.

"Are you riding at the fair, Aunt Fannie?"

"Is that the army horse you got in Miles City?"

"Did you see our new Model T Ford?"

Bertha shooed them away. "Now, you kids let Fannie catch her breath."

"Let them be," Fannie insisted, lifting the youngest, five-year-old Amelia, nicknamed Babe, into her arms.

"I have a Shetland pony, Aunt Fannie," the little girl announced.

"Well now, Babe, we just better take a look at that pony." And the whole crew detoured to the corral before Bertha could get them to the dinner table.

"Looks like things are going well for you," Fannie commented during the meal.

"Had good luck with the cattle," N. D. said. "And quite a few folks are paying to take our boat ride through the Gates. Yesterday, we ferried two fellas who work for the Watkins Company. They sell household products, vanilla and such." He glanced at Bill. "Said they're looking for salesmen."

Bill did not respond to the remark, but the following morning as they left for home, he announced he was going on into Helena to call on the Watkins people. Fannie, pleased with his initiative, trailed the stock to the ranch, turned them into the pasture, and unpacked the wagon while he was gone. Shortly after sundown, he startled her by bounding into the kitchen and playfully slinging his hat onto its peg by the door.

"Mrs. Steele, you're now looking at a bon-a-fide, gen-u-ine Watkins man!"

"Oh, Bill." Fannie put her arms around his waist and hugged him.

"They're letting me use a company delivery wagon with our team to make the rounds, and I start in October after the fair. I'll earn a small salary and a commission on everything I sell."

Bill and Fannie prepare for a trip to town in the new Dodge.

"That's good, Bill," Fannie said happily. "That's real good."

Freezing winds blew in an early snow and while Fannie settled into her winter routine, she learned that the Watkins Company, founded by door-to-door sales of liniment fifty years earlier, offered a whole line of products, from cosmetics to stove polish—all things that sold well to Bill's customers. But he complained of the difficulty of servicing his territory with the team and wagon, and, borrowing from Fannie's cream-and-egg money, he made a down payment on a small, shiny black, Dodge pickup truck.

"Folks'll sit up and take notice now when I come driving in," he said.

Fannie responded, dryly, "Give me a horse any day."

More Bad Luck

23

In the early summer of 1922, two teenage girls, Violet and Margaret Brander, who had ridden bareback from their folks' hardscrabble ranch near Avon, dropped from their scrawny mounts in front of the house on Jackson Creek. They had come to learn from Fannie how to ride bucking horses so they could earn some money riding at roundups.

To Fannie, the two fresh faces and determined personalities were welcome as rain, and she invited them to stay for the summer. The girls, nicknamed Vi and Marg, proved to be just the hands Fannie needed. They helped with the haying, milking and churning, fencing, and other chores. They rode with Fannie and watched her work the string.

"I never saw nobody who can talk to horses like you can, Fannie," Marg said. "How'd you get 'em to understand you like that?"

"I listen to *them*, I guess. I seem to know what they're thinking just from being around them all my life. I feel it in my bones . . . in my heart. I wouldn't know how to tell anybody. You have to get to know them. Takes time. And patience."

The Brander girls rode in a few local stampedes that summer, earning a small amount of prize money, and they stayed to mind the ranch when Fannie and Bill left for the Miles City Roundup.

Camped just outside of Forsyth on the final leg of their junket to Miles City, Fannie noticed Silvertail was gone. The mare had pulled her picket pin.

Fannie saddled Daisy, and with Bill following on Chief, they rode in a wide circle, whistling and calling for the roan. They saw no sign of her.

"We'll have to look for her on the way back," Bill said.

Three days later, on the return trip, they intensified the search for Silvertail—along the river, through thickets, and up and down the countless coulees—but found no sign of her. Then, approaching the railroad yard near Forsyth, they saw a ghastly sight. On a dusty slag heap, a flock of crows were pecking at an animal carcass. Fannie's heart leapt into her throat and she spurred Daisy forward. The crows scattered, scolding as she stopped short before the stinking remains. A roan hide, some exposed bones, a matted flow of silvery mane and tail was all that was left.

Fannie's eyes blurred.

A squat little man in overalls and a brakeman's cap came up behind them from the railroad yard. "You folks own that roan? She ran right in front of the switch engine."

With the brakeman's assurance that the remains would be buried, Fannie and Bill mounted up and started for home.

Their homecoming seemed empty without the favorite mare. Fannie sent the Brander girls to bring in the cows, then sank onto the sill of the open barn door, her heart leaden.

"No use crying over spilt milk." Bill tried to sound cheerful as he went about his chores.

No, Fannie thought. No use crying. No use anything. She buried her face in her hands and tears came. Then a deep agony of sobs. Sobs that reached beyond the loss of the mare. What was it all leading to? What was the use of anything? She wept bitterly.

When the tears stopped, she sat, pale and shaken, gazing across the range as the setting sun skimmed the sage and glinted on the rainbow colors of the horses romping in the home pasture. Vi and Marg came in with the cows, and Fannie, averting her eyes, rose from the barn doorway. But the girls, seeing her sorrow, came awkwardly to comfort her. "We've changed our minds, Fannie. We're staying here. We won't leave you now."

Fannie looked blankly at them. "Were you leaving?"

"We thought we might go to high school. With fall coming on, you don't need us so much, and Ma wants us to get more schoolin'."

"Your ma's right. You should go to school." Fannie managed an encouraging nod, remembering those very words from her own mother many years ago. "I've been working you too hard anyway."

"But we don't want to go now, with you feeling so bad about Silvertail."

"You two have to do what's best for you. Bill and I will manage." She tried to smile. "Having you girls here this summer meant a lot to me—you know you're welcome anytime—and I want good reports on your schoolwork, you hear."

The girls broke into grins, then delighted little squeals. "Oh, thanks, Fannie. You and Bill have been swell. We'll write to you."

Violet and Marg said their final good-byes before Fannie and Bill left for the Three Valley Fair in Three Forks on September 4, where Bill would furnish twenty-eight horses, one mule, a clown act, and a lady bucking-horse rider for the sum of $150.

The Branders later wrote saying they had rented a room in Deer Lodge and found domestic work to keep them while they attended school. Fannie felt more alone than ever.

Bill left on his Watkins route immediately after the fair. His truck had allowed him to increase his territory to include the Bozeman area, and he spent more time than ever away from the ranch. So when he arrived home after a two-week absence, fuming about being stalled on an upgrade with an overheated engine, Fannie felt little sympathy.

"A horse is twice as dependable as that flivver."

"A horse can drop dead on you, too." Bill seemed in bad humor. Sales were down and tire repairs had taken his last dollar. "I have to borrow some money from you, Fannie."

"All I have is the hundred and thirty I got for my pelts last spring. Winter feed and groceries will take all of that." She hated to bring up other needs. "And with cold weather coming on," she said, "I have to get a heavy coat. The wind whistles right through my old jacket."

"You'll get your coat, honey. But I can't make my route without a dime in my pocket. Let me have just twenty?"

Fannie hesitated.

"Tell you what." Bill chucked her under the chin. "I'll go with you to Helena tomorrow. You can get your grub *and* your coat. You won't need to buy feed till the hay runs low, and I'll pay you back before then." He smiled at her expectantly. "We can even go to the picture show. I hear there's a Hoot Gibson two reeler. He's a big movie star since he came back from the war."

They finished the chores early next morning, and Fannie, bundled against the November wind in her old jacket, climbed gingerly into the passenger seat of Bill's little Dodge truck for the trip to Helena. Bill threw the engine crank into the back and jumped behind the steering wheel to gun the throttle. "Ain't this a lot better'n setting a saddle?" He grinned, waiting her approval.

"I don't feel no friendliness under this seat like I do from a good horse."

"Wait till we hit some weather. You'll be just as cozy as if you were sitting in your own parlor." Bill shifted the gears and the truck sputtered away from the log house and headed for the main road.

In Helena, they purchased the grocery staples first, then walked down the street to the Emporium, where Fannie asked the bosomy, gray-haired clerk to see the ladies' coats. Bill followed the two women to the back of the store. Fannie browsed through a long rack of coats, squinting at the price tags, and as she tried garment after garment, gazing disapprovingly at herself in the mirror, Bill perched restlessly on a stool, grousing about high prices. Finally, Fannie selected a warm, sealskin overcoat that covered her from ears to ankles. She counted out the bills from her purse.

"It's a lovely, warm coat." The clerk wrapped string around the huge box. "I know you'll be happy with it."

"She should be," Bill quipped. "It's costing me an arm and a leg."

Fannie, seething at his remark, picked up the box and strode from the store. "I didn't know it was *you* who paid for this coat." Her sarcasm infuriated Bill.

"Look, I'll pay for the blasted coat. I'll buy you a whole damn outfit."

Embarrassed to quarrel on the street, Fannie clenched her teeth. "Here's the twenty dollars you asked for."

Bill's anger faded as he put the money into his pocket. "Honey, listen. I've got an idea I've been saving. Let's go to a cafe and talk about it. Here, put on your new coat." He tore the string from the box. Fannie's heart felt heavier than the sealskin as she changed from her old jacket, leaving the box in the truck, and they walked down the street to the Placer Hotel.

But the new coat perked up her mood. She felt strangely elegant as Bill squired her to a table in the well-appointed dining room, placed the twenty-dollar bill on the table, and ordered two dinner specials. Then he leaned across the table and put his hand on hers.

"Fannie, I been working on a plan. Got a lot of time to think, driving all over creation day after day." He settled back in his chair, looking pleased with himself. "I think I know how I can get away from peddling vanilla and, at the same time, ease you out of the bronc-riding business."

Fannie hadn't seen such confidence in his face for a long time, and she was caught up in his enthusiasm. "What, Bill?"

"Remember that fella we met who has the OTO Guest Ranch down near Gardiner?"

"Dick Randall, the dude rancher?"

"He and his wife take in city folks and show them how to ride, hunt, and fish. Lots of ranchers are making money packing dudes into the backcountry. The way I see it, no reason we can't do the same."

Fannie pressed forward over her dinner plate. "You know, Bill, I think we could. We have all the qualifications."

"Except one." He held up a finger of caution. "Our place on Jackson Creek can't handle dudes. And that's the part I've been working on." He looked more pleased than ever. "I know a guy who'll take it off our hands."

"Oh, Bill, if we *could* sell it, then we could get the place we've always wanted. We could raise horses. And the dudes would give us some income."

"I'd like to go west of the Divide somewhere. Over near Lincoln maybe. Elmer Keith surveyed over that way. Says it's God's country."

"Oh, yes. A pretty spread up in the mountains . . ."

"Good hunting. Plenty of deer and elk. Bear, even. Streams jumping with trout."

"Our pintos could be our trademark."

"With my management and your name and reputation . . ."

"Do you really think we could get folks to come?"

"You just leave that to old Bill."

Fannie looked into his eyes. She had heard him say those words before more times than she could count. But at this moment, to her surprise, she realized she still believed in him.

Dude Ranching on Arrastra Creek

But it was to be three more years before Bill heard about the ranch for sale on Arrastra Creek. Across the Continental Divide, 7 miles from Helmville, the isolated hunters' retreat was nestled among giant pine, fir, and tamarack on a mountain wilderness above the Blackfoot River.

"Oh, Bill, it couldn't be more perfect," Fannie announced on their first visit to the property. She inspected the four-room log cabin—a kitchen, parlor, and two bedrooms—that stood at the edge of a wild meadow. Then she hurried down the slope toward the beaver-dammed lake and a second small cabin in the woods.

"I see deer and elk tracks." Bill picked a handful of wild larkspur and gave it to Fannie. "Welcome home, honey."

She sniffed the tiny blue flowers. "The horses will love it here. And with this cabin and the extra bedroom, we can bunk our dudes."

Bill was equally enthusiastic. "I'll quit my Watkins job and have the main cabin snug by snowfall."

"There's just one thing I don't like." A frown crossed Fannie's brow. "Eighty miles is a long way from the Beartooth."

"Don't worry. Walter and Fleta are looking after your ma," Bill assured her. Walter and Fleta, who had married and started a family, were living with Rachel on the homestead.

"You're my girl, Fannie." Bill gently kissed her forehead, and she smiled through her fistful of larkspur at the only man she had ever loved.

By mid-August everything was ready for the move, and Fannie accepted a farewell-supper invitation from Arley and Jack Burt, their Jackson Creek neighbors.

"Tonight, I'm putting my callow youth behind me," Bill told them. "From now on, I'm a respectable rancher. Ain't that right, honey?" He draped his arm across Fannie's shoulders as he retrieved a bootlegged bottle of whiskey from his hip pocket. "Let's have some glasses here. We're drinking to the W. S. Steele Dude Ranch. Finest fishing and hunting in the heart of the Rockies."

Arley brought glasses and Bill poured small shots of whiskey into each.

Jack raised his glass. "Not many folks have the guts to start out on a new life at your age."

"At my age!" Bill roared. "Hell, I'm only fifty. Got half my life ahead of me."

"Wish I had your spunk," Jack said.

"I wish I had your wife," Arley countered. Then, turning to Fannie she said, "You've been a fine neighbor, Fannie. I don't know how I'll get along without you."

"It's more the other way around," Fannie said, relaxing into Arley's comfortable Morris chair, her boots up on the footstool. "But you'll stay over when you come to visit. We may need some help corralling those dudes."

"You gonna keep ridin', Fannie?" Jack asked.

"Nope. After the Bozeman Roundup in September, I'm hanging up my spurs." The sound of her own voice saying it made it seem real at last. "At thirty-eight, I need to keep whatever I still got to run our new operation."

"The cowgirls' bucking won't amount to much without you."

"Not many women in bronc riding these days anyway." Fannie grimaced at the strong taste of her whiskey. "Most of the stampedes—or rodeos, they call them now—have quit the cowgirls' bucking-horse event." Fannie stretched her strong, still-youthful figure into the soft cushions and hunched her shoulders, mugging a comic, quizzical expression. "They say the sport is just too dangerous for women."

Next day, their procession—Bill's truck, two heavily loaded wagons, the

Fannie's mother, Rachel Sperry, still sitting pretty in the saddle in her late seventies.

string of thirty horses, and two milk cows—headed out from Jackson Creek toward the Continental Divide. Bill and Jack manned the truck and wagons, followed by Fannie, riding her mother's mare Pumpkin, and Arley, on her own horse, trailing the stock. "Take Pumpkin with you," Rachel had insisted. "You need a good trail horse, and I'm not riding her much anymore." Fannie, perhaps wanting to take along something of the Beartooth, had agreed. "She'll like it up at the new place, Ma," she had promised.

The trek to Arrastra Creek took four days across nearly 90 miles of rugged mountain terrain and over Stemple Pass. Each day Bill drove on ahead, setting up camp at designated spots to have meals waiting when the others trailed in. They rode through the main street of Lincoln, then continued west along the Blackfoot Valley, skirting Flathead National Forest, and, finally, swung north up the last 3 miles of wooded mountain on a narrow rocky road bordering the shallow but swift Arrastra Creek.

Fannie paused at a point where the precipitous waterway branched away from the road. "Used to be an old mining operation up there with an arrastra wheel." Arley peered up into the cool shadows of the gully as they passed. The horses followed single file behind Daisy, their pinto colors dappled by patches of sunlight filtering through the high branches. Rounding another bend, they came onto an open meadow fenced with lodgepole rails. Beyond the meadow the mountains rose to a craggy rim against the sky.

"This is it!" Fannie beamed at her friend.

"Golly." Arley gazed in awe at the beauty of the land, then at the log cabin tucked among the trees at the far side of the meadow. She waited while Fannie opened the gate to let the stock onto the lush meadow. The horses trotted single file into the deep grass, then kicked up their heels and frolicked across their new pasture. The milk cows began to graze.

Just then the cabin door flew open and Bill emerged, coughing and sputtering, followed by a cloud of black smoke, which he fanned with a flapjack turner. "The damn stove ain't working right," he called to Fannie. The others laughed, but Bill saw no humor in the situation. "Stovepipe won't draw. We can't cook on that thing."

"How about a campfire, then?" Fannie suggested. "We're starved. We can set up our own stove tomorrow." She dismounted and pulled the saddle off the tired Pumpkin, who started off to join Daisy and the other stock.

"It's so pretty here." Fannie leaned back against her saddle before the campfire and breathed in the evergreen fragrance. "I don't care if I never go inside." After the meal, they sat listening to evening birdsongs and chatting happily while shadows crept up the mountainside to the east, and the last rays of sunlight tipped the crest. No one suggested moving into the cabin. The twilight was too lovely. But when fatigue finally overtook them, they set up the beds in the cabin and fell gratefully into them.

Toward sunup, a light rain began to fall, and Fannie awakened to find her bedroll damp from a leak in the roof above her. Bill was already up and swearing. "Damn rain is pouring in around the stovepipe." She pulled on her boots and joined him in the kitchen, where another rivulet trickled in below the warped door frame.

"This place is a blasted sieve," Bill growled, scowling at the soot-covered ceiling above the stove.

But Fannie felt too happy to let a little rain dampen her enthusiasm. "It ain't a palace," she said. "But it'll soon be home."

After helping to set up the stove, sweep out the cabin, and put the meager furnishings in place, Arley and Jack Burt left for Jackson Creek. Bill drove the little Dodge truck to Lincoln to pick up repair materials. In the days that followed, while he worked on the cabin and shed, Fannie cut and stacked the meadow grass and trimmed lodgepoles to mend the fence.

Bill applied for a license as an outfitter and guide, and on September 25, 1925, while Fannie fulfilled her commitment to ride in a bucking exhibition at the Bozeman Fair, he arranged for the printing of a brochure promoting the ranch.

Enjoy rugged western beauty: mountains, canyons, creeks, streams, lakes, clean fresh air and cool nights. A large picture of Bill in angora chaps and his big Stetson, crouching before a set of elk antlers, adorned the brochure cover. Inside, photos of Fannie and Bill on horseback flanked more copy.

We want you and your friends to know that when you come to the Steeles' ranch on Arrastra Creek, you'll be right amongst Nature's virgin wilderness. What a thrill you'll get in going after rainbow trout with rod and line. Our place is as handy to the finest deer and elk hunting as it could possibly be. This Blackfoot country is pretty big, and we can take you to plenty of spots where we know the hunting is good in the fall.

The beautiful summer passed all too quickly, and when autumn temperatures grew colder, Fannie and Bill drew closer to their stove during the evenings. Bill brooded about the dearth of paying guests. "Guess I didn't run our advertisements soon enough," he reasoned.

"The word is out," Fannie said. "We're sure to get a bunch next season."

At night they slept soundly in the profound silence of the mountains, waking each morning to a fringe of ice in the wash basin, and grateful that the pump provided a reliable water supply for the stock.

By Christmas, snow lay deep around the cabin. "Oh, Bill, the fence is down again and the horses are gone." Fannie's announcement became a frequent one, and she and Bill learned quickly where to find the wayward band in the subzero temperatures. Hiking the hills on snowshoes, they would come upon two or three pintos sheltered in a clump of pine, or foraging among outcropping rocks, perhaps others looking for water near the creek. Spotting a naturally camouflaged pinto on a snowy, wooded landscape required a keen eye. As soon as Daisy was located, Fannie would slip a bridle on her and climb aboard. Getting the others was easier then. Once Butterfly remained lost for several days, returning on her own, gaunt and weakened, and Fannie fattened her with an extra daily ration of the feed Bill had trucked from Helmville after the county snow crew plowed out the road.

Returning from one such trip to pick up mail, Bill came into the cabin waving a packet of letters. He danced into the kitchen like an excited schoolboy. "We got our first dudes! Two sisters from Milwaukee. Norma and Irma Dean, their names are. They want to come out in July. And here's one from a family named Briggs. They sent a check."

With the coming of spring, 1926, Fannie cleaned and furnished the lakeside cabin with secondhand beds, a table and chairs, and a small heating stove. Then she began training her pack string, Snowball, Jiggs, and Gus, who would pack supplies for them into the mountains. She fit the sawbuck pack-saddles to each animal, adjusting cinches, breeching, and breast collars in preparation for the heavy loads they would carry. With small rocks giving weight to the packs, she worked with the animals, leading them over the rough terrain to work out any problems downed timber and steep slopes might present.

"Snowball and Jiggs get along fine," she reported to Bill. "But Gus always wants to run to the top of every upgrade as fast as he can. He crowded Snowball off the trail twice today."

"Horses think a mountain is only as high as the next knoll." He chuckled as he soaked the new manty ropes with water and stretched them between two fence posts to fuzz them up for a tighter wrap on the packs. "Gus doesn't realize the slope goes up more than five miles. He'll learn to pace himself."

"We're crazy about the Old West," Norma Dean said, alighting from the truck, which Bill had shined up to fetch the girls from the Drummond railroad station 35 miles to the west. She gazed up at the tall trees, then down toward the lake. "Look, Irma, a real log cabin."

"Oh, it's fabulous!" Irma agreed. Attractive girls in their early twenties, their hair bobbed and permed in the latest style, they hurried toward the meadow to see the horses and help Fannie bring in the two milk cows.

"Do cows *like* to be milked?" Irma asked, observing thoughtfully as Fannie began the milking. Amused, Fannie fielded all questions. Then, as the girls carried the two full pails of milk onto the porch, a Model-A Ford sedan honked at the meadow gate.

"Must be the Briggs family." Bill stepped from the porch, waving the car forward. It pulled up next to the shed, and Eugene Briggs, a pudgy, well-barbered man, climbed out, walking gingerly in spanking-new cowboy boots.

"Howdy." Bill extended his hand. "I'm Bill Steele."

"Rugged country you got here, Bill," Briggs drawled. Behind him, two boys about twelve and fourteen, carbon copies of their father except for their tousled hair, sprang from the backseat. Both wore knickers and boots laced to the knee.

"Our boys, Jimmy and Chuckie," Briggs said. "And this is my wife, Hazel." Mrs. Briggs, a tiny wisp of a woman dressed in a bright print dress, emerged from the car carrying a cowboy hat. She wore her straight brown hair bobbed at the ears.

How sensible, Fannie thought, tossing her own braids behind her back. Then, seeing Hazel's silk stockings and dainty high-heeled shoes, she allowed a wide smile to serve as her greeting. "I'm Fannie Steele."

Hazel Briggs shook Fannie's hand. "Fannie, I've admired you ever since my daddy took me to see the Irwin Brothers Wild West Show some years ago."

"That does go back a ways," Fannie said.

"I just can't see Jimmy and Chuckie growing up without knowing a hack-amore from a sawbuck." She smiled as she put her arms across the shoulders of each boy, displaying them for Fannie. This is a nice woman, Fannie thought. She likes her boys. And they look like good kids, too. But she can't know much about ranches with those shoes.

"We'll give the boys a workout," Fannie promised. "Come on, I'll show you where to bunk." She helped carry their luggage to the lake cabin.

When the Briggs family appeared for supper, Hazel wore a pair of men's trousers and comfortable boots, explaining, "I always wear pants for riding." She found a perch on the porch railing, swinging her legs, her boyish haircut fluttering in the breeze.

"It's cool for summer, isn't it?" The Dean girls, who had the spare bed-room in the main cabin, climbed up beside her. "Your haircut, I mean. We just had our hair bobbed, too, this spring. Everyone in Milwaukee is doing it."

Hazel touched her short locks. "Eugene doesn't like it much." She glanced at her husband, who was helping Bill place extra chairs around the kitchen table, then giggled. "But who cares? It feels good."

Fannie shrugged, tossing her long braid over her shoulder, and led the way to the kitchen. By the time the supper of venison stew and hot biscuits was on the table, she felt as if Hazel Briggs and the Dean sisters were old friends.

Up before dawn the next morning to bring in the pack string, Bill did chores, milked, and cooked a ranch breakfast for their eager tenderfoots, while Fannie readied supplies for packing. She placed the 8-foot-square canvas manties on the ground in pairs and arranged food, cooking gear, bedding, and personal items to be wrapped in them, plus the two tents— all necessities for their coming week in the wilderness, and all to be transported in two panniers of equal weight on either side of each packhorse's sawbuck.

"You're going to be comfy as can be," she assured Snowball, Jiggs, and Gus, who stood quietly, docile models of deportment, as she hefted the first manty onto Snowball's sawbuck and tied it with a diamond hitch. The Briggs family, coming sleepily from the cabin, offered to help, but Fannie insisted on attending to the packs herself. "The britchen has to be just right—loose enough so the horse can stride uphill, but tight enough so the saddle won't slide forward on the downgrade," she explained.

"I know," Hazel agreed. "You get that cinch ring too far up, it can stop the horse's circulation. A poorly cinched packsaddle," she instructed her sons, "can rub an open sore on a horse's hide in less than half a mile." Fannie grinned at Hazel. This little woman knew a thing or two about packhorses.

"And the cinches will all have to be adjusted again," Fannie said, "when these little devils slim down later in the season. They're fat as butterballs, now." She secured the fishing poles atop Jiggs's load, then slipped her Winchester into the scabbard. She assigned Nifty and Pansy to the Briggs boys, Butterfly and Red Cloud to the Dean sisters. Hazel adopted Pumpkin, and Eugene was given a gelding called Paint.

"What about that big one?" He pointed to Chief in the corral. "A big guy like me maybe should ride a bigger horse."

"Chief stays here, today," Fannie said. "Daisy may be inclined to do a little flirting just now, and we don't want to have to cope with a romance on the trail." Eugene laughed and stepped up into Paint's saddle.

"Now don't tangle with any grizzlies," Bill teased, waving them off. Then he did a double take, staring in astonishment as Fannie tipped her hat to reveal her new haircut, bobbed to the earlobes.

The big sky hovered brilliant blue with just enough breeze to keep riders and animals comfortable. Fannie, on Daisy, led the packhorses, which

Fannie (left) and Bill (right) ready a packhorse for their first dudes, Norma and Irma Dean, at their Arrastra Creek ranch.

were roped together single file and in front of the line of riders, with Eugene bringing up the rear.

"Keep an eye on Gus," she called back to Hazel. "He may decide he wants to get there before the rest of us."

"How could he get past Snowball and Daisy on this narrow ledge?" Irma Dean looked down over the rim toward the valley stream far below.

"He'll find a way." Fannie said.

"Maybe we could tie a rope to his tail, and I'd hang onto it," Chuckie Briggs suggested.

"Don't be silly." Norma Dean sat tall in her saddle just as she'd seen Tom Mix do in the movies. "He'd pull you right off the edge."

"Nifty wouldn't let him do that." Chuckie patted his mount's neck. "Nifty likes me. Don't you, Nifty?"

The riders chatted happily through the morning. After their brief noon picnic, the trail brought them to the steepest part of the ascent and they settled into silence, their bodies protesting the hours in the saddle as the horses strained beneath them to climb the rocky trail.

Nearing the crest of a knoll, Gus suddenly made a run for it, edging past Snowball and snapping the breakaway ropes that anchored him to the other packhorses. "Gus, get back there." Fannie caught his lead as he forced her precariously to the outer edge of the narrow trail. But Daisy held her ground, and Fannie was able to dismount, back Gus into position, and redo the break ropes. Inspecting his load, she discovered he had scraped one of his packs against the rocks. It now hung off balance.

"I'll have to repack this booger," she announced, "or we'll have gear strung from here to kingdom come." The others dismounted to stretch their legs while she retied the manty ropes on Gus's load.

At the clearing where they would camp for the night, everyone pitched in to help set the two tents, gather wood, build a fire, open cans of food, and prepare the meal. Horses were watered at the nearby stream, then brushed and curried before being left to graze. Fannie picketed Daisy to a lone fir tree in the middle of the clearing and then walked among the other horses, petting and offering them sugar lumps. She had extra sugar for Gus.

"These folks are green yet," she murmured to the animals. "But you all did a fine job today. Sorry to have to picket you tonight, Daisy, but we don't want you taking a notion to spend the night with Chief and lead the others back to the ranch while we sleep." Daisy nosed Fannie's hand.

Repeating the procedures the next day, they reached Heart Lake by sundown. Jimmy Briggs caught the first fish, and the fresh trout served with Fannie's home-baked bread perked up the saddle-weary riders. The guests helped with many of the routine camp chores, but Fannie still packed the manties and loaded the packhorses herself.

All during that first season at Arrastra Creek, Fannie's prime goal became guiding her guests and the animals safely along the trail. She taught the inexperienced to feel the partnership between themselves and their horses, to sense the contentment in this unique way of life, and to revere the beauty of the wild country. She felt confident in her new role. Sun-drenched skies by day and star-sprinkled heavens by night marked the weeks of serenity and renewal.

And profit. Net income from the first two pack trips totaled $62.50.

"Don't seem like much," she remarked to Bill as she worked over the books. "I thought charging forty dollars a week per person would give us a nice profit."

"Just too many expenses getting set up," Bill said. "We'll make more money next year."

While in Helena getting supplies for hunting season, Bill dropped by the office of the Department of Forestry Service, which had written him expressing interest in buying or renting horses for surveying the backcountry. When he left an hour later, he had been hired by the Montana Fish and Game Department to stock area streams and lakes with fish for a modest but steady income. He would begin the following spring by planting fish in a stream called Meadow Creek.

Their second quiet winter at Arrastra Creek brought 3-foot drifts around the cabin. Bill kept paths shoveled so Fannie could milk and put down hay for the stock, keeping an eye out for a big bull elk that seemed to think her efforts were for him. Only Chief, Pumpkin, the team, and the two milk cows stayed the winter. The rest of the horses had been pastured down the mountain near Helmville. As always, Fannie followed coyote trails to set a trapline, and Pumpkin proved to be good company as well as capable help in packing back an occasional carcass.

One frosty morning, with the thermometer outside the window registering twenty-nine below zero, Fannie bundled up against the biting wind to go out to pump water into the horse trough. "I swear it takes longer to get dressed than it does to pump water." She chuckled as she pulled two pairs of Bill's old wool trousers over her long union suit, then topped a wool shirt and jacket with her heavy sealskin coat. Felt-lined rubber pacs over two pairs of wool socks, fur mittens over lighter gloves, and a raccoon-skin cap that Bill had made, the fur inside for warmth, completed her ensemble.

The horses stood waiting near the pump, their frosty breath hanging in clouds of vapor, but the pump was frozen, its usual gush of water replaced by the hollow scrape of the metal handle. The creek and lake, too, lay frozen solid under the deep snow.

She fetched a teakettle of hot water to pour into the pump. No luck. After several tries, she told Bill, "We'll just have to melt snow." They filled the washtub with snow and melted it on the kitchen stove. Throughout the cold spell, they took turns refilling the tub and carrying the water in buckets for the four horses and the two cows to drink from.

When a warm snap blew in, bringing the temperature above zero, they were able to thaw the pump. And when the county crew once again plowed out the Arrastra Creek road, clearing a track through the gate and up to the buildings, Bill made his usual trip into Helmville to pick up supplies and mail.

After watching his truck disappear down the mountain between the high banks of piled snow, Fannie decided to check her trapline. But Pumpkin was not among the other horses. She saddled Chief and had ridden quite a distance along one of the coyote trails when she saw the golden buckskin lying across the trail. All around, the tramped snow glistened red. The bleeding mare, a foreleg nearly severed by a coyote trap, lay dying.

Fannie fell into the snow beside the injured animal and held the fine head in her arms. Chief lowered his head to sniff as his fallen friend's breathing weakened, then stopped.

"Oh, Pumpkin. I'm sorry. I'm so sorry." Fannie wept, kneeling beside the dead mare until her legs and feet numbed with cold. Then she rose and trudged back to the cabin, leading Chief. She sat in the darkened kitchen until she heard the Dodge coming along the plowed road. Then she got up and lighted the lamp as Bill entered the kitchen, bringing with him a blast of cold air.

The look on Fannie's face alarmed him. "What's wrong, Fannie?"

"Pumpkin's dead." Her voice was dull with grief.

"What?" The lamp flame cast an eerie glow on his startled face.

"She stumbled into one of the coyote traps. Cut an artery."

"Christ! What next?"

"I should have watched her better," Fannie said, tears brimming. "But I didn't think she'd go clear up there where I set those traps."

"It wasn't your fault. These things happen."

"But if I'd found her sooner . . ."

"You couldn't have saved her. Not with a cut artery." Bill unbuttoned his coat, and Fannie heard a strange, tiny whimper. "Here, I brought you something." He lifted a small, furry ball of black and white from inside his vest, a fluffy pup, and held it out to her. "He needs a good home."

She reached for the tiny creature. It squirmed and squeaked, blinking its eyes in the lamplight.

"He's part collie," Bill said. "Let's get him warmed up." They pulled chairs close to the stove, Fannie cradling the pup, Bill's arm around them both. "Look how his little tail curls over my finger. Let's call him Curly."

They sat in silence for a while. Finally Bill said, "I sure feel bad about

Pumpkin. I know she was your ma's favorite." He stroked the sleeping pup on Fannie's lap.

"Why does it hurt so when they go?" she murmured. "I always feel as if I've lost a member of the family."

"They're the only family we got," Bill said.

Packing into the Wilderness  25

The old grizzly sow growled and reared on her hind legs, breath steaming in the November dawn. Fannie pulled up short, her hunting party of three vacationing doctors close behind. Panicked at the sound and sight of the bear, Daisy snorted and skittered off into the deep snow, while the packhorses broke loose and scattered. Dr. Baines, his spectacles knocked askew by his army-surplus parka, fumbled with his Winchester.

"Don't shoot!" Fannie whispered. "She has cubs."

Behind the sow, two young grizzlies scampered onto the trail. The sow swung her head toward them, then bared her teeth, a low growl escaping the heavy throat.

Motioning the men back, Fannie slipped her rifle from its scabbard and released the safety, holding a bead on the bear's brow while the men moved back into the shelter of the trees.

"Why don't you shoot?" rasped Dr. Lukins, a heavyset man with graying hair. Sweat glistened on his ruddy face as he gripped his weapon anxiously. Dr. Anderson, a lean six-footer, tensed to make a run for it.

Fannie put a finger to her lips to caution the men to remain silent. The sow dropped to all fours and turned toward her cubs. When the grizzlies had moved off through the brush, Fannie relaxed her aim and replaced her rifle in its scabbard.

"I can't see leaving a fine trophy like that," Lukins grumbled.

"We don't want to orphan those cubs," Fannie explained. "Besides, that old she-bear can do forty miles an hour in a stiff headwind. She might take a notion to rough up some of us before we could bring her down." Fannie trudged among the snowy trees to round up the scattered packhorses.

"Fannie's right." Baines struggled to catch Snowball's lead rope. "We were lucky to get out of there."

Regrouped, they rode across the white-mantled mountain with Fannie leading the pack string. She had guided a steady stream of hunters and fishermen into the backcountry all during the season. Many were seasoned outdoorsmen who made the trips pleasurable for all. But many were rank dudes who had never hunted or ridden a horse. Fannie felt a strong responsibility not only to see that her hunters got their meat and returned safely, but also that they experienced adventures they could relate with enthusiasm to other potential guests.

Now, with the temperature at freezing and the overcast sky threatening more snow, Fannie picked up a fresh trail and signaled the men to circle downwind. Below them on the mountain slope, they spotted a five-point bull elk in a clump of scrub pine. Baines raised his rifle to take it. The Winchester cracked, and the elk went down, hit in the right flank. But instantly, the animal was up again and off down a snow-filled gully.

"Those old bulls are tough," Fannie said, "But he's not going far with that 220 slug in him." She led the way on foot through the crusted snow. The bull moved at an awkward run. Baines fired again, this time into the shoulder. The elk went down again, then staggered to its feet once more, sidling in a wide arc.

The wounded animal slowed, then stopped about 200 yards below them. Baines crept forward until he was less than 20 yards from his target. As he raised his rifle, the bull whirled and charged. Baines pulled the trigger, and the bullet hit the elk square in the bulge of the neck. The animal dropped.

Fannie showed the men how to bleed and gut the kill. Then they dragged the carcass back up the mountain to where they had left the horses. There, Fannie skinned and quartered it for transporting.

Gus sometimes objected to packing game, and Fannie knew she would have to fool him if he was to hold still for the wild-scented cargo. The men helped her roll the elk quarters in manties and balance them on Gus's and Snowball's sawbucks. Jiggs, the most experienced, would carry the head and hide. He skittered a bit as they secured the antlers, then settled down under his load in his usual position behind Gus. But Gus took one sidelong look at the antlered pack behind him and bolted up the trail, bucking and kicking to dislodge his cargo of flopping hindquarters.

Fannie glared after him, disgusted. "I'll go get him and meet you in camp," she told the men.

But she never caught up with the determined Gus. Just short of where they'd had the morning encounter with the grizzly, he veered off into the forest and up a steep embankment. Fannie kept to the camp trail, confident he was headed back to the ranch.

As she approached camp, she sensed something amiss. The bear and cubs had paid them a visit. Fannie's tent hung in tatters. Leaving Daisy at the edge of the clearing, she chambered a round, and listened. No sound. No movement to indicate intruders still in the tent. After a confirming wait, she crept closer and peered through the ripped canvas. Inside, scattered canned goods littered the ground. Each can had been bitten into, and corn, beans, and tomatoes were splattered everywhere. A large lard can was licked clean.

Fannie stepped into view when she heard the men approaching. "Looks like that grizzly came by to pick up a few groceries." The men dismounted and stared at the remains of their chuck.

Anderson peered about the camp. "Let's get out of here." The others agreed they had spent enough time in this particular spot.

"We have to go back to the ranch to replace our grub anyway." Fannie tied the salvageable gear atop the mantied elk quarters on Snowball's and Jiggs's packsaddles. "Without that lamebrain Gus, you two'll have to do his share, too," she apologized to the two packhorses as they braced, stiff-legged under their heavy loads.

The party headed for the ranch, and at dusk, after a supper of fresh elk steaks, they made camp a good distance from the tree where Fannie suspended the meat high out on a limb. Near the men's tent she spread her bedroll on the remains of her own tattered tent, tucked her rifle beneath it, and slept under the clear November sky.

They arrived back at the ranch before noon the next day and saw Gus, sleek and sassy as ever, among the horses on the meadow. Bill came from the shed to meet them. "Gus was here when I got up this morning," he reported. "Delivered the two elk quarters just as nice as you please."

"Lucky he didn't lose the meat, the way he lit out through that timber."

Baines chuckled as he pulled the antlered head from Jiggs's sawbuck. Bill held the bridle to steady Lukins's mount as the saddle-sore doctor dropped to the ground.

"We had a run-in with a grizzly," Fannie said. "Had to come back for a new load of grub."

"I thought we were goners when that sow reared up out of nowhere," Baines began. And the men related all there was to tell about the encounter with the grizzly and then some.

That night, snug in their comfortable bed, Fannie told Bill she planned to invest in a .375 Hoffman. "I doubt I could have slowed that big grizzly sow with my Winchester," she said as she drifted off to sleep.

In the seasons that followed, business flourished at the Arrastra Creek ranch. A Model-A Ford four-door sedan now transported guests from the station, and a high-wall army tent and kerosene stove helped facilitate the pack trips. Fannie and Bill cut and hauled lodgepole pine to build another guest cabin near the lake, and Walter offered to come to help put it up. Fannie, happy to have Walter around, invited him to bring Fleta and their two young sons the next time he came.

"Wish I could, but the kids and Ma are a handful for Fleta. It's hard for us to get away. I can see you have your work cut out for you here, too."

"Carrie's kids are coming to help out. Florence and Bea will do the cooking this summer, and Nick and George will mind the place while I'm packing in." The oldest of Carrie and Joe's twelve children, now in their early twenties, liked nothing better, when not hired out elsewhere, to come "over the mountain," as they called the Great Divide, to lend a hand. Aunt Fannie and Uncle Bill were always good for room and board if not always for wages. Bertha and N. D.'s four hard-working teenagers also came in shifts. All were welcome. And needed.

"Don't Bill pack in, too?" Walter asked.

"His job with the Fish and Game is hard on him, toting those containers of new-hatched fish into the backcountry. He's not as young as he used to be."

"Reckon none of us are." Walter continued to spit roofing nails to meet the blow of his hammer.

One evening as Fannie sat at the kitchen table writing a letter to her mother, Bill wearily added a few sticks of wood to the crackling fire in the stove and then sank onto a chair opposite her. "Fannie, I want to try to find my boy." When she raised her eyes to look at him, she saw that his face seemed drawn.

"I've been thinking about him, too, lately," she confessed.

"He'd be in his twenties now, I guess."

"But where will you look?"

"Don't know exactly. But I've got to try."

During their 1930 Christmas visit to the Beartooth, he went on into Helena to contact a lawyer. Fannie, glad that Bill wanted to find his son, was stunned by her mother's failing health. The once bright-eyed and energetic Rachel had become sunken and helpless, with a worsening senility that made it impossible to leave her unattended. Fannie could see the burden she had become for Walter and Fleta, who had added a baby daughter, Laura, to the family. Still, Fannie knew she could not keep her mother with her at Arrastra Creek through the packing seasons, let alone the difficult winters.

Because of the responsibility for Rachel that she had to bear, Fleta seemed curt and distant. The visit was not a pleasant one, and the Steeles left as soon as Bill returned from Helena. As he gunned the Model-A back over the snowy Divide, he reported on his mission. "I talked to a lawyer about Ivan. He'll get in touch with a detective agency in Kansas City."

When winter weather began to moderate, Fannie's nephews came to build a third cabin to bunk the growing number of hunters. Carrie's son Nick, a soft-spoken lad with a firm square jaw and powerful hands, brought the mail from Helmville. One day Bill opened an envelope postmarked Kansas City.

Glancing at the signature, he looked up in surprise. "It's from Ivan!"

"Already . . . ?" Fannie's voice trailed off as Bill read aloud.

Dear Dad. I sure didn't think I'd ever hear from you. I've been going to dental school and plan to set up a practice in California when I graduate. My wife, Mickey, has worked to put me through. We named our baby Ivan, too, but we call him Van so as not to get him mixed up with me. I'd like to visit you when I can. Your son, Ivan Steele.

"Bill, you're a grandfather!" They looked at each other in pleased amazement. "And Ivan's going to be a dentist. Oh, I can't wait till they can come."

"I'm not waiting," Bill said. "I'm going to Kansas City now, before our season starts." Next day, Fannie drove him to Drummond to take the train to Missouri.

When Bill returned, his report of the reunion was brief. "He's a smart boy. His wife works hard to help him. She's a good woman. And you should see the baby, Vannie. He's a cute little fella. They say he looks a lot like me."

"Will they be coming out?"

"I hope so."

Bill's stomach began to bother him after his trip to Missouri, and when Fannie took time out to ride Chief in the Fourth of July parade in Lincoln, he felt too ill to go. In August, nearly doubled over with pain, he admitted to Fannie, "Darned if I don't believe maybe I need to see a doc." Fannie drove him the 40 miles to Missoula in record time.

The doctor looked grave as he joined Fannie in the waiting room of the hospital where Bill had undergone tests. "Your husband is a sick man. I don't want to alarm you, but there's a possible malignancy. He needs immediate exploratory surgery." Fannie caught her breath. "We'll operate first thing in the morning," the doctor told her.

Fannie hurried down the hall to Bill's room, where he lay ashen with pain despite the sedatives. He turned and tried to smile as she pulled a chair close to the bed and sank into it, clasping his hand in hers.

"Well, champ," he murmured, "we sure drew a rank bronc this time."

"You'll be all right, Bill. Doctor says we're not to worry till we know for sure what it is."

"Fannie, I want to make out a will. I want to be sure Ivan gets what's rightfully his."

"You know I'll share with Ivan."

"I did wrong by him, and I want to make it up to him before it's too late. I may not pull through this, Fannie," he whispered.

"But you have to, Bill." Struggling to hold back her tears, she leaned close, her hand touching his face. "I'm not much without you. You know that." But his eyes were closed, and she wasn't sure he heard her.

Presently, he spoke again, almost inaudibly. "Get me some paper, Fannie. For the will."

Perhaps he was right. It was good to have a will. Just in case. She summoned a nurse, who tore a leaf from her notebook and gave it to him along with the pen from her pocket. Fannie propped the pillows and held the page on a tray so he could scratch a few lines.

I hereby give my share of the Steele ranch at Arrastra Creek to my son, Ivan Steele.

Beneath, he scrawled his signature, *Wallace S. Steele.*

Fannie spent a sleepless night at his bedside, and three endless hours pacing the corridor during the surgery the next morning. Bill has a lot of good years left, she thought. He's only fifty-four. A young man, really. Maybe I should have taken better care of him. I shouldn't have let him drink so much. All those bucking horses. He took his share of spills. Broken bones. Dislocated shoulders. But he's been healthy . . . till this. "Possible malignancy," the doctor had said. Did it mean . . . ? No. She refused to think of that. He *would* get well. He had to.

The doctor, still in his white surgical gown, came toward her, removing his face mask. "Your husband is doing well," he said. "He's going to be all right." Tears of relief filled her eyes, and the doctor took her hand. "He's had a serious operation, but we found no cancer. It's ileitis, an inflammation of the intestine. We had to remove part of the bowel, but he'll be good as new in a few weeks."

Fannie heard herself thank the doctor, then, trembling, she sank onto a bench. He's going to be all right! The rush of relief brought sobs that drained some of the tension of the past two days.

Shortly after Bill came home from the hospital, Ivan wrote that he was sorry his dad had been ill, and since he was packing up his wife and baby for their move to California, they would come through Montana to visit. Anticipating their arrival, Fannie slicked up the house and yards, groomed the horses, and laid in a supply of special groceries. She trimmed Bill's hair, and they both dressed in their best shirts and pants. When they finally saw the small rumble-seated coupe bumping toward the cabin, she helped Bill down the porch steps to greet the visitors.

"Say, you're hard to get to." Ivan walked toward them, a tall young man wearing glasses. Fannie saw at once his resemblance to Bill. He shook hands with his father, then with her.

"Welcome to Montana, Ivan." Just calling him by name had a strangeness to it. Like eating a food you'd often heard about but never tasted. You had to get used to it.

"Thanks." Ivan stretched his long arm toward the woman emerging from the coupe carrying a child. "This is Mickey." Mickey's reddish hair was permed and pinned back behind her ears. She proudly displayed the baby.

"Vannie's fifteen months old," she said. The little boy's large, blue eyes darted about the new surroundings, then settled on the cattle in the meadow. He pointed a tiny finger, his apple cheeks dimpled in delight. Fannie's heart melted. Little Van seemed more beautiful than any picture-book baby she'd ever seen. He looked somewhat like his mother. But he had Bill's eyes.

Ivan turned to Bill. "How are you feeling?"

"Not too bad." Bill would never admit how weak he felt.

"When we heard you were ailing, we thought we'd better come this way and cheer you up." Mickey smiled the broad grin of a girl who wanted to be liked. "Vannie came to see Grandpa, didn't you, Vannie?" She smoothed the boy's rumpled romper.

"You're just in time for tomorrow's trail ride," Fannie said. "Got a couple of dudes to entertain. Ever do any riding, Mickey?"

"Only as a kid. Ivan might like it, though, wouldn't you, Ivan?"

"Afraid I'd get saddle blisters. We can't stay long anyway. You go ahead, Fannie. We'll stay here and keep Dad company."

Two days later, shortly after Fannie returned from the pack trip, Ivan and his family left in the little roadster, almost as abruptly as they had come.

"It was good of Ivan to drive all this way," Fannie said.

"Probably thought I was going to kick off." Bill's voice was hard.

"Bill, what a thing to say."

"I want him to feel I'm his dad. But . . ." He turned his face away, his lips set in a grim line.

"But what?"

"He called me a sonofabitch and said it was about time I acted like a father."

Loved Ones Lost  26

The bleak winter blew in heavy snow, and Bill was frequently out of sorts. Fannie lavished attention on him, preparing his favorite meals and seeing to his comfort. Toward spring, while she prepared for the pack season, he gradually resumed his correspondence and was able to apply his growing strength to minor household chores. Fannie arranged for her nephew George Hilger to help out during the pack season, which proved to be an especially busy one with an overflow of guests week after week.

Between pack trips, even with her energetic niece Florence Hilger there doing the cooking, Fannie worked long hours mending clothes or tack, baking bread, tending stock, and helping George build a new chicken coop.

One late-June afternoon, when George had gone to Drummond to pick up a party of dudes, Bill offered to help the women by making biscuits for their supper. Hardly had he begun when he fell to the floor, out cold, the overturned batch of biscuit dough beside him.

Fannie knelt beside him, checking his breathing.

"What's the matter with him?" Florence anxiously hovered over them.

"He just keeled over." Fannie tried to keep calm while she hurried to wring a cloth in cool water from the water bucket and place it on Bill's forehead. His eyes opened. He seemed confused as he struggled to speak. "You fainted," she told him. "You've been overdoing." He seemed unable to use his right arm and leg but, by supporting him on either side, Fannie and Florence managed to get him to the bedroom and into bed.

"You rest now," Fannie soothed, covering him with the tattered wedding quilt. "We'll bring your supper in." Bill lay back and closed his eyes. Fannie motioned Florence outside and closed the door.

"What made him faint, Aunt Fannie? Is he sick again?"

Fannie walked silently into the kitchen and began to clean up the ruined biscuit batter. "I think he may have had a stroke." Though her voice remained steady, her heart pounded with fear.

In their concern, they failed to notice the sound of a saddle horse approaching and the rider's footsteps on the porch until a voice called out. "Anybody home?" In walked an athletic-looking woman in jodhpurs and riding boots and carrying a basket. Her windblown hair formed a bright, golden halo around her face in the late-afternoon light. "I'm Lois Parker, your new neighbor."

Fannie got to her feet, brushing the floury biscuit dough from her hands. "I heard someone bought the ranch down yonder. Pleased to meet you. I'm Fannie Steele, and this is my niece Florence."

Lois grasped their hands. Her wide, engaging smile produced similar responses from Fannie and Florence.

"We just had a little accident here." Fannie went back to wiping up the floor. "My husband don't feel too good."

"I heard he had surgery." Lois's smile changed to an expression of concern. "I hope he's doing all right. Folks in town speak highly of you both."

"He's resting." Fannie was too upset to go into the whole story.

"I couldn't wait to get acquainted, so I brought you some homemade deer sausage and a bowl of potato salad. There's some huckleberry jam here, too."

"Well, you're an angel in disguise." Fannie said. "We got people coming tonight and nothing ready to feed them. Florence, let's get this meal together before George gets back with the dudes. Maybe Lois will stay for supper, too."

"I'd love to," Lois said. "My husband, Lloyd, works for the railroad, and he's gone a lot." Lois not only stayed for supper, she stayed the night as well, first helping Fannie settle the guests, then helping organize supplies for the next day's pack trip. When everything was ready, she and Fannie sat up talking until nearly midnight. Fannie poured out her anguish about Bill's health, though he seemed fine after the fainting episode, and his right arm and leg had returned to normal.

"If you need help," Lois offered, "or just moral support, let me know.

With Lloyd away so much, I get lonesome."

"I know what you mean," Fannie said.

"As much as I like my horses," Lois confessed, "I feel isolated out here. With no children to come and visit, we don't see many people. I envy your busy life, Fannie, with your guests and all."

Fannie chuckled. "Well, it does keep me hopping. No time to feel blue. Least not in the summertime." Then she added, "If I do, Curly, here, cheers me up." She patted the black-and-white dog at her feet. "He's a smart one. Understands everything I say."

"I want to meet those high-school horses I've heard so much about."

"You bet. And wait till you see Young Daisy's pretty new colt. I've named her Princess." Talk centered on horses until the two women could no longer keep their eyes open. Lois spent the night on the living-room couch. Next morning, Fannie and her fishing party hit the trail, their bellies warmed by Lois's special flapjacks and the remainder of the deer sausage and huckleberry jam.

Bill's health improved, but Fannie now received regular urgent pleas for help from Carrie, who went daily to assist Fleta in caring for their mother. Rachel, her rationality gone, fought all efforts to make her comfortable.

"Just bathing her is more than we can manage." Carrie's letters repeated the difficulties in detail, and Fannie was troubled at not being able to help. With Bill dependent on her, she couldn't leave him to go over the mountain that winter, yet she couldn't bear not being able to be with her mother, the dear, wonderful woman who had given her so much and who needed her now.

Fannie was even more tied down with dudes during the spring of 1934 and on through summer and fall. That season, at the peak of the national depression, railroads offered special rates to passengers bound for Montana and Wyoming guest ranches, joining with the Dude Ranchers Association to induce easterners to travel to the wide-open spaces. Hard times, having hampered travel to Europe and other more costly vacations, seemed to spur lengthy visits to western ranches.

Though unable to do heavy work or packing, Bill never tired of entertaining their guests with his tall stories—nor of the profits that topped all previous years.

Around Thanksgiving, Rachel took a turn for the worse and Carrie urged Fannie to come at once. She hurriedly bundled a few things and drove the 80 long miles over the Divide to Carrie's homestead, where Rachel Sperry lay dying. Entering the small, back bedroom, she saw her mother lying, fragile as ashes, under her quilts. "Hello, Ma."

The senile woman opened her eyes and looked wildly about the room. "It's Fannie, Ma. I've come to take care of you."

"Fannie . . ."

"Yes, Ma." As she clasped the parchment hand, Rachel sighed deeply and closed her eyes. Fannie sat beside the bed for a long while. When at last she rose and went into the kitchen, Carrie met her gaze with tears in her eyes.

"She had a real bad spell yesterday. She thought Fleta and I were trying to hurt her. She said if it weren't for Dad's rupture, he'd take a stick to us. Oh, Fannie." Carrie wept on her sister's shoulder. "I'm so glad you're here."

December snow swept across the Beartooth, then lay on the land as silent as the tiny form of the dying woman lying in the back bedroom. Fannie slept on a cot beside her beloved mother, who never recognized her after that first glimmer of response the day she arrived. Three days before Christmas the final flutter of the eighty-nine-year-old woman's breath faded into the stillness.

When Bertha came, the three sisters cried together. Tears of grief for the lost Rachel. For their lost beginnings. Walter and Fleta cried with them, their tears also expressing sad relief from the burden they had borne the past few difficult years. Fannie's heart went out to Fleta, and she hoped they could be better friends.

On Christmas Eve, Rachel Schrader Sperry was laid to rest beside her husband in the small cemetery north of Helena.

The following summer, 1935, Ivan wrote that his dental practice in Apple Valley was doing sufficiently well to allow him, Mickey, and little Van a Montana vacation. Fannie was overjoyed. Vannie was now going on six.

Bill, too, welcomed them eagerly. Ivan had grown more mature, Fannie thought. More meat on his six-foot-two frame. But his hands were soft and white. Like a dentist. She smiled at the thought. Mickey looked wonderful in her California sports clothes. Vannie delighted them all, running first to the shed, then to the meadow, then checking out the stock, the chickens,

Curly, and the cats—all the new excitement of the ranch.

"Your practice going good?" Bill passed Ivan the platter of beef and browned potatoes as they seated themselves around the supper table.

"Can't complain." Ivan's response was as curt as Bill's question.

"Well, I got three horses just itching to take you up to Copper Lake," Fannie said. "I hope you brought your riding britches."

"We sure did." Mickey took dainty portions from the heavily laden platter. "I want Vannie to learn to ride."

"Can I ride Chief, Grandma?" the little boy asked.

Fannie chuckled. "Not Chief. But I think your Grandpa has a surprise for you."

"A surprise for me, Grandpa?"

"Well now, let's see." Bill pretended to be studying the boy. "If you're as good a cowboy as I think you are, I just might have a pinto pony for you. And a little saddle, just your size."

"For me?" The keen blue eyes sparkled. "Oh, boy!"

"That's right, young fella. Right after supper you can ride him."

"You shouldn't give him a pony," Mickey said, obviously pleased. "You'll spoil him."

"But I want to." Bill beamed at the little boy shoveling down his supper as fast as he could.

Ivan sat stony-faced.

"Isn't that wonderful, Ivan?" Mickey said. "A pony for Vannie."

"That's more than he ever gave me." Ivan stood abruptly and left the table.

Mickey tried to smooth over Ivan's behavior. "He'll be all right. He's moody sometimes."

Vannie took to the pony with great delight, and under Fannie's supervision he was soon loping across the meadow and back, bouncing along in the tiny saddle.

"Why don't you let Vannie stay with us for a while?" Fannie suggested on the last day of the tense visit as Ivan loaded suitcases into the car. "He likes it here, and we sure would enjoy having him around."

Mickey looked expectantly at her husband.

"No, he's too young." And almost before proper good-byes could be said, Ivan had herded his family into the car and shifted it into motion across the meadow. Fannie and Bill stood watching it pass through the gate and out of sight down the mountain. They gazed after the visitors for a long moment, as if not moving would somehow bridge the unexpressed emotion between them and those now on their way back to California.

Finally Bill spoke. "I gave him the will, Fannie."

"What will?"

"The one I wrote out in Missoula . . . giving him my share of the ranch. I thought it might . . . well, might bring us closer."

The realization brought a sinking feeling to the pit of her stomach. "Does that mean he owns half the place now? Has half the say so?"

Bill nodded. "Right now he's too busy to think about anything but building up his practice. He likes you, Fannie. He says he'll do right by you when I'm gone."

Fannie stood stunned, the full impact of Bill's action too unsettling to acknowledge. "You're not going anywhere, Bill, for a long, long time."

"I've hurt him, Fannie. I don't think things can ever be right between us. But at least he knows I care about him. That his dad isn't some saddle tramp who can't leave him anything."

In the following weeks, Fannie hardly had time to sort out her ambivalent feelings, and there was no further mention of Ivan's legacy, though the fact hovered ever present. Bill seemed dispirited and ill. Sometimes he sat in the kitchen all day waiting until it was time to make biscuits or peel potatoes for supper.

Still, he kept up with the rodeo news in the newspaper. "Says here the Brander sisters rode in the annual World's Championship Rodeo in Chicago. They've made quite a name for themselves."

Fannie smiled. "Those two ragtag kids." It gave her special pleasure to recall the excitement of a bucking horse twisting beneath her, the roar of the crowds. That roar was the most beautiful sound in the world. One she would never forget.

Anna Pauls came for a visit. Having shed her first husband and worked as a cook in Alaska for a time, she had remarried and settled in Seattle. Looking at the short, plump body of her old friend, Fannie couldn't imagine her bounding on and off a relay horse. They reminisced, laughing and joking. After Anna left, Fannie, perhaps inspired by the visit to bring back the old days, rode an exhibition bronc at a Helmville rodeo. At fifty years old, she was as lean and fit as she had been when she rode to fame as one of the Montana Girls thirty years before.

One evening, Bill insisted he didn't feel up to making the biscuits for supper and asked Fannie to make them. Fannie, getting supplies ready for a pack trip the next day, said she didn't have time. "Besides, you never liked my biscuits," she added. But she gave in, tossed all the ingredients hurriedly into a bowl, slopped the batter with a big spoon onto a pan, and jammed the doughy blobs into the oven.

At supper, an expression of amazement came over Bill's face as he tasted the unexpectedly delicate biscuits. "These are the best I ever ate," he said.

Fannie chuckled. "I think I've found the secret. You have to make biscuits like you just don't give a darn." From that day on, Bill never made another biscuit.

Lois Parker became an invaluable friend, providing a ready ear and helpful hands when Fannie needed them. Carrie's third daughter, Viola, came to help out, too, along with Hallie, her youngest.

One hot day in August of 1940, Fannie and Hallie, who had been stacking hay, paused for their noon meal. As they entered the house, they found Bill struggling to breath. "Help me, Fannie," he gasped. His hands clutched at her overalls, his face distorted.

With pounding heart, Fannie reassured him. "Just take it easy. We'll get you to the doctor." She looked desperately at Hallie. "Hurry, get the car!"

Hallie's face turned white. "George took the car to Lincoln to be worked on!"

No car. Fannie knew that the Parkers weren't home and there was no one close by who could help. "Take Warbonnet and ride into Helmville," she directed. "Find a telephone and call your pa."

Fannie propped Bill with pillows to ease his breathing. But it was more than two hours before Joe Hilger came speeding across the meadow, and they began the terrible trip to Helena. Joe drove at breakneck speed over the mountain roads while Fannie held her husband in her arms, murmuring words of comfort he never heard.

That night in a Helena hospital, Bill Steele died.

Life with Beloved Horses  27

The country cemetery lay on the summer-browned flats, a small patch of green bordered by tall pines that hovered above the scattered tombstones and shaded the automobiles clustered on its dusty road.

Fannie avoided looking at the coffin, the plain box of polished pine that held the still body of her heart's partner. Instead, she focused on two small stone markers beside the gaping grave. Datus E. Sperry, 1842–1914. Rachel S. Sperry, 1845–1934. Soon another would rest beside them. Wallace S. Steele, 1876–1940. Such small stones to commemorate such precious lives.

"Bill Steele was a famous rodeo clown in his day," someone murmured.

"The best," another said.

Yes. A rodeo clown. And yes. The best. Fannie bit her lip to hold back the tears. Oh, why did he leave me here all alone?

Fleta gently placed her gloved hand over Fannie's work-roughened fingers. "Why don't you come home with us for a few days?"

"Thanks, Fleta, but Ivan is driving me home."

Ivan took her arm and guided her toward his big, green Buick. He had come immediately when she called. She appreciated that. He was family after all. Bill's son. He helped her into the car and they drove from the cemetery.

"He suffered terribly before he died," she said when they had driven for some time in silence. "Almost an invalid toward the end. I tended him like a baby."

"I know, Fannie. It's a blessing he's at peace." Ivan had cried during the service.

Fannie's eyes welled up again. "When you tend someone like that, that person becomes even closer and dearer. It's hard to let go."

Ivan nodded, his smooth white hands gripping the wheel. "Have you thought about getting some permanent help at the ranch?"

Fannie shook her head.

"I think you should, Fannie. Walter mentioned a fellow who's looking for a job. Says he's a good foreman. Name's Homer Reinoehl."

Fannie remembered the words of Wild Bill Revelle many years before in New York. As her Bill lay in the dust after being thrown by a bronc, Wild Bill had remarked to Guy Weadick, "Bill Steele could be dead and in heaven, and Fannie would still ride those broncs." A sad smile tightened the corners of her mouth. Wild Bill must have been something of a prophet. Of course, she must carry on. No time for grieving. Hunting season was almost upon them. Much needed doing. She managed an appreciative nod for Ivan. "I'll write to Walter and have him send this Homer around."

But her heart was heavy as they came up the Arrastra Creek road. She felt the aching beauty of the mountain, of the pines and tamaracks pushing toward the sky, the grazing horses coming to alert as the car approached. Only it all seemed different now without Bill. They pulled up to the meadow gate, and Fannie got out to open it as she had done countless times before. As she released the latch, grief flooded in. Clutching the gate post, she wept. Bill was gone. His life, her life . . . What had it all meant?

Ivan came to her from the Buick, and she recovered her composure, dabbing her eyes with her crumpled handkerchief. "I'm all right," she said, swinging the gate wide. Ivan got back in his car and drove through, but she waved him on. "I'll come on by myself," she called. She closed the gate and walked across the meadow toward the house, her attention drawn to the crest of the mountain where the setting sun caught the tops of the pines like a halo of hope.

When Lois came running out to meet her, Curly at her heels, Fannie shrugged off her embrace. "Lois, where's my red hunting cap?"

Lois grinned. "Hanging behind the kitchen door where it always is."

"I'll have to apply for an outfitter's license. Do you think they'll give one to a woman?"

"They'll give one to you," Lois said.

A few days later, at age fifty-three, she became the first woman to be licensed as a wilderness guide in the state of Montana. Despite her grief and loneliness, she pitched in to preparations for the coming hunting season. She would need her guests now, more than ever, along with the old friends and fans who continued to stop by.

Homer Reinoehl arrived just before the hunters. A tall, rugged man in his late thirties with wayward, brown hair and gentle gray eyes, he carried a lumpy duffel bag.

"Walter said you needed a hand." He set the bag near the shed where Fannie worked at replacing shoes on the pack string. "My gatherin's," he said, nodding toward the duffel.

"Do you know horses?" Fannie looked at his large, gnarled hands.

"Ain't nothin' I know better."

"Good hand with a rifle?"

"Yes, ma'am. Brought my .30-30." Again, he nodded toward the duffel.

Fannie liked his straightforward manner. "I'm getting ready for hunters. Think you could finish up on Gus here?" She handed him the hammer.

After getting her approval on Gus's well-shod feet, Homer helped milk and separate before washing up for supper. "You got a nice place here," he said, joining Fannie and Lois at the table.

"There's none better," Fannie said. "Where you from, Homer?"

"Been ramroddin' operations of one kind or other around Montana. Came from Canada originally. It just never seemed to work out that I could stay in one place."

Fannie noticed he didn't lack for a healthy appetite. "I need someone for the season."

Homer's earnest gray eyes conveyed dependability. "I'd be much obliged to have the job." He patted Curly, who sat wagging his tail beside Homer's chair.

"Got a hunting party coming in tonight," Fannie said, "and I'll be hitting the trail early in the morning. After morning milking, you could clean the manure out of the shed, then we need to start laying up wood." She indicated an axe standing in the corner. "I've cut all the downfall close by, so you'll have to go back up the hill a ways."

Homer nodded.

"And the fence needs bracing on the far side of the meadow." She pointed across the broad expanse behind the haystacks.

"Yes, ma'am." Homer grinned.

"Hate to start you right out cutting wood, but what needs doin' needs doin'."

The hunting party, two couples from Missoula, arrived after supper. Fannie acquainted them with their cabins, then invited them to sit a spell in the front room to enjoy some of Lois's popcorn. Homer joined the group, carrying a guitar. "Fannie, what would you think of me singin' some songs for the folks?"

"Well, that'd be real nice." Fannie introduced him to the guests, and he strummed a few chords. "If you folks know these songs," he said, "you just help me out." Then he began to sing "Red River Valley." His melodic baritone soon had the Missoula couples joining in on the choruses.

Fannie and Lois stood listening. As he launched into "When the Work's All Done This Fall," they looked at each other with raised eyebrows. "I think you got yourself more than a ranch hand," Lois whispered.

In the weeks to come, Homer's songs and good humor went over well with the guests. And his efficiency around the place impressed Fannie. He handled the horses nearly as well as she did. "Don't know how I got along without him," she told Lois.

"He's good company for you." Lois grinned. "And did you notice something else? Even Curly likes him."

After hunting season ended, Fannie and Homer sat down to settle accounts, and she paid him his wages. "Don't leave much to show for a busy season, does it?" She spread the remaining cash on the table. "With thirty ponies to winter down the mountain at three dollars a head, that's ninety dollars just for those little devils. Looks like I won't be able to start the new barn this year."

"Can't you cut expenses somewhere?"

"I've already cut to the bone."

"Buildin' that new barn makes more sense than paying pasture rent. If I get to work on it, we could store enough hay to keep the horses *here* next year."

"Truth is, Homer, I can't afford to pay you over the winter."

His weathered cheeks crinkled with good humor. "I don't have nothin' else to do. I could help you out through the winter just for my board and room."

"Homer, that's good of you, but . . ."

"No buts. You're a fine woman, Fannie. I reckon it's my job to see that you don't winter-kill." They laughed. "Now, about the barn," he went on. "Maybe I could lend you a little for materials so we can get the thing started."

"Why, I couldn't take your money, Homer." Fannie sat silent for a moment. "But I tell you what. I got a fine saddle. Hand tooled and silver mounted. One of those Missoula dudes wanted to buy it. Made me a good offer."

Homer frowned. "Not the one you won at Calgary?"

Fannie nodded. "I reckon I need a barn a whole lot more'n I need that saddle." She turned in early that night.

When December snows stopped work on the new barn, Fannie and Homer selected a meadow site for the second well they planned to put down. They made plans for other improvements, too, while sitting at the kitchen table each evening after supper until Homer retired to the lakeside cabin.

"We'll give you colties a better winter this year for sure," Fannie promised her horses that spring. But she and Homer packed almost continuously all season, and progress on the barn was slow. By December the structure still lacked two walls and a roof, and the heavy snow cover forced Fannie to again trail the horses over to Drummond for the winter, keeping only a few at the ranch. Parting from her pintos each year was hard for Fannie. Young Daisy's filly, Princess, a well-marked piebald, was one of the prettiest yet, and she made plans to begin breaking her in the spring.

As she rode back across the meadow, Homer came running from the cabin in his shirt sleeves. "The Japanese have bombed Hawaii!" he shouted. "President Roosevelt just declared war."

Homer left the next day to enlist in the army. "I'm sorry to leave you to winter by yourself, Fannie, but it's something I have to do." His usually jovial face looked grim as he shook her hand and said good-bye. "This war should be over by spring."

Losing Homer seemed a sacrifice for the war effort that Fannie was willing to make. She knew he'd be back as soon as it was over. Her niece Vi, now a young woman of eighteen whose dark hair and blue eyes showed the family resemblance, came to spend the winter. Fannie enjoyed her company, and they lavished attention on the few remaining horses and on the dog, Curly, who could close the door on command and perform many other tricks requiring surprising intelligence and devotion to his mistress. In return, Curly received the bulk of Fannie's affection, along with the horses and an assortment of cats.

Christmas Eve, having been unable to get through the snow to buy Vi a present, Fannie wrapped two new gray kittens in a large box for her niece. Unaccustomed to such individual attention in her large family, Vi beamed with delight when she tore off the wrapping and out popped the two kittens. One had a red bow around its neck with its name "Merry" printed on it. The other had a green bow labeled "Christmas."

"Oh, Aunt Fannie." Vi hugged the kittens, then Fannie, then the kittens again. "This is the nicest Christmas I ever had."

Christmas morning, under a heavy sky, they snowshoed up the mountain and brought back three grouse for their dinner. Ivan and Mickey had sent a Christmas card, but Fannie did not receive it until the county plowed the road in mid-January and she was able to get through to Helmville to pick up her mail.

Despite the war, Fannie's reputation as an outfitter grew. Once again the affluent, unable to travel abroad and limited by gas rationing, found the railroads, though crowded with servicemen, convenient transportation to western dude ranches, and Fannie's summer and fall seasons continued fully booked. Florence and Bea had married, and while nephews George, Nick, Matthew, and Charles served their country on the western European front, Fannie depended on nieces Betty, Hallie, and Vi, along with Lois Parker, for much-needed help on the ranch.

The war dragged on, and winter again brought the tranquil quiet of heavy snows. Fannie whiled away the long evenings writing to Homer and her nephews in the army, her sisters, former ranch guests, and old friends whose letters rekindled the warmth of times they had shared as stampede performers. The hours she spent at her correspondence became a treasured time, and when the roads drifted full and she could no longer get through to the Helmville post office to receive her mail, she began to keep a diary.

NOVEMBER: *Had a kind of young blizzard last night. Wind drifted my trail in so me and Princess had to break it out again. Snow is knee-deep here. Rains and chinooks don't seem to take it down much. The canyon was all ice last time I was down.*

FEBRUARY: *If Warbonnet does have another colt it would be from Sundog, but she always carries quite a belly, so there might not be any coltie. Echo's won't come until April. Might be good to get her away from Warbonnet, who'll try to steal a colt from its mother if she can. When Red Cloud was only a few days old, she ran right in between Goldie and him and kicked the dickens out of Goldie. Kept the colt on the opposite side. Was cute to see, but afraid she'll kill the colt if it gets in the way of her heels. Ponimay is another one crazy about colts. Last fall she'd follow that yearling Shetland around and wouldn't let any other horses come near.*

DECEMBER: *Old Daisy don't look very good. This hay is so dry and hard, she can't eat much of it without teeth. Only takes the ground feed I got for her. Belle and Goldie are down the valley being fed. They both look like they'll have twins. When I harnessed them I had to walk around to snap the quarter strap. Couldn't reach it underneath them.*

As the years passed, Fannie made occasional entries in her diary, noting the month but not the year.

APRIL: *Coyote hides are sure down.*

OCTOBER: *Matthew and Charles must be prisoners of war, or Carrie would have heard by now. I feel fine except for a little rheumatism.*

MARCH: *Star's colt arrived on Sunday. It's sorrel and white, marked a good deal like Warbonnet only with glass eyes. Sure pretty. Bonnie's came yesterday evening after I put her in the shed. It's a mouse color with a big star that covers his whole face, with a white front and hind foot on opposite sides. Two hours later, Princess had her new colt. Black and white. About half as big as the others. She can walk right under her mama's flanks without bending, but her legs are long enough so she can get her meals. Think she'll be a race horse. Bonnie's colt must be from Ribbon. Looks just like him. Wish he'd stay blue, but suppose he'll shed off black.*

JANUARY: *Eight more inches of snow. Shoveled twenty inches off the shed roof. Went and got my two milk cows because one was ready to freshen. Got a black heifer calf. Pumping water is the worst, but I ought to be glad there's water in the well to pump, I guess.*

MARCH: *Glad Carrie finally heard from Charlie overseas. Tomorrow I'll walk to Lubecks and see if he'll bring 500 pounds of oats, five gallons of honey, a gallon of coal oil, and some block salt and leave it at the fork of the road below the gate. Then I'll have to figure out how I'm going to bring it the rest of the way through the snow. Can't do much with the team when the colts are so young, nor Old Daisy either. Flash is too darn poorly to use much. I think it's her teeth. Don't know how I can fix them alone. Two hands aren't enough to hold her and file her teeth at the same time. Sure got trimmed when I traded for her.*

DECEMBER: *Maybe I'll hitch up the Shetlands to the sled and bring the grain up that way. Wish I had that black work mare I sold. It's hell to be afoot with five horses on the place.*

Broken Promise

28

Homer came back from the war just before hunting season in 1945 and picked up where he'd left off nearly four years before. Once again the partnership blossomed. One evening he sat down to supper in a jolly mood. "Fannie, I'm tired of looking at that half-done barn. I think I got the answer."

"What's that?" Fannie felt in high spirits now that Homer, with his easy-going manner and dependable help, was back.

"I saved some money while I was overseas. Why don't I chip in some every month and manage the place for you? Call it a lease if you want. You're a strong woman, Fannie. But you're not as young as you used to be. You should be slowing down a little."

"Fiddlesticks. My ma rode horses till she was past eighty. I've a notion I will, too."

"Riding is a darn sight easier than outfitting and guiding. Packing's backbreaking work. Not to mention riding herd on hunters." He paused, awaiting her answer. "How about it, Fannie? Why don't you let me handle all that? You'll have a regular monthly income, and I'll carry most of the work-load."

"But I don't see what's in it for you. This ranch ain't going to make any-body rich."

"The way I look at it, it'll be an investment in the place—in my future here. You'll still have the run of the place. But when you want to slow down, then I'll take over."

He's young and strong, she thought. And we get along so well together— working, sharing. We even think alike. I like him. And I need him.

"Can't think of anyone I'd rather have take over when I'm gone." She reached across the table and patted his big paw of a hand. "I'll draw up a lease arrangement."

The lease arrangement worked extremely well for several years, during which time Fannie was able to lessen her workload while continuing to enjoy her horses and the life of a dude-ranch operator. Then, on a midsummer morning in 1952, Fannie rose before dawn to bring in the horses and prepare breakfast for a group Homer was packing to Copper Lake. He had saddled eight horses and mantied supplies for the four-day trip onto four pack animals. The riders were mounting up in front of the cabin when Fannie noticed a big car coming through the gate.

As the black Chrysler neared, she recognized the driver and ran to meet him. "Ivan. What a surprise!"

"Hello, Fannie." He got out and gave her a quick peck on the cheek. "How are you?"

"Still in the saddle."

"Good to see you looking so well. Mickey sends her love."

"Well, where is she? And Vannie? Couldn't they come along?"

"Not this time. This is just a quick business trip."

"You got business in Helena?"

"No, not exactly." Ivan glanced at the mounted dudes who waited for Homer's signal to head out. "Fannie, could we go inside and talk?"

Fannie searched his face for a clue to this mysterious visit, then led the way into the kitchen.

"Fannie, I'll come right to the point." Ivan pulled out a chair and sat, protecting the knife-sharp creases of his pants. "I want to buy you out."

"Buy me out?" Fannie was puzzled. "But why? You know this place is half yours, and you're welcome to come anytime."

"It's more than half mine, Fannie."

"More than half? What do you mean?"

"Under the laws of this state, a wife inherits only one-third of her husband's property. When Dad made out that will giving his share of the ranch to me, legally he gave me two-thirds of the place. You own only a third."

"What are you talking about?" Fannie sank onto a chair, her eyes fixed on Ivan's. His expression remained businesslike.

"I have the majority interest. I can do what I want with the property."

Fannie stared, not believing her ears.

"I want to do right by you, Fannie. You're a nice lady, and you've always treated me fine. But . . . well, I need to get my finances in order. And frankly, this whole thing weighs on my mind."

"Weighs on your mind?" Fannie stood, her voice also rising. "I've put my lifeblood into this ranch, built it year by year into what it is today. You've no right to tell me what to do."

"I'm afraid I have. Fannie, I'm trying to be nice to you."

"Nice?" Fannie shouted.

Homer, uneasy about Ivan's visit, had delayed starting the pack trip, and hearing the loud voices, he came hurrying into the kitchen. "What's going on here?"

"Thank goodness you haven't gone yet." Fannie moved toward her trusted friend. "Ivan says . . ."

"Homer, maybe you can make Fannie see reason. I've offered to buy out her small share in this place." Ivan repeated the explanation he had given Fannie.

"God O'Mighty!" Homer's face reddened with anger. "You'd do that to Fannie?"

"It has nothing to do with my feeling for Fannie. Sometimes hard necessity forces an issue, and this is one of those times. I have to have this place in my name so I can borrow against it to put my finances in order. Fannie can stay on the place and continue to operate the pack business. It's just that total ownership will be in my name. Either that or you can buy me out."

"No, Ivan, I won't sell and I don't have the money to buy you out." Fannie left no doubt that she meant what she said.

Homer stepped forward. "I'll buy you out, Ivan."

"You?" Ivan looked at the rough cowhand. "You got the money?"

"Part of it. And I can get the rest. Or I can pay you in payments."

"No, I need it all. Now." Ivan put his hand to his forehead in exasperation. "Don't you see, I stand to lose everything if I don't get my hands on some cash right away."

"Be reasonable, man. What's your rush?" Homer glanced out the window at the waiting riders, eight paying guests growing restless for their pack trip.

"Homer loves this place as much as I do," Fannie pleaded. "He's worked harder here than anyone. He deserves to buy it. You have no real interest in it."

"That isn't the point. I've invested in a string of Laundromats that aren't doing too well, and . . ." He raised his voice and whirled to face Homer. "Damn it, either you get me the money today, or I buy Fannie out. With the title papers to this ranch as collateral, I can borrow on it to get the cash I need."

Anger now flushed over Homer's ruddy cheeks. "What's the matter with you, Ivan? Can't you see those folks out there waitin' for me to pack 'em up to Copper Lake? I'll be back in four days. Then I'll get you a down payment."

"No down payment. It's one hundred percent cash or nothing."

Homer made a gesture of futility. He went out the door, took up Warbonnet's reins, and led the group of riders across the meadow toward the forest trail.

Ivan took a packet of legal papers from his pocket and spread them on the table, placing a pen beside them. "I've had the ranch appraised at twenty-one thousand six hundred dollars, Fannie. That's a fair price, don't you think?"

"Well, it may be a fair price, but . . ."

"That makes your share worth about thirty-six hundred. This paper is drawn up stating that I'll pay you fifty dollars a month for the next six years." He searched her face. "Fannie, this is very important to me. I'll lose my Laundromats if I don't get my hands on some cash."

Fannie studied his eyes. So like Bill's. He *was* Bill's son. And he needed help. "If I sign, you're saying I can stay and operate the place same as always?"

"That's right."

Bill would have wanted me to help Ivan, she thought. And this regular income would help me get through the winters. "But Homer had his heart set on buying the place someday," she told Ivan. "I can't sell him out for a bunch of washing machines."

"Fannie, be realistic. Homer will never come up with the money. He's a dreamer. He'd need more that eighteen thousand dollars to buy me out."

"That's a lot of money," Fannie murmured.

"Trust me. I have your best interests at heart. And Homer's, too. You can both go on operating the place as long as you want. I won't bother you. Believe me, Fannie. You know Dad wanted me to have the ranch someday." He held his finger to the dotted line for her signature.

Maybe Ivan was right. With tears welling, she picked up the pen and signed her name.

Ivan prepared to leave the ranch immediately, refusing Fannie's offer of a bite to eat. "I want to get to Helena and have these papers recorded," he said. As he crossed to the door, Curly crouched low and growled.

Good Lord, what have I done? Fannie thought. Even Curly thinks there's something fishy about all this.

But Ivan was across the porch and moving toward his car. Fannie followed, raising her hand as if to stop him from carrying her heart away. Ivan now owned the ranch, the thing most precious to her in this world. At the car door, he turned. "Don't be so glum, Fannie. Nothing has changed. I'll send your check the first of the month, every month." He got into the car and started the motor. The smooth hum of the engine hurried her questions.

"But when will you be back again? How is Vannie? Is he getting big?"

"We'll try to come when we can. Good-bye, Fannie." He turned the car and sped across the meadow. Fannie watched as he stopped to open the gate, drove through, and closed it behind him. Then the Chrysler moved down the road and was lost in the trees.

When Homer came out of the mountains four days later, Fannie avoided looking at him. Facing a wild bronc was nothing compared to having to tell the gentle Homer that his dream of owning the ranch had been dashed. He, too, seemed to avoid her until the packs had been unloaded and the dudes settled into their cabins for the night. Then he came into the kitchen, where she sat waiting. He placed his hat on the table and sat down. He said nothing, merely looked at her, waiting for her explanation of what had taken place after he left. Fannie bit her lip. Words were hard to form.

"Guess it's bad news," Homer said.

Fannie nodded.

"Damn that Ivan." Homer exploded. "What right does he have to come barging in here?"

"None, really." Fannie gazed beyond the distressed Homer and out the window into the gathering darkness. "But now he's got the ranch."

"You sold out?"

Fannie nodded again.

"Damn you, too, Fannie. How could you do a thing like that?" Homer swept his hat from the table and stood abruptly.

Fannie looked at him, pleading for him to understand. "Don't you see? He already owned most of it. What say would I have in anything, anyway?"

"We could have got a lawyer or something."

"No, Homer. It'll be all right. He says we can stay here as long as we want. We'll go on operating the place. And we'll have the extra fifty dollars every month."

"I suppose he wants his cut, then."

"He didn't say anything about that. He simply wanted to get his financial affairs in order."

Homer's skeptical gaze held hers as he sank onto his chair once more.

"Homer, Ivan is Bill's son."

"I don't like the way he handled this whole thing."

"Well, nothing is changed, really. And now with the extra money, we should be able to finish the barn and make other improvements."

"No, Fannie. Not now. It wouldn't make sense to put my heart and soul into somebody else's place." Homer sat for a long moment without speaking. Finally, he raised his head and looked at her.

"I'm going, Fannie. I can't stay here now. There's no future in it for me." For a moment, she thought he was joking. But she could see he wasn't.

"Homer, you can't leave. I can't get along without you."

"I've been drifting all my life, Fannie. I got to get settled somewhere. I'm sorry. You're about the finest woman I ever knew. I wanted this to be it."

Fannie felt leaden. Numbed. She wanted to reach out to Homer, to hold him there. But she had no right to do that. An owl hooted somewhere up on the mountain. A lonely sound.

"I'll be going, then, right after hunting season." He took his hat from the table and moved across the kitchen toward the door. Like the motion in a dream, Fannie watched him push open the screen. He stepped out on the porch. He walked into the night. What was left of her heart went with him.

Survival and Contentment  29

Spring returned to the mountains, rekindling Fannie's wonder at the great renewal and strengthening her belief that each plant, each creature, was an important link in the grand scheme of things—lowly moss to towering tamarack, timid field mouse to fearsome grizzly. She walked the forest, discovering wood violets and jack-in-the-pulpit, savoring the rich, moist smell of humus. The ranch seemed a world in itself, its meadow, lake, woodland, and mountainside unfolding nature's endless variety of surprises.

With the lazy sounds of summer came the pleasant whir of the sickle mower; Otto Eder had come to cut the first hay. Otto, a stocky German with a flourishing mustache, and his wife, Jennie, a comely Flathead Indian woman, owned a ranch in the valley near Helmville. Fannie was readying packs for a fishing party when a car drove up and a young man in a seersucker suit got out.

"I'm looking for Fannie Steele." He puffed on a small pipe as he eyed the packhorses and the fishermen mounting up. Fannie stepped forward.

"I'm Fannie Steele." In her old fishing clothes, the sixty-six-year-old woman was indistinguishable from the rugged anglers she guided.

The young man looked surprised. "I'm from *Life* magazine. I've read some newspaper stories about you, and I'd like to do an interview."

"Can't right now." Fannie picked up Paint's reins. "I'm packing in a bunch to Meadow Creek. You fish?"

"No, and I have to get back, so I'd appreciate it if you could talk with me now. The interview should only take a couple of hours."

Fannie stepped up into her saddle, ready to start off.

"You don't understand," the young man persisted. "I want to do a feature on you for *Life* magazine." He enunciated the magazine name as if Fannie hadn't heard him the first time.

"Maybe some other time, sonny. Got guests here." She nudged Paint, and the reporter was left standing in the corral looking after the string of mounted fishermen that followed her up the forest trail.

A few minutes later, Otto noticed Fannie coming back, leading a packhorse. "That city fella's gone," he called.

"I didn't come back for him," she fumed. "This knothead keeps trying to shed his pack."

Otto watched as she led the packhorse into the corral and untied his load. Scouting about for several rocks, the biggest she could lift, she wrapped them in the manties and lashed them to the packsaddle. The disgruntled animal bucked and kicked, groaned and heaved, twisted and shook, gamely trying every trick he knew, plus some he learned on the spot, to shake the weight from his back. Fannie sat quietly by until he tired, his defiance spent. Then, she released her hitches and dropped the rocks to the ground, repacked the original load, and rode off after the fishing party leading the now-docile packhorse.

Otto smiled under his mustache. He had an amusing story to tell Jennie that night.

Fannie's grandnephew, David Lake, teenage son of Carrie's daughter Florence, came to help out that season. Bright and interested in all that went on, the slim, sandy-haired youth became a ranch regular. Between pack trips, Fannie liked to round up her pintos every few days to make sure they remained in top shape. Dave, riding Smoky, made a good wrangler and, with Fannie on Paint, they searched the mountain, through forests and across rocky terrain, until they found all the horses.

"Ain't they some beauties," Fannie remarked as they came upon Caesar, Nifty, and Butterfly grazing in the shade of a rocky overhang. Still higher up they found Easter and Red Cloud on an open grassy park, then Taffy, Silvertip, Echo, and, down in a ravine near a spring, the handsome piebald, Princess, granddaughter of the first Princess.

"Aunt Fannie, I think they're glad to see you." Dave watched her ride among the animals, greeting each one with friendly pats and kind words. Princess nuzzled her hand, then followed along as Fannie moved among the others.

"Princess wants to know what I want her to do," Fannie said. "I tell her and she tells the others. She's the boss lady."

Dave chuckled. "I can't see how you know where to find them. They're scattered over thousands of acres of forest and mountains. But you seem to know just where to look." They started down the trail, Princess heading the string of twenty-eight horses, and Fannie and Dave bringing up the rear.

"Well, I'll tell you." She saw a trace of resemblance to Walter in this special young man. "You know they're not going to be where the horseflies are bad right now. They'll be where the grass is greenest and longest. Just good horse sense. You have to think where you'd like to be if you were them."

Dave chuckled again. The pintos strung out along the trail, their sleek sides gleaming, their colors flashing in the sunlight as they moved at a good trot down the slope. "They sure are a pretty sight."

"None prettier," Fannie said.

Secured in the corral, the horses stood like patient children being groomed for school. Fannie inspected each for ticks and checked their hoofs, ears, and teeth. "Looks like Echo's been kicked." She bent to examine an abrasion on the mare's flank. "Shame on you, Echo. Fighting again?" Echo tossed her mane, then sniffed Fannie's hand. "Dave, bring some of that salve from the shed." After doctoring Echo's scrape, they curried and brushed each coat, mane, and tail, chatting with the horses as they worked.

Darkness had fallen and a full moon flooded light over the mountain before Fannie felt satisfied that each horse had gotten its share of care. Then she opened the gate. "Take 'em back now, Princess." The piebald snorted as she reeled around the fence line and through the gate. The other pintos followed, whuffling softly in their eagerness to be off for the high pastures again. They galloped playfully across the meadow, their white patches luminous in the moonlight, and followed Princess onto the forest trail. Fannie stood listening until the sound of their hoofbeats faded. When she turned to Dave, the crinkled lines at each side of her weathered face framed the sparkle of pride in her eyes.

A few evenings later, while milking the two cows in the shed, they heard a car horn. Fannie continued the steady pull, pull of her hands on the cow's teats. "See who it is, Dave."

A familiar voice from the past said, "Why don't you look up and see for yourself?" She peered around the cow's hind leg. There in the open door, stood Guy Weadick and his wife, Florence LaDue.

"Well, if you two ain't a sight for sore eyes." Her hands continued the steady pull, pull.

"We saw a story about you in the Calgary paper," Guy said. "We were coming through Helena, so we thought we'd look you up."

"It's good to see you, Fannie." Looking pretty as ever in a becoming flowered dress, Florence bent forward to get a look at the woman behind the cow. Fannie finished her milking, picked up the full pail, and poured milk into a basin for the cats. Then, wiping her palms on her overalls, she stepped forward to shake hands with the Weadicks.

"Excuse the hands. Just good clean cows' milk."

"You haven't changed a bit," Guy teased.

"And you still know just the right thing to say. Why, I feel twenty years younger just looking at the two of you. Come on in the house and tell me what you've been up to." The old friends moved into the kitchen where, after a hearty fried-chicken supper, they talked long into the night about the early days when rodeos were still called stampedes and women rode right along with the men. The flamboyant era of women rodeo riders, at its peak in the thirties, had floundered with the coming of the war. Cowgirl bronc riding was no longer a featured event, and the expense of maintaining and trans-porting a string of horses, with little hope of adequate remuneration, had killed relay racing.

"Things just aren't the same now," Weadick mused. "Women riding these days are a new breed. Men, too, for that matter."

Before the Weadicks left the next morning, they invited Fannie to attend a reunion honoring those who had performed in the first Calgary Stampede in 1912. The event was to be held at the High River Rodeo in Alberta, Canada, in September. Fannie promised she'd be there.

"They still remember me in the rodeo world," she said to Dave as the Weadicks' car headed down the mountain.

"You bet they do. Don't I bring an armload of mail every time I go to Helmville."

Fannie shows her contentment with life at Arrastra Creek, about 1955.

"That's from friends. I'm talking about old-timers who don't even know whether I'm still alive. Guy says they ask about me."

Fannie came back in high spirits from the High River reunion, where thousands cheered the guests of honor—Guy and Florence, Fannie, and cowboy-champ Ed Echols—veterans of the first Calgary Stampede forty-four years before.

With the first snow, Fannie trailed her horses down the mountain to the pasture she had rented for them on the McDonald ranch, and after visiting overnight, she rode back without them up the Arrastra Creek road, dwarfed by the giant, white-frosted forest. She loved the majesty of winter despite its hardships, but when she closed the meadow gate behind her that November day, for the first time she faced the arduous season alone. Except for Princess,

Paint, Warbonnet, three colts, Curly, twenty-seven cats, the wildlife, and the whispering tamaracks.

The deepening winter's profound solitude wrapped her in its cocoon, its brittle cold held at bay by the warmth from her stove. The midnight crack of freezing pine branches contrasted with the purr of napping kittens on the sunny windowsill. The peace of her contentment layered with the depth of her loneliness.

During the long evenings, she again took up her diary.

DECEMBER: *Blizzard night before last. County didn't come up with the Snow Cat yet. Rode up to the stack. Isn't much hay up there. No elk in sight, but their tracks look like I been feeding cattle up there.*

A guy here in the valley lost five steers in the river. Broke through the ice all at once. He pulled them out while still warm and cut their throats, thinking he could sell the meat. He said they bled good, but the inspector at Missoula condemned them. So he's out the price of five steers. Eighteen below yesterday, but only eight below today, so it won't be bad riding down to meet Nick. Glad he's coming. The woodpile is awful small. Spent Christmas day with McDonalds. Had them up here for New Year's.

JANUARY: *Princess's colt, Marbles, thinks she's pretty smart. When she wants more hay, she comes over to the house and paws on the doorstep. Old Daisy used to do the same thing when the water trough was empty.*

A big six-point bull elk came into the hay corral by the house. I opened the door to see how many points he had. He just stood there, so I stomped my feet and yelled at him. He never made a move. So I came in and put on my coat and overshoes and started walking toward him. Then he trotted over to the fence, jumped over, and was gone into the brush. If the darn things were only that tame in hunting season.

FEBRUARY: *Been busy canning my bull elk. Don't think I'll ever want to look an elk in the face again. He had two broken ribs so I sawed the broken part out and boiled the meat off to see what the bones looked like. They hadn't knit together. Had only gristle holding them. Wonder how they do that. Must do it fighting or bumping into trees when they run.*

MARCH: *Hay is $25 a ton, and I had to pay $9 a ton to have it trucked up here. Lloyd asked a saw-mill guy what they wanted for planed two-by-fours per thousand. He said $240. The best. No knots. A person has to be a millionaire to buy lumber these days.*

I broke Echo's little coltie yesterday, and he led in no time. Smart as can be. Warbonnet's colt took twice as long to get to lead. A guy came along claiming he got $50 to halter-break

Arabian colts in Oregon. I had a swell birthday, big feed with neighbors, cards, and presents.

APRIL: *Had a heifer down on McDonald's pasture. He said she'd freshen April 19, but when I went over there the calf was already two weeks old. Don't know why they didn't let me know. Thought they knew I wanted to milk her. She may hold up her milk now. My colts down there look pretty tough, too. He fed them out with the other stock, and I doubt they got water enough as he had to chop the creek open. The ice was thick and the water down deep. They were probably afraid to go after it.*

MAY: *No feed up in here so had to pasture the horses two weeks more. Cost me $8 a head over at Jens, and four cents a day each where I have them now. Wintering costs me about $450 a year. And had to shoot Warrior, second best horse I had, after paying $8 pasture bill on him. He was nearly blind. One eye went bad last winter and the other one this winter. Nifty's two-year-old cream-and-white colt is missing. Either died or somebody took him.*

Had one hell of a time bringing the horses. Got off on the wrong trail into three feet of snow on an icy hillside. Red Cloud got into a bog hole up to his neck, and we had to borrow a 75-foot cable and an inch rope to pull him out with the Jeep. He was a mud-colored horse when we got through with him. Took us half an hour to wash alkali mud out of his tail. It's a terrible place to have to look after them. Six sections of land is too much to cover on foot with four to eight inches of snow to track through.

Worked on the lower irrigation ditch. I've shoveled a ton of rock, dirt, and sand, and there still isn't much water coming in. Brought up two cows that had calves. Put both calves on one. She's too hard for me to milk with my bum fingers. I'm going to get me a little pig this spring so I can have some good old pork next winter.

AUGUST: *Hay isn't much. Have been trying to get wood and fix up the old fences. Found the last pinto, Spot. She was up at Cameron's, three miles this side of Lincoln all winter, then got into the woods. They called me to come and get her. She was so gentle, I thought somebody had broke her to ride. But when I put a saddle on, she blowed up and about the third jump missed the ground with her feet and landed full length. Then she got up and turned it on harder. Never seen a horse go faster with as many crooked jumps as she did and stay with it. Wish she had been broke, she's pretty and seems so nice—the little two-faced hellion.*

SEPTEMBER: *Built fence up to haying time. All the animals I want in get out, and the ones I want out break the fence down and come in.*

Trying to tame three broncs so we can pack them. Rainy's back comes up like a rainbow as soon as the cinch tightens, and he starts crow hopping. He doesn't buck, but he's a spooky devil.

OCTOBER: *Busy as a cat in a straw pile since hunting season opened. One party of six each got their elk, and a man and wife that I took to Lost Pony each got theirs. Another couple failed to get their meat, but no fault of mine because they could see elk from camp nearly every day. Just couldn't seem to find them when they'd go out after them. They were in there two weeks, too. It's been raining every day since hunters started riding in. The corral is sure a mess. All the ropes and saddles and pack blankets are wet. Trail wet and sloppy all the way.*

NOVEMBER: *Had sixteen hunters in Meadow Creek. Only got one elk cow and calf, and the cow spoiled because they wounded her late in the evening and didn't find her till morning. Never saw so few elk tracks in there. Short on elk and long on bear. Another damn grizzly tore up my big tent. It was too cold to sleep anyway.*

Two hunters just stopped by. Dissatisfied with their trip with Copenhaver's outfitters. They're looking for a place for next year. I'll have to buy hay even if I only keep two saddle horses, a cow and calf. Ponimay's colt don't look so good, nor does Echo's, so would like to keep them here and feed them a wee bit of oats.

Rented four horses to Deer Lodge hunters this morning to ride up Arrastra Creek. I asked if any of them had packed before and one said yes. When they got back just after dark, one pack had the rigging tore out of it and they had the cinches fastened with rope. Two pack saddles had a side strap broke. Breeching and two halter ropes broke. They said one of the horses went on the wrong side of a tree, but I know better. It looked like they might have had them all down. Looked like it happened after elk was loaded. Next time, I'll go along.

DECEMBER: *Eighteen inches of white Christmas. May have to go out by horsepower. It's a cinch Princess won't high center and have to be shoveled out. I'm pumping water, packing hay to the animals, baking some of that meat-scraps bread for the cats, splitting wood. Got two cows, five calves, and five horses with me. Only intended to keep four, but Golddust had a different idea.*

APRIL: *Horse wrangling yesterday. Stormy and windy but warm. Found fourteen more. They were feeling what little green grass they found and took off up the hill on high, old Paint in the lead. Finally caught up with them. Easter's old bones show up pretty good. The yearlings look better than I thought they would. Couldn't find the rest. The pasture is so darn big.*

I'll go after the heifer and calf tomorrow. McDonald said I could use his trailer, but he tried to bring a heifer of his in it, upset, and spilled her out. I could tie the calf in the back of the Jeep. Mac said my heifer went on the prod and put him up in the hay rack. So we may have some fun dodging her round head when breaking her to milk. Nothing like a little excitement. Gets awful dull up in here when there's nothing doing.

Two feet of snow. Five feet at Kid Young's cabin six miles up Arrastra Creek. Went up there last week. Saw four fresh lion tracks. Hunters have already killed six right around here. First it's bear, then cats. Saw a bob cat not far from the house.

OCTOBER: *I've given up hope of ever getting a roof on my barn. Guess I'll just have to move when the old shed falls down. The bronc buster I hired turned out to be a fizzle. May have to sell those colts. I have too darn many horses.*

Wintering at Arrastra Creek, Fannie and two companions haul wood.

NOVEMBER: *Saw ten head of elk on Bugle Mountain. No hunters in there this side of East Fork when I came out with last party. Old Paint looks bad. Don't think she'll make it through the winter.*

APRIL: *When I got up this morning, Goldie had got down on her back in a hole with her front feet and one hind leg through the fence and the other doubled up against the wire. Must have been down a couple of hours because she was shivering, and snow was melted under her. At first, I didn't know how to get her out by myself, and I knew Echo couldn't pull her. Then I thought of my Jeep. I used a chain with a short piece of rope around her feet, and by helping her what I could, she just made it and that's all. She was a pretty sorry-looking pony, skinned up some, with a big sore on the hip bone where she laid. Think it got frosted. I fed her oats today. Hope she don't lose her colt.*

I'd like to get the others up here if there's any grass by the middle of May. The pasture bill is $300, cow feed down there another $300, and hay $100. I better go out of the livestock business. Get me a dugout somewhere, and let old Uncle Sam keep me.

MAY: *It's raining. There are eight white-tail deer on the meadow. Haven't see any elk this spring. The loggers are still hauling timber out. The horses we brought home are all down along the river bothering the neighbors. Wish I had my ten head of broncs broke to ride, but horse breakers are scarce as hen's teeth these days. Folks over here herd their cattle with Jeeps and pickup trucks instead of saddle horses.*

SEPTEMBER: *Went to Helena with the Parkers looking for pasture. Got a place for the horses at $2.50 a head. Don't know how good it'll be. Joins Brian O'Connell's on the west.*

All the cows got out again. Took me all afternoon to build three new sections of fence. Had to drag heavy old green poles by hand. Not as good a work mule as I used to be. Better get busy and answer a couple of hunter's letters. Looks like I won't have too many this year.

MARCH: *My elk herd is getting tame. Last week, the big bull was eating in the feed lot between the shed and where the old mowers are parked. He's a big devil and probably old as the hills. He's been in my hay every winter for fifteen years. The game warden promised to bring lumber and fence the stack, then later said he'd bring hay to replace what the elk eat. I haven't seen either one yet. Coyote and lynx are thick as fleas around these parts. They're coming down the creek out of the deep snow.*

Lois gave me a birthday party again. Sure cooked up a swell feed and had the table all prettied up. Had the Coughlins, McDonalds, the Greys, and Herb Zimmerman. The Greys are the ones from Ohio who visited the Parkers last fall. Liked Montana so much, they came back to stay.

APRIL: *Guess I'll have to try the red-pepper cure on my rope-chewing knotheads. Have to tie old Brownie with a chain or he'll chew himself loose. Helen McDonald Clark and her husband have stayed at Copenhaver's this winter. She's a real good writer. She got pictures from me and all the dope on my rodeo days. Had a story about me in the Great Falls* Tribune. *Olive Henry wrote one for* Out West Magazine *before that. It's real good, too. Mrs. Clark has sent another one to the Deer Lodge paper, the* Silver State Post, *but it hasn't come out yet. She says she's going to write a more detailed one for* Western Horseman. *I'm getting quite a few letters from the first article.*

The county plowed up to my gate again so guess I'll drive the Jeep into Helmville to refill the grub box. I always wave to let the road crew know I'm okay. They say when they don't see me, they look for smoke coming from the chimney. Where there's smoke, there's life.

JUNE: *Still no word from Ivan and Mickey. Had hoped they could come this summer. Guess Ivan's busy with his practice and his laundromats. Vannie never writes either. His pony's getting the rheumatism.*

AUGUST: *Awful dry summer. Poor pasture all over. Dave's laying up wood for me. He's going to college.*

Fannie, well into her seventies, rides one of her favorite pintos to oversee her Arrastra Creek ranch.

SEPTEMBER: *Looking for pasture. Everything so high priced around here. Will have to buy oats for Echo, too. Her teeth are going bad. Have to cook it for her so she can eat.*

OCTOBER: *No choice but to trail my colties over the Divide to the Beartooth. Can't have them dying of pneumonia in some strange pasture. Carrie wants me to come for Thanksgiving. Guess we'll all come. All thirty-three of us.*

Hitting the Trail for the Last Time

30

Swirling white snow sifted around the string of pintos as the three mounted figures bundled in scarfs and heavy macintoshes prepared to trail the horses across the Divide to the Beartooth for the winter. Fannie, on Princess, squinted against the large flakes at the spotted horses trotting through the gate. Niece Vi, riding Marbles, and Bryan, Bertha's youngest son, on Butterfly, headed two frisky yearlings after the others.

"Are you sure it wouldn't be easier to move 'em with the Jeep?" Bryan nudged the stragglers after the others.

"Not those colties." Fannie gazed lovingly at four born the previous spring, noting resemblances to former favorites. All the great ones were long gone now. Napoleon. Chief. Blaze. Sultan. The two Daisys. Old Princess. All passed away of old age, and new horses had taken their places in Fannie's heart. Once in a while, to weed out a "snake" or to get some needed cash, she sold or traded one. But most of Fannie's pintos lived out their lives in her tender care.

By midday the continuing heavy snow covered the Lincoln road to a depth of several inches, and the wranglers could barely see to keep the horses together. Fannie tried to keep spirits high. "Just think of that good old chicken your ma will roast for our Thanksgiving dinner."

Vi grimaced into the blowing gusts while scanning the whiteness for the traces of the snow-laden fence posts along the road. "Are you sure we're going the right way?"

"We got to be. My guess is we're about five miles out of Lincoln," Fannie shouted above the howl of the wind. "We'll be at the Grantier ranch by nightfall."

She took the lead, giving Princess her head, trusting the horse's instincts as much as her own. They reached the Grantier ranch mid-afternoon in the already gathering darkness and turned the horses into the corral. That night as guests of the Grantiers, they slept warm and cozy with full stomachs.

In the morning the thermometer registered twenty degrees below zero. But the snow had stopped, and a pale, cold sun shown on the dazzling whiteness. Mrs. Grantier expressed concern. "Don't you want to stay here till the weather breaks? You could freeze out there on the trail."

"Much obliged, but Carrie wants us there for Thanksgiving," Fannie explained. "Besides, the sun is out today. We won't get lost."

Another day's trailing through the drifts and intense cold got them as far as the Nettleton ranch near Canyon Creek, where they again spent the night in warm hospitality, arriving at the Beartooth the next forenoon in time for Carrie's Thanksgiving dinner. They had trailed the horses more than 80 miles, and Fannie, vowing to start before snowfall next year, was pleased to see that all of the animals had come through in good shape.

Two days following the Thanksgiving festivities at Carrie's, the curious string of pintos lined up along the fence to watch Fannie saddle Princess for the return ride. "I'll be back for you in the spring," she told them. "You behave yourselves."

The weather had warmed some. Twenty degrees above zero seemed mild to Fannie after the rigors of the trip over. With a last look at her beloved horses, she started on the long, high road over Stemple Pass and back to Arrastra Creek, where she would again winter in solitude.

Fannie's Jeep gradually became her link with the outside world. She complained that it balked now and then, but she accepted its efficiency at hauling supplies and transporting new calves.

One afternoon in 1962, when making a hurry-up trip to Helmville before she was to guide a fishing party into the wilderness, she turned from the highway onto the Helmville road directly into the path of another car. A screech of brakes. A sideswipe of vehicles. The Jeep skidded out of control into the shallow ditch, and Fannie felt a sharp crack as her knee struck the dashboard.

The man in the other car, unhurt, came on the run. "What the hell are you doing, lady? You turned right in front of me."

"I'm sorry." Fannie tried to move her leg and felt a searing flash of pain. She grimaced. "I didn't see you. Guess my mind was on something else. You okay?"

"Yes, but my grill's bashed in." His scowl softened when he saw she was injured.

At that moment, Otto Eder pulled up in his pickup. "Got some trouble here, Fannie?"

"It's my knee, Otto. Can't move it. Must be broke."

Otto and the other driver lifted her into the front of the pickup for the ride to a doctor in Lincoln. Her kneecap was indeed broken. Walter and Fleta came that evening to check on her, along with their son Ed, who volunteered to guide the fishing party the next day. Walter looked relieved when Fannie explained that the broken kneecap was the worst of it.

"First broken bone I ever had. Imagine that. After all the broncs I rode. Always said cars are more dangerous."

"Were you thrown out?" Fleta asked sympathetically.

"Nope. Rode it to a standstill," Fannie quipped.

In the following months, the injury aggravated the advancing arthritis in her knees and limited her participation in ranch activities. She depended more on grandnieces and grandnephews, plus an occasional hired hand, to guide the trickle of hunters and fishermen who still came.

Otto Eder often rode halfway from his ranch to a spot where he could see smoke curling from Fannie's chimney, hidden among the trees up on the mountain. "Fannie will go on forever," he would invariably remark to Jennie after these excursions.

But her knee injury was not the most crushing blow she was to suffer. In the autumn of 1965 a letter came from Ivan.

Dear Fannie,

I'm sorry to have to tell you that I've sold the ranch. The new owner, Mr. Thompson, will be coming to see you soon.

No tears this time. Fannie folded the letter, placed it in a drawer, and began packing her belongings. September hovered over the mountain, spreading a golden crown of warm yellows on the tamaracks and soft, autumn-fragrant browns over the meadow grasses. The horses were hairing up already, too. Probably a cold winter ahead. Loving trips back and forth between house, cabins, and shed served as her unspoken good-bye.

Princess snuffled as Fannie saddled her, preparing to trail the pinto string over the Divide for the last time. Carrie and Joe had offered her the use of the homestead cabin they built in 1903 shortly after they were married, now standing vacant on their ranch under the Beartooth. "You're going to like your new place," Fannie reassured the old mare.

She gazed across the meadow toward the familiar mountain trail. How many times had she ridden that trail, packing dudes, looking for frisky ponies? Too many to count. Her memories she would take with her, and in days to come she would ride her pintos up the familiar trail in her mind's eye. Just as she would put up the meadow hay each summer. Cuss the old bull elk at her haystack each winter. Rebuild the fence year after year. And plan to finish the barn come spring. It would all be with her always.

The rumble of Dave's truck sounded from the Arrastra Creek road. He had come for the furniture and boxes, packed and ready in the cabin. Nieces Susan, Babe, Betty, and Hallie waited to begin the long ride. The horses stood ready to trot through the gate one last time.

Fannie peered across Princess's saddle. This would be the last time she would scan the meadow and beyond the gate into the trees for an approaching visitor.

Dave braked the truck beside the porch and jumped out. "Aunt Fannie! Here's a special-delivery letter for you. I met the mailman down on the highway."

Fannie took the letter. She read the address, then the postmark. "Who do I know in Oklahoma City?" She rubbed the envelope between her fingers as if to sense the identity of the sender.

"Open it, Aunt Fannie."

She tore the end from the envelope, took out the letter, and read the few

Fannie trails her pinto string back to the Beartooth for the last time.

lines of type. Astonished, she looked at Dave, then the girls.

"Well, what is it?" they asked in unison.

A warm glow flowed over her. "It says here I've been chosen a charter life member of the Cowboy Hall of Fame."

"The Cowboy Hall of Fame!" Dave let out a whoop.

"That's a high honor." Babe, grinning from ear to ear, dismounted and ran to hug her. Susan and Hallie followed.

"You bet it is." Babe also hugged Princess's regal head as if to relate the good news to the faithful mare.

Fannie smiled fondly at them all. "They remember," she said.

Eyes shining with pride, her body straight as an arrow, the seventy-eight-year-old woman swung into the saddle. "Princess, let 'em ramble." The old mare stepped out, leading the lively ribbon of paints, piebalds, and pintos across the meadow and down the mountain toward the Beartooth.

Epilogue

Fannie Sperry Steele lived on the homestead beneath the Beartooth until age eighty-seven, when, in 1974, needing care, she entered a nursing home. Though afflicted with arthritis in her hands and knees, she remained lively in mind and spirit, surrounded by her extended family, receiving old friends who remembered her heyday, and reliving the life she believed to be the finest she could have had. Fannie died on February 11, 1983, six weeks before her ninety-sixth birthday.

Fannie Sperry Steele, age 95, sits for a portrait shortly before her death in 1983.

To the yesterdays that are gone, to the waddies I used to know, to the bronc busters that rode beside me, to the horses beneath me—I take off my hat. I wouldn't have missed one minute of it. I lived when I wanted to, the way I wanted to, and that is saying a lot for one mortal.

Fannie Sperry Steele
(Helen Clark interview,
True West magazine, 1976)

About the Author

A native Nebraskan, Dee Marvine built a career as an editor for corporate clients and publishers in Chicago before moving to Montana to devote full time to writing. Her published books include: *Last Chance* (hardcover, Doubleday, 1993; paperback, Leisure Books, 1998; audio, Books In Motion, 2004), which was nominated by Western Writers of America for their 1994 Best First Novel award; *Sweet Grass* (Five Star, 2003); and *All Aboard for Paradise* (Five Star, 2004). A member of Western Writers of America and a founding member of Women Writing the West, she lives in Big Timber, Montana, with her artist husband, Don Marvine.